D1171694

Dixie Dharma

The University of North Carolina Press · Chapel Hill

Dixie Dharma

Inside a Buddhist Temple in the American South

JEFF WILSON

Publication of this book was supported by a
grant from Bukkyo Dendo Kyokai America.

Designed by Jacquline Johnson
Set in Arno Pro
by Tseng Information Systems, Inc.

The paper in this book meets the guidelines for
permanence and durability of the Committee on
Production Guidelines for Book Longevity of the
Council on Library Resources.

The University of North Carolina Press has been a
member of the Green Press Initiative since 2003.

Library of Congress Cataloging-in-Publication Data
Wilson, Jeff (Jeff Townsend)
Dixie dharma : inside a Buddhist temple in the
American South / Jeff Wilson.
p. cm.
Includes bibliographical references and index.
ISBN 978-0-8078-3545-6 (cloth : alk. paper)
1. Buddhism — Southern States. 2. Southern
States — Religious life and customs. I. Title.
BQ739.U6W55 2012
294.30975 — dc23 2011036322

16 15 14 13 12   5 4 3 2 1

Contents

Illustrations

Acknowledgments

Acknowledgments are often the final words that we write as we finish our books, but it is appropriate that they go at the front, because it is only through the assistance of others that our projects ever get set in motion. In my case, I am immeasurably indebted to the community at the Ekoji Buddhist Sangha of Richmond, which through nine years, countless religious services, hundreds of hours of interviews, and much bonhomie has provided me with the data that forms the core of this work. On my first research visit to the temple, I wasn't yet a graduate student; on my final visit, I was a full-time assistant professor of religious studies. At each stage of my development, the members have shown gracious tolerance and warm welcome. In my commitment to maintaining the anonymity of my informants, I will not name those who particularly went out of their way to share their thoughts and feelings with me (not to mention, in some cases, their spare bedrooms) — but they know who they are. Y'all have my deepest thanks. I hope you will find this an interesting, insightful, and fair representation of your experiences.

Many others in the Buddhist community of Richmond beyond Ekoji also helped me with this research, including folks at Hue Quang Temple, Vien Giac Temple, Richmond Vipassana Group, the Richmond chapter of Soka Gakkai International–USA, Cambodian Buddhist Association of Richmond, Still Water Zen Center, Won Buddhist Meditation Center of Richmond, Chrysalis Meditation Group, Richmond's Unitarian Universalist Buddhist group, and the Richmond Tzu Chi chapter. More broadly, the interactions I have had with Buddhists in many hundreds of temples and groups from Hawaii to Massachusetts over the past fifteen years have shaped my observations about regional differences and American Buddhist practices. To anyone who has suffered through a site visit or been nagged for information by me (they are legion), I give my thanks.

On the academic front, I have benefited from many mentors. At the earliest stages of this research, it was ably shepherded by Thomas Tweed and Yaakov Ariel of the Department of Religious Studies at the University of North Carolina, and Richard Jaffe of the Religion Department at Duke

University. Glenn Hinson of UNC's Folklore Program guided my initial forays into the field and taught me the basic fieldwork methods that I have deployed ever since. Early research presented at the American Academy of Religion received helpful feedback, especially from Charles Prebish and Paul Numrich, who showed great patience with a very junior scholar. Another section of this work was premiered at the Buddhism without Borders conference at the Institute for Buddhist Studies. I received feedback there from so many colleagues that they are too numerous to list, so just let me say thank you to all and give special appreciation to Scott Mitchell and Natalie Quli for organizing that event, which I believe will be looked back on as a milestone in the study of Western Buddhism. Useful feedback also came from the members of the 2010–12 Young Scholars in American Religion program run by the Center for the Study of Religion and American Culture.

Several early stages of this research were supported by summer grants from the Pluralism Project. I thank Diana Eck and the Pluralism Project for the funding and moral support they provided my various projects on southern Buddhism during my graduate school years. The archives and libraries that I consulted for this book are numerous, but two deserve special mention. I thank the staffs at the Library of Virginia in Richmond and the Japanese American National Museum in Los Angeles, where the Buddhist Churches of America archives are housed.

I want to express my appreciation to Elaine Maisner at the University of North Carolina Press, who saw both potential and plenty of weaknesses in this project, and whose efforts to push me have resulted in a stronger final product. I am also in debt to two anonymous readers who critiqued the project on behalf of the press.

Finally, I thank my friends and family who supported me during the many phases of this work. My late grandmother provided the home base for this research during the final years of her life and deserves special mention. My in-laws Patrick and Sandi Macnamara also allowed me to use their home as a launching pad for further research toward the end of this project — without their help this book would not have come to be. Above all, my wife, Kristen, and more recently our children, have had to sacrifice in order for me to carry out this research and get it published. I cannot fully express how much I have received from their love and support.

Dixie Dharma

The world is places.
— Gary Snyder, "The Place, the Region, and the Commons,"
   The Gary Snyder Reader, 1999

Introduction

ENCOUNTERS AT A MULTIDENOMINATIONAL
TEMPLE IN THE SOUTH

"Heart Sutraaaaaa." The sound of our chanting dies away as we finish reciting a famous Buddhist text, our fading voices an expression of the emptiness that the sutra celebrates.[1] Martin, a white-haired gentleman with an
equally white mustache and a look of calm concentration, strikes the dark
bowl-bell, which rings once and then slips back into stillness. For a moment,
the small room here at the temple is quiet with anticipation, the silence broken only by the muffled rush of cars in the wet street outside and the rain
tapping out its own syncopation on the windowpane. Huddled on our black
cushions, we wait for the next signal. Then the wooden fish drum lets out a
hollow yelp as it is hit by Li, a Chinese American man dressed in jeans and
a loose white shirt, and we all launch into nianfo, the continuous recitation
of Amitabha Buddha's name.[2]

"Na-mo-O-mi-to-fo, Na-mo-O-mi-to-fo, Na-mo-O-mi-to-fo" — the
sacred words of the Buddha's name fill the temple. Li's fish drum cries at
each syllable, insisting that we stay on beat. Amitabha stands before us on
the altar, his skin blackened by fire, his robes and nimbus blazing gold in the
half-lit room. The cloud of incense that surrounds him tickles my nostrils
and tastes like sawdust in the roof on my mouth, the sensation constantly
renewing itself as air moves in and out with each new devotion.

As the Buddha's name spills out of me, my chest and back begin to tingle, as if energy is gathering and circulating. The drum seems to fade into the distance, like a tree branch tapping far away. The other ten people in the room begin to lose their individuality as we function like a single organism — our minds, voices, and bodies suffused with the Buddha. The walls disappear as my peripheral vision dissolves — there is only us and the Buddha, only the name and the breath between the name, only this moment now without past or future. "Na-mo-O-mi-to-fo, Na-mo-O-mi-to-fo, Na-mo-O-mi-to-fo, Na-mo-O-mi-to-fo . . ." Minutes pass unheeded — we have forgotten the world and it has forgotten us, as for a few moments we chant the Pure Land into being here in the sanctuary of the temple. Now it no longer even seems as if it is we who are doing the chanting. Volition and thought drop away. There is only the name speaking itself, announcing its presence from its hiding place behind every thought and deed in the waking world of form.

Sitting here in this same place the next morning is an entirely different experience. Another group has gathered to meditate, not chant, and unlike yesterday afternoon's mixed-race gathering, nearly everyone here today is white. Now instead of facing the Buddha, I am staring at the pale greenish wall of the temple, just eighteen inches from the end of my nose. My eyes are half-closed, and my attention is directed inward, counting my breaths one after another. When I reach ten (or, as often happens, twelve or thirteen), I return to number one and begin the process again. Silence and noise have achieved an uneasy truce here in the midmorning light — no one speaks, but the quiet itself makes me preternaturally aware of everything around me: the fridge humming to itself in the kitchen, the mourning doves sobbing outside, the gurgling stomachs of my fellow wall-gazers. My aching left leg implores me to shift my position, but the discipline of the others sitting straight and solid like mountains keeps me from fidgeting. Not allowing ourselves to be moved by passing thoughts or temptations, we are emulating the Buddha's famous triumph over the evil god of desire Mara on the day the Buddha achieved his awakening.[3]

A bell sings a lone, low note, and we bow slightly on our cushions. With gratitude for the chance to move, I kneel and ritually fluff the round zafu that has been my support, trying to do so mindfully, respectful of its role in my practice.[4] Next I ritually brush away imaginary dirt from the black zabuton mat beneath it, and fold the mat back out of the way.[5] Soon I am standing with the other fifteen participants in a line that snakes around the room to meet itself again behind me. The bell sings again, and with stately drama we put one foot forward. And wait. A breath passes. Slowly, we take another step. And breathe. With the dignity of utter attention to our actions, we gradually circumambulate the room, hands held clasped at the chest, eyes cast down, breath sweeping mind. Elsewhere in Richmond at this hour others are receiving the Spirit with joyous enthusiasm, reciting their adherence to the Nicene Creed, or testifying to the power of Jesus' blood to wash away sins. But here in this temple a few blocks up the street from the Confederate Memorial Chapel, our gentle pace is taking us steadily down the Eightfold Path of the Buddha.

These disparate experiences took place at Ekoji Buddhist Sangha of Richmond, the "Temple of the Gift of Light" (as the Japanese name Ekoji translates in English), located in Richmond's Museum District.[6] This attractive, human-scaled neighborhood is an important part of the Virginia capital's proud southern identity. Dogwoods and magnolia trees line nearby Monument Avenue, watched over by statues of Robert E. Lee, Stonewall Jackson, and other heroes of the Confederacy. At the end of the street are the venerable buildings that housed the Congress of the Confederate States of America and the home of Confederate president Jefferson Davis. While the Confederate past has ceased to be as important as it once was, other long-standing patterns persist—Richmond (and the South as a whole) remains a region of strong evangelical dominance in religion and concerted effort by traditional constituencies to hold on to their social and political prerogatives. Therefore, for many Richmond would seem like a surprising place to find a Buddhist temple. But this mixing of Asian East and American South has been occurring for close to thirty years, as Buddhism and other non-Western religions proliferate in the old strongholds of the Methodists and Southern Baptists.

Ekoji is notable not only because it is located in the South, where Buddhism has rarely been remarked on by historians and ethnographers, but also because it houses five distinct groups practicing in separate lineages, as my differing experiences with chanting and meditating partially illustrate. Under one roof groups representing the Pure Land, Soto Zen, Kagyu, and Vipassana lineages of Buddhism have sought refuge together as a single community, as well as a Meditative Inquiry group largely informed by Buddhist thought and practice. Several different groups sharing a temple would be a highly unusual situation in modern Asia, so this novel arrangement has implications for the development of Buddhism in Richmond and beyond. It is from this meeting of traditions that one of the observations of this book emerges: the close proximity of Ekoji's groups requires them to differentiate themselves through various means but most obviously in bodily and spatial practices and the medium of material culture. Intersectarian contact among Buddhist groups in North America is not just about cooperation and exchange — diversity is always an opportunity for conflict and identity-making as well. At the same time, however, groups and individuals at the temple are certainly influenced by their contact with each other and with forces beyond the temple, such that Ekoji's groups demonstrate noticeable hybridity, even in the face of their attempts to create themselves along specific sectarian lines. The result is a highly pluralistic Buddhism, which prizes commonality and contact among multiple Buddhist lineages, though not without instances of ambivalence.

Pluralistic attitudes toward Buddhism can be found in many parts of the United States, but it is no accident that this unusually institutionalized example of Buddhist pluralism emerged in the South, where practitioners are relatively isolated from the American Buddhist strongholds in the North and West and must work together in order to maintain a presence on the landscape. The exceptional degree of pluralism at Ekoji was the first unexpected sign to me as a researcher that I needed to pay attention to how regional specificity affects Buddhism in America — and once I started down that road, many additional insights arose from following it. Thus I am especially concerned, initially, with discussing how regionalism may manifest in relation to American Buddhism, in the hope that such analysis will increase our understanding of Buddhist phenomena in North America overall and offer an analytical tool that other researchers can use in their specific case studies. In pursuit of this first exploration of American Buddhist regionalism, the South will be my main example, with Ekoji Buddhist Sangha of Richmond serving as the primary case study. Therefore this book is an exploration of two themes — pluralism and regionalism. Different chapters focus more strongly on one or the other, but both are intertwined throughout because they are fundamental facts of where my fieldwork was carried out. In grounding a study of pluralism in a specific place, I am trying to move discussion of Buddhist diversity beyond the abstract into an examination of how pluralism is actually experienced and enacted by Americans through the physical media of bodies, ritual implements, images, texts, and buildings. This is part of my larger argument that places in their local and regional specificity — not just their national and transnational generality and connection — need to be more closely attended to by scholars of Buddhism beyond Asia.

Peter Williams, a historian of American religion who has studied the nation's sacred architecture, has observed that "in both their general patterns of construction and distribution as well as in their individuality, churches can be interpreted as markers of a community's social, cultural, and historic identity. To understand their significance, one must learn to *read* them—to see them not just as generic icons of religiosity but rather as particular embodiments of that cultural impulse, simultaneously unique and representative."[7] In this book, I attempt such a reading of Ekoji, as revelatory of the identities of certain types of American Buddhists. The question immediately arises as to what sort of "document" is being read: Is it a book, a newspaper, a website, a love letter? As I conceive of it, the built space of Ekoji can be read as a sort of map, with the various architectural and ornamental elements serving as signs and landmarks that point to the community's varying identities. The objects and images of Ekoji are important marks on the map. Nonetheless, a map is not useful unless one knows how to read it—so I have consulted the members of Ekoji as my expert guides through its terrain. As they explained their personal cognitive mappings of Buddhism, Richmond, the South, and Ekoji's shared space, the alternate ways the temple is used to construct identity came into clearer focus, as well as the ways they live as Buddhists and as southerners.

If I may take the cartographic trope a step further, it can be seen that regardless of how one draws a map, people may take diverse routes as they traverse the same space, and thus have dissimilar—and illuminating—experiences of that place. Ethnographers of southern religion Ruel Tyson, James Peacock, and Daniel Patterson have pointed out that "members live their religion by doing it, acting its rites, restating its memories, speaking its hopes, obeying its commands, thus gaining an identity and a world to live in."[8] This acting and doing will receive close scrutiny in this book, as I attempt to discern how bodily practices serve as paths through the shared space of Ekoji and the streets of Richmond, revealing further information about identity formation and expression. As I will show, each group charts a particular path through Ekoji, yet their trails frequently intersect and merge. This contrasts with the parallel model of congregations at American Buddhist temples advanced by Paul Numrich in his groundbreaking *Old Wisdom in the New World*, whose case subjects in Chicago and Los Angeles follow noticeably divergent paths despite sharing the same sectarian tradition.[9] The five groups at Ekoji are different sectarian paths from disparate Asian homes that nonetheless move toward greater cooperation and shared identity—the dominant story which most participants tell about their routes through Ekoji is one of intersecting, not parallel lines. They are not all following identical paths through the Buddhist landscape, but on the whole they do feel they are walking together with one another toward a common destination.

Peter Williams extends his analysis beyond Christian churches to encompass Buddhist temples as well. As he notes:

> Buddhist temples in North America vary considerably, given the wide variety of ethnic groups which practice particular sorts of Buddhism as well as a multitude of native converts usually attracted to Zen or Tibetan varieties. A Zen meditation center will generally have no images but feature an open space for the practice of *zazen*. Temples in traditions that emphasize devotion rather than meditation may feature a prominent image of the Buddha on a central altar, which becomes a focus for chanting. Flanking this central figure often are subsidiary images of various "saints" such as arhants and bodhisattvas.... Tibetan temples may have prayer wheels as an aid to meditation. The interior of some older Pure Land temples may resemble a Christian church, with pews, an organ, and hymnals, although the image of Buddha Amitabha and murals of the Pure Land, though similarly placed, differ markedly in content from those that might be found in a Christian church.[10]

Indeed, but what happens when these things come together in a single place? Pushed up against one another, forced to work within an identical framework, the differing strategies that various Buddhist groups employ to produce appropriate religious spaces are thrown into high relief. The situation at Ekoji is such that we can often discern what these strategies are, uncovering insights that can be applied to less contested spaces.

This introduction lays out the focus of the book and the methods I used to investigate the subject. Chapter 1 presents an overview of my approach to studying regionalism in American Buddhism. I provide a brief history of how regionalism has been used in American religious studies and suggest possible regions that we may be able to discern in Buddhist America. That studies of American Buddhism have so far ignored the long-standing American historiographical trope of regionalism is surprising and suggests that American religious history as a discipline needs to be mined far more extensively by scholars working specifically on Buddhism outside of Asia.

In the second chapter, I provide the history of Ekoji — how it was founded and when each group joined. I pay particular attention to the modifications that were necessary to convert the former residence into a Buddhist temple. Ekoji's history is unusually complicated, and a clear understanding of the temple's past is necessary to understand its present. I provide a general description of the building, which sets up the discussion in chapter 3 of how each group uses the space. Chapter 2 also examines the pivotal Ekoji founder Takashi Kenryu Tsuji, using him as an example of a Buddhist circuit rider in the South and a modernist Shin priest in American Buddhism more generally. I also examine how distribution patterns play into the study of Buddhism in the South.

Chapter 3 concentrates on each of the current groups at Ekoji in turn. Defining each group's lineage and describing how it conducts its services, I consider how each group creates its own particular identity. They all more or less use the same basic elements in their services: for most the meeting hall is the same, the altar and statue are the same, and the same cushions, mats, and chairs are used. Thus, differentiation among groups occurs primarily in *how* they use the same place and objects, including the embodied practices of the participants. Surprisingly, each group has managed to carve out its own identity by use of the same elements, such that no group uses the same artifacts in precisely the same way. Discussing the way orientation in space informs religious identity, the geographer of religion Thomas Tweed has noted that "where we *stand* names who we are."[11] As I show, for Buddhists in America this insight might well be extended to observe that where and how they *sit* names who they are. Members of the Pure Land group face Amida Buddha on the altar, their central object of worship, whom they venerate in chant. Members of the Zen group face the wall, turning their attention away from the savior toward themselves, locating their practice in their own minds. Members of the Vipassana group face the altar, but they keep their eyes closed and perform no group liturgy; their lineage emphasizes that ultimately one treads the spiritual path alone. Members of the Meditative Inquiry group studiously act as if the statue is not even there, other than as an obstacle to be avoided during walking meditation. And members of the Tibetan group have relocated to a different room in the temple, the better to create their own unique aesthetic. Differentiation and competing uses of the shared space of Ekoji will be the informing concepts of this chapter. I believe this provides valuable insight into how these various traditions relate to place, ritual, and self-identity.

In chapter 4, I seek to complicate the picture of Ekoji as five clearly distinct, self-defining groups. The guiding concept here is permeability, as I trace how groups and individuals are affected by each other. Both consciously and unconsciously, the five groups at Ekoji find themselves assimilating aspects of each other's practice, doctrine, and material culture into their own even as they seek to assert the stability and coherency of their tra-ditions. Thus, the Pure Land group sits on Zen cushions placed before sutra benches crafted by the Tibetan practitioners, and it incorporates significant periods of silent, eyes-shut meditation. Contrary to traditional practices of their parent Theravada lineage, Vipassana practitioners bow to a Mahayana Buddha and pour tea over the baby Shakyamuni at the springtime celebra-tion of his birth.[12] I assert that Ekoji represents a particular form of Bud-dhist community, which I term a "pluralistic temple." I identify factors that may result in similar arrangements and amalgamations in other American Buddhist communities: lack of residential leaders, limited resources, low membership, contact with other Buddhist lineages, converts' need to imag-ine and create an unfamiliar religious practice, and a deemphasis on creedal approaches to religion, and I discuss how regionalism may affect some of these forces.

When I first arrived, I was surprised to find four separate groups (the Meditative Inquiry group is a more recent development) sharing what is really a rather small building. In this situation I looked for sectarian rival-ries and racial divisions and tried to discern tensions between "converts" and "cradle" Buddhists and those emphasizing meditative versus nonmedi-tative practices. Most of the literature on Buddhism in America that was available when I began my investigations in 2002 suggested that I should have found these sorts of rifts in the Buddhist community.[13] But while such separations are not entirely absent, and people do tend to sort themselves into preferred groups based on practice types (and perhaps race and eth-nicity), there seems to be a very low level of friction among and within Ekoji's groups. The temple's board scrupulously works to ensure that it in-cludes representation from all groups at Ekoji, and temple-wide events are always designed to include input from the different traditions. I rarely heard negative opinions expressed about other forms of Buddhism, and my attempts to draw out unspoken feelings were largely unsuccessful. It may be that I have missed significant incidents during my research, or that some of my consultants held back their less charitable opinions.[14] Sharing space at a single temple, participants must find ways to get along, if only for the sake of practicality. However, I believe that the general absence of signifi-cant rancor at Ekoji despite its many different groups can more easily be explained by examining the reason that my consultants frequently offered: they claimed to value diversity, believing that it adds something to their knowledge and practice of Buddhism, and that it helps them live Buddhist principles of tolerance, patience, and nondualism. They were grateful that they could practice in a place that supported their affirmation of Buddhist pluralism. As one informant put it, "I feel proud that we have all the groups here and they all get along."[15]

Because *pluralism* will be a prominent theme in this text, it is important to lay out precisely what I mean by this term. I employ this word to refer to two different phenomena found at Ekoji Buddhist Sangha. First, pluralism denotes the fact of multiplicity: Ekoji is a plural temple because it houses five different types of groups. Second, I also treat pluralism as a religious ideal. William Hutchison, a prominent historian of American religion, defined pluralism as "acceptance and encouragement of diversity."[16] Following this understanding, I use the term to refer to a pervasive attitude that I encountered at Ekoji: that multiplicity may be more desirable than singularity, even when it involves certain compromises in the way that a group is able to perform its practices. Particularly in chapter 4, I foreground the positive value attached to pluralism by many of Ekoji's members, and I suggest that this pluralistic ideology both results from and informs the evolution of the group's shared space.[17]

In chapter 5 I consider Buddhism within the context of its location in the American South. No scholarly work concerned with Buddhism in the South has ever been published. What we think of as "American Buddhism" is largely the Buddhism of California, the urban Northeast, Hawaii, or, less often, the Chicago area—not some sort of truly representative phenomenon that adequately accounts for Buddhist practice in every region of the country. To practice Buddhism in Richmond, Virginia, is to face challenges and confront an environment significantly different from that of San Francisco or Honolulu or New York City. Buddhists do not react to this environment uniformly, and I display the very different ways—positive, neutral, and negative—that Buddhists in the same temple may experience what it means to be Buddhist in the South.

A single ritual is the subject of chapter 6. The slave trade meditation vigil was held in Richmond in 2008. It provides a glimpse of a very specific southern Buddhist form of practice, where the history and environment of the region combined with more recently introduced religious ideas to produce a public event that acknowledged and resisted certain aspects of Richmond's past and present. In examining how local, regional, national, and international currents intertwined in this ritual we see that the regional operates in a nexus of forces that are also operating at more micro- and macroscopic levels. It is not my argument that all Buddhist activities in America are regional in nature, even though they do indeed all occur in specific places, or that region is always the most important aspect of any given practice. Nor is regionalism of equal importance in every corner of the country. But regionalism is important in certain times and places, and to the extent that it is overlooked (and in the study of American Buddhism, it has indeed been largely ignored) we miss forms of interpretation that can be illuminating.

In the conclusion, I provide final thoughts on American Buddhist places based on the evidence presented in this book, and I suggest possibilities for future research.

Movement and Places

I debuted this regionally based research at a conference at the Institute for Buddhist Studies in March 2010. While it was well received, I could not help but notice that everyone else seemed to be seized by a passion for looking at Buddhism on an international scale. It is an impulse I can understand. I live in Canada, but the year or so during which I wrote this book found me in over a dozen different American cities, as well as in Peru, Ecuador, and Japan. In most of these places I observed local Buddhist phenomena. Not counting connecting flights, I flew into or out of more than twenty airports. In certain ways, however, I never left home. I was online nearly every day, and I communicated with people in my own town and in every part of North America, as well as overseas. No matter where I was, I could almost always find a familiar fast food restaurant, watch CNN, listen to my iPod, argue via e-mail with my colleagues throughout the world, and enjoy the pleasures — dubious and genuine — of our globalized modern world.

And yet, the excitement and confusion of our ever more globalized reality is not the only important part of the story of contemporary religion. Scholars in my field — broadly defined, cultural studies; narrowly defined, modern religious studies; most specifically, the study of Buddhism in North America — are in danger of losing sight of the specific embodied and emplaced experiences of the people we study. Buddhism anywhere is indeed now connected in some fashion with Buddhism everywhere, but that does not mean that it is the same thing to practice Buddhism in Hilo, Hawaii, as it is to practice in Bozeman, Montana: not at all. During the past fifteen years I have closely observed Buddhism in New York, Virginia, North Carolina, Los Angeles, and Toronto, and, less systematically, in nearly every part of Anglophone North America (as well as in many parts of Asia). And as much as these places share commonalities and exist within mutually entangling webs of national and transnational connection, they are also distinctive places with their own cultures, and, I will argue here, Buddhisms.

The issue is that while most people are impacted by transnational developments, few of them live truly transnational lives. We may be losing sight of the places amid all the motion. Most people live in specific places, and the majority of their movements are within their own regions. When they do go further, it is *travel*, and they are usually moving *from* their own places. The places they travel from and return to are not all the same as one another no matter how many long-distance connections they may share, and the reasons they travel are not the same. For example, Buddhists in the South are more likely to travel outside their region in order to temporarily pursue Buddhist practice than are Buddhists in Hawaii or California.

In this book I use the South as my primary case study for concentrating on a particular region within American Buddhism. I was born in the North to southern parents, and have spent considerable time in various parts of the South. I have also lived in different parts of the Northeast, in the West, and outside the United States. I thus have experience with the South and the non-South, enough, I hope, to do the South justice and to not romanticize it. The most important point of this book, however, is not about the South per se, but about the places in which American (and by extension, all Western) Buddhists pursue religion. Every Buddhist sits, chants, or reads in a specific place and is impacted by that place in ways we may be able to discern, as well as others that escape us. Even the globetrotting Buddhist (as well as the scholar of Buddhism) is from somewhere and does most of her practice in a certain place. While the study of Western Buddhism must attend to national and transnational flows, it also must—I believe—pay sustained and sophisticated attention to the regional and the local, the sites where the butt meets the cushion, so to speak.

My motivations in writing this book arise from my desire to speak to several different audiences. First, to those involved in the study of Buddhism in the West, I think it behooves us to pay greater attention to regional phenomena, and especially to observe the stories that are unfolding in places where we have failed to cast our gaze, such as the South. What we have been calling "American Buddhism" may very well be mere regional phenomena, while Buddhism in other parts of America proceeds with somewhat different characteristics and experiences. We need to diversify our field studies in order to determine precisely what phenomena are truly national and what are actually local. This applies as well to Buddhism in other Western countries than the United States, of course. At the same time, greater attention to specific places will help put flesh on the bones of our studies of various trends in North American Buddhism, such as pluralism.

Second, to those who study American religious history, and especially to the southern historians, I think it will pay dividends to bring increased awareness to the phenomena of Asian religions. American religious historians have moved partially from a metanarrative of Protestantism and its discontents toward a more complex model based on multiplicity and contact, but as Thomas Tweed has recently observed, there is still considerable work to be done in this area.[18] And in the South in particular there has been little attention to Buddhism; indeed, there is resistance in some quarters to the study of southern religious diversity beyond black and white, as if to acknowledge it would mean that the South was no longer distinctive, thus obviating the very need for contemporary southern anthropology and sociology. In the historiography of American religion (especially in the South), regionalism and pluralism have often been conceptualized as enemies locked in a struggle: either America is a collection of discernibly different cultural and religious regions—diverse between regions but not within them—or it is a homogenous blur of national diversity, where everything is mixed up and nowhere is all that different from anywhere else. What is missing from such antagonistic narratives is the observation that pluralism, rather than being the antidote to regionalism, is yet another factor to explore in the production and maintenance of enduring regions. All regions are more diverse than they once were, but pluralism differs both in degree and in meaning among different parts of the country, and the experiences of those who contribute to the diversification of regions are by no means identical in, say, the Pacific Northwest and the South. Thus, I believe that proponents of research on the South will find that the addition of Buddhists to their narratives does not signal the death knell for their field but rather a new chapter in an ongoing regional story that changes and complexifies but nonetheless continues robustly on.

For the sake of immediate clarification, I should say that my use of the term "the South" in this book differs at different points, which I believe should be clear in context. Fundamentally, my presentation of the South encompasses the geographic territory of North Carolina, South Carolina, Georgia, Alabama, Florida, Mississippi, Louisiana, Texas, West Virginia, Tennessee, Kentucky, Missouri, Arkansas, Virginia, and Washington, DC. I group these fourteen states and the District of Columbia into the South because of a shared southern identity, history, and culture, while recognizing that there are other ways of drawing the lines around the South. They largely, but not completely, overlap with a second South that I refer to, which we might call "the Buddhist South," which is a region distinguished primarily through attention to local Buddhist phenomena. The most notable difference is that I exclude the Virginia suburbs of Washington, DC, and the District of Columbia itself from this South. The parameters of this South are explored in chapter 1, but I also complicate this category by breaking it into two subregions, the Coastal South and the Inner South.

While I use Richmond as my specific case study (since I have done almost a decade of work there), my thinking on Buddhism in the South is also informed by site visits to scores of other Buddhist sites, both in Virginia and other southern states. The South is anything but monolithic, and the same should be said about the Buddhism one finds there: even within just North Carolina, my work with temples in the mountains, the Piedmont, and on the coast revealed clear subregional distinctions to me (though the differences were small compared to the similarities). At the same time, if we offer *only* microstudies then we lose the ability to make larger arguments as scholars. In part, I use this large category of "the South" because my fieldwork has convinced me that while the South can be quite different for the average southerner living in one place or another, the variety of southern experiences for the average *Buddhist* fall into a number of patterns which are, I believe, substantially similar regardless of subregional location (when other factors that I discuss later, such as metropolitan size and proximity to kinship networks, are accounted for). And these common regional experiences differ in meaningful ways from the experiences of the average Buddhist in another region such as the West Coast, Midwest, or Northeast. In other words, the region is created in part by the experience of the group under study, and it does not merely exist in an uncomplicated manner "out there" on the landscape as a fully given entity.

Methods and Positions

Before proceeding, I should say more about my methods of investigation. Most important, I have relied on eighteen months of intensive participant-observer ethnographic fieldwork conducted at the temple from January 2003 to March 2004; June 2006; and May to June 2008. This fieldwork included more than one hundred site visits to services at the temple and was augmented by approximately a dozen other visits in 2002 and 2005. From 2003 to 2011 I conducted lengthy structured interviews with forty-two Ekoji participants (over half of the temple's membership) as well as additional interviews with key nonmembers in the wider community. Beyond the regular structured interviews, I interviewed a dozen lay leaders at the temple additional times over the course of nine years of research. I also analyzed data collected from a questionnaire about Ekoji members' religious practice and sectarian identification distributed in 2004; this questionnaire had a 92.5 percent response rate from the fifty-three members of the temple in 2004 (more information is provided in the appendix). To complement and contextualize my analysis, I consulted archival materials and printed sources related to Ekoji's history (including the temple's newsletter, the *Dharma Wheel*), and I drew on innumerable casual conversations with Ekoji participants at the temple, in local restaurants, cars, parks, museums, movie theaters, grocery stores, and at their homes.

My interpretations are primarily attempts to judiciously represent what I saw and heard during my field study. Portions of this material appeared in my 2004 M.A. thesis on Ekoji for the Department of Religious Studies at the University of North Carolina, but most of it is newer work that I have produced as I did further fieldwork and my thinking changed over the last several years, and even the overlapping material has evolved since I have received further feedback from informants and they have amended or modified their discussions with me. During the summer of 2004 I received a grant from the Pluralism Project to study the other Buddhist groups in Richmond. I visited each of them multiple times during this period or in later follow-up trips, talking with clergy and laity and participating in practice sessions whenever possible. The regularity of my visits to Ekoji and the other temples of Richmond was sometimes impacted by outside developments, such as three months of unrelated dissertation fieldwork in Japan during 2006; during such periods and up until this manuscript was produced in 2011 I was nonetheless in regular e-mail and phone contact with Ekoji members and received electronic bulletins and discussions from several of the groups, as well as general temple news, providing me ongoing connections to the evolution of the temple. Finally, my thoughts on regionalism and American Buddhism are augmented by observations and research at many hundreds of Buddhist temples in various parts of the country starting in the 1990s, especially but not only my investigation of Buddhism in other parts of the South, in the Northeast, the West Coast, and Hawaii.

My initial ethnographic training took place in the Folklore program of the Department of American Studies at UNC, and it strongly emphasized the reciprocal relationship between the researcher and his informants. Thus

I did not hide my interests or interpretations from the people I studied. Rather, I discussed my findings at each stage with many of them, and sometimes shared chapters or vignettes from my work with interested informants who provided me with feedback. I also donated copies of my M.A. thesis to the temple and encouraged the members to read it and tell me what I got wrong. When possible, I gave them transcripts of our interviews and allowed them to modify them to be sure their meaning was clearly expressed. At times, they steered me away from interpretations that were misguided or difficult to defend; at other times I stuck to my guns on interpretations that they as insiders were uncertain of, but which I as an observer felt were accurate reflections of the larger picture. Whether I accepted their feedback or not, I appreciated all of their contributions, and I hope that those of them who choose to read this book find it to be a fair interpretation of their religious views and activities. Of course, ultimately I am responsible for all of the material presented here, especially any mistakes. In order to maintain my informants' confidentiality in their small religious community (and in Richmond, where many are not public about their Buddhist practice), I have employed pseudonyms throughout this book, except in the few cases of truly public Buddhist figures, such as the teachers Takashi Kenryu Tsuji, Josho Pat Phelan, Lama Norhla, and Taigen Dan Leighton.

Historian Donald Mathews once rightly observed that "the writing of southern history has often become in itself a religious expression of the author and a moral Rorschach for the reader."[19] Quite so, but such has not been my intention here. Nonetheless, while I have attempted to the best of my ability to approach my subject as a disinterested scholar examining a particular historical phenomenon, it is incumbent on me to discuss positionality. Like my "informants," I am a Buddhist, although that is not the only religious label I wear, and the particular sect which I affiliate with is not currently represented at Ekoji. From the beginning of my research I identified myself to everyone at Ekoji as both a researcher and a practitioner. This gave me entrance into the interior life of the temple, as I meditated, chanted, bowed, discussed, and offered incense with the other participants. Although I was often accompanied by a notepad, tape recorder, camera, tripod, or video recorder, and I remained alert to capture any information that might help me better understand the temple as I encountered it, it would be incorrect to think of me as an unimportant and uncomplicated outside observer. My presence as a researcher and a practitioner *both* altered the situation in discernable ways — and surely in unrecognized ways as well. As I sat in on discussions and queried the participants, discussions sometimes turned away from the book or topic of the day to questions of identity, differentiation, and the use of the temple facilities. And as a fellow Buddhist I was frequently called on to share my opinions or experiences; eventually, I was even asked to occasionally assist services at some of the meetings, a conflicted intersection of practice and research that I discuss later in this book when it becomes especially relevant. While I was still struggling to find the line between participant and observer, many of my consultants had already erased the dividing line and taken me into the heart of the temple as one of their own. For a new ethnographer, this lack of boundaries was at times terrifying. And yet it was directly from these boundary-breaking experiences that many of my most important insights ultimately derived, as some of my conclusions will suggest.

Thus, my complicated position is something to remember throughout the tale I narrate here. When I note numbers of participants at specific events or the average attendance of various groups, I do not include myself, in part because the relatively small numbers at Ekoji are easily distorted when an additional body is added to the mix. And, outside of this introduction, I have not taken pains to call attention in the text to my presence, as I was most often a silent participant listening as others discussed their interests and concerns. Nevertheless, I was always a factor, whether minor or significant, in how each activity proceeded—researchers and observers *always* alter their environment in some manner, and no ethnographer should fail to take notice of this fact. There may have been information withheld because of my status as a researcher, or stories given a certain spin because my consultants knew my interests and background. It would be foolish for me to assume that my gender (male), race (white), relatively young age (I was twenty-six the first time I visited Ekoji), and other characteristics never influenced my informants at Ekoji, or that—despite my best attempts at objectivity and dispassionate analysis—these and other factors have not been operative in my interpretations and presentations of my research. In the end, the experiences recounted herein remain only a partial view, sighted from a single cushion, of the richness that is Ekoji.

Geographical diversity is the hallmark of religion in the United States.
—Mark Silk and Andrew Walsh, *One Nation, Divisible,* 2008

Chapter One

BRINGING A REGIONAL PERSPECTIVE
TO AMERICAN BUDDHISM

Before proceeding to a discussion of Buddhism in the South—primarily taken up in the later chapters of this book—it is necessary to lay the groundwork for a regional approach to the subject of American Buddhism. Fortunately, there is a long and fruitful history of regional analysis in the study of American religious history. But why has Buddhism not been a part of this analysis?

American Buddhist Historiography: The Lack of a Regional Awareness

American religious history is in some senses inherently a regional project: it looks at religious phenomena within a certain geographic and national area: the United States of America. As long as people have been describing the religious history of the New World, they have noted the importance of place, and furthermore, they have often singled out specific places for investigation. Perhaps the first true work in this area was Cotton Mather's 1702 tome *Magnalia Christi Americana, or, The Ecclesiastical History of New-England.*[1] Nearly a century and a half later, regionalism as an interpretive motif was still considered relevant, as seen in Robert Baird's 1844 *Religion in America.* Published just before the entrance of Buddhism onto the American scene, Baird's examination paid attention to the major geographic areas of America, to the ethnic and religious origins of the settlers of various places, and noted distribution patterns for an already diverse America's different denominations.[2] And when American religious history began to coalesce as an academic field in the early twentieth century, regionalism was a major analytical key, whether it was the contrasts between North and South or East and West, or the influence of Frederick Turner's frontier thesis and the development of new forms of American Christianity.[3] A perusal of current introductory textbooks on American religious history quickly reveals that regionalism remains an ongoing strategy for discussing the historical interaction between various religious groups and the wider culture.[4]

And yet, regionalism is an interpretative approach that has been applied haphazardly, with many religious traditions and issues never receiving adequate regional attention. Regionalism has never been applied robustly to my own primary field of research: Buddhism in North America, especially the United States. American Buddhism has been an occasional object of scholarly study since the mid-twentieth century, began to produce important foundational works in the 1970s, and since the late 1990s has emerged as an increasingly coherent subfield. It has developed various topics of intense academic discussion, such as the contrasts and continuities between Asian and American Buddhisms, the number of Buddhists in the United States, how to determine whether one is or is not Buddhist, Buddhist contributions to the wider American culture, and issues of race and ethnicity. Yet in 2012 we find that major forms of interpretation such as regionalism from one primary related discipline — American religious history — remain nonetheless widely neglected. Among the implications of this inattention to regional phenomena is the possibility that we may know less about "American Buddhism" than we think we do — we may, rather, know mainly about West Coast, Northeastern, or Midwestern Buddhism, not American Buddhism per se.

Among the various important studies that have appeared in the past fifteen years, nearly all have been based on work in a few restricted areas that are nonetheless held up as representative of American Buddhism on a national scale. In American Buddhist studies, California, the urban Midwest, and the Northeast are somehow transformed into the entirety of the United States. Consider our major book-length ethnographies. The first of these was Paul Numrich's 1996 *Old Wisdom in the New World: Americanization in Two Immigrant Theravada Buddhist Temples*. Numrich's pioneering study was carried out at sites in Chicago and Los Angeles.[5] In 2001 Eve Mullen published *The American Occupation of Tibetan Buddhism: Tibetans and Their American Hosts in New York City.*[6] In 2004 Wendy Cadge's excellent *Heartwood: The First Generation of Theravada Buddhism in America* and Sharon Suh's *Being Buddhist in a Christian World: Gender and Community in a Korean American Temple* appeared. Cadge's work was done in Boston and Philadelphia; Suh's ethnography was carried out in Los Angeles.[7] More recently, Carolyn Chen looked at both Buddhists and Christians in *Getting Saved in America: Taiwanese Immigration and Religious Experience.* Released in 2008, it looks at Taiwanese immigrants in the San Gabriel Valley just outside of Los Angeles.[8]

We can also see similarly restricted patterns in more general interpretive works, such as James Coleman's *The New Buddhism: The Western Transformation of an Ancient Tradition* (2001), whose argument about an emergent convert-based, pansectarian neo-Buddhism homegrown in America has been widely influential, if also often criticized. The seven sites for Coleman's fieldwork were four California centers (three of them in the San Francisco Bay Area); one in Boston; one in Rochester, New York; and one in Boulder, Colorado.[9] The large majority of other studies, such as journal articles, book chapters, or M.A. theses and Ph.D. dissertations replicate these trends — indeed, California alone accounts for a significant proportion of all the study sites examined to this point. Time and again, the lion's share of work on American Buddhism is done in a few specific locations, but is then extrapolated to somehow represent phenomena at the national ("American Buddhism") or even international ("Buddhism in the West") level. Meanwhile, relatively little attention is paid to how the specifics of the local environment impact the particular sites under study, or how these Buddhist temples affect the differing regions in which they find themselves.

Descriptions of Buddhism in America rarely convey in-depth presentations of Buddhism's differing manifestations in various parts of the country. Most often, American Buddhism is depicted as a broad continental movement, diverse in terms of groups but with little indication that there might be more Vipassana meditators in Boston than in Phoenix, or more Chan Buddhists in Houston than in Chicago, and no consideration of the differing experiences of Buddhists in these separate places. This was true of initial works in the field, such as Emma Layman's *Buddhism in America* (1976) and Charles Prebish's *American Buddhism* (1979), and perhaps is to be expected of early descriptive works.[10] But it remains just as true for later texts, including Prebish's *Luminous Passage: The Practice and Study of Buddhism in America* (1999) and Richard Seager's *Buddhism in America* (1999), which even includes a chapter titled "The American Buddhist Landscape" succinctly describing elements within American Buddhism without addressing the issue of regional differences.[11] Nor does attention to region appear in the major edited anthologies that have helped drive the subdiscipline, such as Prebish and Kenneth Tanaka's *The Faces of Buddhism in America* (1998), Duncan Williams and Christopher Queen's *American Buddhism: Methods and Findings in Recent Scholarship* (1999), Queen's *Engaged Buddhism in the West* (2000), Prebish and Martin Baumann's *Westward Dharma: Buddhism beyond Asia* (2002), and Numrich's *North American Buddhists in Social Context* (2008).[12] Usually, all the reader can hope for is that an author may gesture toward Buddhism as an especially West Coast (sometimes subtly coded as "hippie") or Northeast (occasionally implying "intellectual") phenomenon, without analyzing the specifics of which Buddhisms exist on the West Coast versus the Northeast versus any other region of the country, and what these differences might mean. And the South in particular remains a huge blind spot for commentators on American Buddhist phenomena. No major studies focused on Buddhism have ever been conducted in the southern states.

Ironically, the partial exception to this typical pattern of neglect is found among historians of general American religion who do not focus on Buddhism specifically. Well familiar with the regionalism trope, they sometimes make a small-scale attempt to indicate that Buddhism is in some ways a regional religion. For example, Laurie Maffly-Kipp, in "Eastward Ho! American Religion from the Perspective of the Pacific Rim," in Thomas Tweed's revisionist anthology *Retelling U.S. Religious History* (1997), uses Buddhism's West Coast origins to argue her regional thesis that Buddhism has often spread from West to East, reversing the usual directionality assumed in American religious narratives.[13] Edwin Gaustad and Philip Barlow, in their fabulous county-by-county *New Historical Atlas of American Religion* (2000), display a similar Western focus for Buddhism, though their data from circa 1990 is unfortunately now quite outdated for analyzing American Buddhism, which has spread and diversified considerably in the intervening two decades. Bret Carroll, in his more classroom-oriented *Routledge Historical Atlas of Religion in America* (2000), demonstrates the largely Western nature of the Buddhist Churches of America (BCA; also alluded to by Maffly-Kipp, this is one of the few groups to receive extended coverage by Gaustad and Barlow).[14]

Among a great many options for including Buddhist examples, the BCA is repeatedly singled out for attention by scholars because it is organized into discrete temples operating on a congregational model, saddled with the comfortable "church" label, and has a central authority that is easily queried for statistics. All of this makes it a convenient and seemingly familiar organization to work with for scholars more used to discussing American Christian history. That this particular organization is the one that is almost invariably gestured toward by the nonspecialists perhaps illustrates the scant level of penetration of research on American Buddhism into the field of American religious studies more generally. And unfortunately this inclusion of a single Buddhist group in surveys of American religious regionalism almost hurts as much as it helps, for while it opens the important question of American Buddhist regionalism, it shuts it as well by allowing one institution to stand in for the hundreds of Buddhist lineages operating in the United States. Worse yet, it merely confirms an unvoiced suspicion, that Buddhism is a California thing, obscuring the possibility of southern, northwestern, or other significant Buddhist regional phenomena.[15]

Why has American Buddhist regionalism been overlooked? It is hard to know for sure, but a few conjectures can be offered. First, the scholars who work on American Buddhism, especially those who do ethnographically based research, have tended to be housed at universities in those few northern and western areas already identified. There are exceptions of course, such as Thomas Tweed, who has spent his entire teaching career in various southern locations, but on the whole this generalization holds true.[16] If scholars working in the field are mainly only exposed to a few selected parts of the country, naturally they may be less likely to develop theories about how Buddhism differs in other areas. Second, a significant number of the scholars who have worked on American Buddhism have come to it originally from Asian or Buddhist studies, and thus while they bring to bear impressively sophisticated approaches from those disciplines, they have a relatively lower exposure to modes of interpretation developed in American religious history as a specific discipline. Third, researchers understandably look for large groups, and in earlier periods the West Coast and Northeast did indeed have some of the largest Buddhist communities. Fourth, scholars who focus on American religious regions have typically overlooked Buddhism as a potential object of study. This is most noticeable in the case of the South, which boasts the most robust regional focus of any American area—no significant works have been produced looking specifically at Buddhist phenomena in the South, perhaps because, despite its growing presence, Buddhism does not fit the traditional narratives of the subdiscipline, which focus on evangelical culture, interregional rivalries, and the legacy of slavery, Civil War, and segregation.[17] And fifth, there has been a tendency to look for some sort of uniquely American form of Buddhism as necessary for the justification of the subfield in the first place. Scholars working in this area are often marginalized by both more traditional Buddhologists (who focus on Asia, and are often textually rather than ethnographically oriented) and Americanists (who focus on Christianity, and are often concerned with earlier, comparatively less religiously and ethnically diverse historical periods). In reaction, researchers who combine the two fields have tried to weave a narrative about the exceptionalism of American Buddhism and thus the legitimacy of it as an object of interest. This defensive maneuver makes it more important to assert a national set of characteristics to carve out a significant new plot of academic ground rather than to argue in the opposite direction against the idea that there is indeed some general thing that can be called American Buddhism. Breaking America down into regional units could be threatening to the whole project of American Buddhist studies in the first place.

But I think the time has come to recover regionalism and apply it in a more systematic and sophisticated way to the various Buddhist phenomena of the United States. Regionalism can serve both creative and critical functions in our studies. For example, it can generate new avenues of research that expand our understanding of the issues that have already been identified within the subfield. One of these common topics is how Americans seek to explicitly Americanize Buddhism, so that it loses aspects of its Asian heritage (often described negatively as trappings or baggage) and is adapted in new forms to a specifically American cultural environment. Attention to regionalism might lead us to inquire whether this process takes different forms in different parts of America. After all, no one really lives in "America" as a whole—we live in Oakland, California; Salt Lake City, Utah; Denver, Colorado; San Antonio, Texas; Kansas City, Missouri; Rockford, Illinois; Waynesville, North Carolina; New Britain, Connecticut; or elsewhere. America looks different to the people who live in these separate places, and while they share much, they have particular regional understandings of what America is and what it means to be American—and often people in these specific places are more concerned with local issues and problems than with developments on a fully national or global scale. All of these places also have Buddhist communities, and surely these regional self-understandings and concerns will have some impact on how they pursue the holy grail of Americanized Buddhism.

Just as one example, consider the Cambodian American monk who is the leader of a Theravada Buddhist temple in Mechanicsville, Virginia. A

Monk and main altar at a Cambodian temple in the Richmond suburbs, with September 11 subaltar and sign supporting George W. Bush.

member of a racial and religious minority in a relatively conservative and nondiverse area, he has helped his temple to Americanize by taking on aspects of the local civil religion that memorializes the September 11 attacks, proclaims a unique destiny for the United States, sanctifies the country's leaders, and justifies the use of military aggression in the name of American values. Thus the worship space of the temple includes a prominent sign declaring support for the president; below that is an altar dedicated to the memories of the September 11 victims (complete with an image of the burning twin towers), and to the side is an American flag. This is a vision of America as chosen nation united in righteous action, a common conceptualization in the surrounding religious and secular culture of Virginia. Such domestications of Buddhism, I argue, are sometimes linked to the specifics of where various Buddhists are practicing.[18]

At the same time, discerning what is regional and what is shared throughout the United States will help to reveal what is truly "American" about American Buddhism. For example, we find many Buddhist groups in the South that are highly interested in silent, seated meditation practices. This matches observed trends from studies carried out in other parts of the country, and it confirms that one type of countrywide American Buddhism is meditation-oriented practice, dominated by people first exposed to Buddhism as adults who are primarily white, tend toward the middle and upper middle class, and mostly live in cities and suburbs.

Regionalism in American Religious Historiography

Before applying regionalism as an interpretation to American Buddhism, it is necessary to look at how regionalism has been applied in American religious and cultural studies more broadly. What criteria have researchers used in their various approaches? The classic work in this area is Wilbur Zelinsky's "An Approach to the Religious Geography of the United States," in *Annals of the Association of American Geographers* (1961). Zelinsky used census data on church membership to plot out the relative concentrations of various denominations on the American map (Catholics and Jews were each treated as single categories, while Protestants were broken into twenty different categories). He then combined this data to create a map of seven "major religious regions," with five subregional areas: New England, Midland, Upper Middle Western, Southern, Spanish Catholic, Mormon, and Western. Alaska and Hawaii were not included. For Zelinsky, immigration, migration, and missionary patterns accounted for the regions, but on the whole he was much more interested in the "what" of American religious regions than in the "why."[19] This early map has proven to have considerable staying power—nearly forty years later Carroll used it for his atlas of religion in America.[20]

Another major study was Raymond Gastil's *Cultural Regions of the United States* (1975). In looking at religion specifically, Gastil retained Zelinsky's general map but further divided the West into Southern California, Central California, and Pacific Northwest. But Gastil's analysis went well beyond religion to also consider politics, architecture and housing patterns, language, crime, education, and other factors. He thus breaks the country into thirteen different cultural regions: New England, the New York Metropolitan Region, the Pennsylvanian Region, the South (inclusive of three subregions: Lowland, Upland Mountain, and Western), the Upper Midwest, the Central Midwest, the Rocky Mountain Region, the Mormon Region, the Interior Southwest, the Pacific Southwest, the Pacific Northwest, Alaska, and the Hawaiian Islands.[21] Another book that looked beyond religion was Joel Garreau's *The Nine Nations of North America* (1981), which also looked beyond national boundaries to include Canada, Mexico, the Caribbean, and even (despite the book's title) parts of South America.

Garreau considers religion, economics, language, politics, climate, topography, and other factors in drawing his borders, but there is also a certain amount of "gut feeling" to his project. The nine regions he discerns are New England, the Foundry, Dixie, the Islands, Mexamerica, Ecotopia, the Empty Quarter, the Breadbasket, and Quebec. Alaska is part of the Empty Quarter in Garreau's vision, but Hawaii is simply lumped into a catchall category called "Aberrations."[22]

Sometimes researchers are eager to look at religious variation on the American map but reluctant to define actual regions. This is the approach taken by James Shortridge in his studies in the mid-1970s. Using information on ratios between Catholics versus non-Catholics, liberal Protestants versus conservative Protestants, church members versus total population, and local dominance by particular religious groups, Shortridge produced maps showing the varying concentrations of these ratios. However, he did not attempt to produce a master map that combined all of these maps into a basic national differentiation of particular regions, and he did not even hazard to provide standard names for the regions at which his research gestured. Nonetheless, some interesting findings arise from his approach—for instance, he is the only researcher to dismiss New England as a useful and clearly defined area in American religion.[23]

A more recent study focused on American religion specifically is the Religion by Region project helmed by Mark Silk of the Leonard E. Greenberg Center for the Study of Religion in Public Life. Between 2004 and 2008 Silk cowrote or coedited nine books on American religious regionalism. The seven regions his project identified are New England, the Midwest, the Pacific Northwest (including Alaska), the Pacific Region (including Hawaii), the South, the Southern Crossroads, and the Middle Atlantic Region.[24] Silk and his fellows carve up their regions based on denominational demographics, variations in the unchurched population and those claiming to have no religion, distinctive regional relations between religion and public culture, and spiritual styles, such as a more mix-and-match approach attributed to the Pacific Region.

Among these various studies, different approaches have also been taken in how the borders of regions are determined within American religion. Zelinsky, Gastil, and Garreau tend to ignore state borders, drawing regions that to varying degrees flout state lines (Gastil is most ambitious in this respect). Silk does cluster states into his regions, using their political borders to define regional edges. Shortridge, meanwhile, uses counties rather than states as his basic measurement. Gaustad and Barlow and Carroll are more concerned with showing the various ways the map can be drawn than with defining regions — thus Gaustad and Barlow also focus on county-by-county statistics, while Carroll uses state borders when assessing numbers and ignores them when displaying religious migration and similar developments.

Using Regionalism to Investigate American Buddhism

If we are now going to carry out our studies of American Buddhism with expanded attention to region, what are the approaches that we should take to the subject? I suggest five specific modes of investigation that will help us produce a more nuanced understanding of the Buddhist regions of the United States: (1) regional distribution patterns within American Buddhism, (2) impact of regions on Buddhism, (3) Buddhist impact on regions, (4) regional differences within the same Buddhist lineage, and (5) difference between built environments. These by no means exhaust the possible approaches to American Buddhist regionalism, but given the very preliminary nature of such studies at this point, I believe these five areas of interpretation will provide fruitful projects that can begin to lay the foundation for yet other and more sophisticated projects to come.

The natural place to start is with distribution patterns for various Buddhist groups and phenomena within the United States: essentially, we need to produce maps of Buddhist regions within America. That is, we need to look at what groups are represented in different areas in varying concentrations, and why this is so. Scholars of American Christianity know that Mormons cluster in the West and that Unitarian Universalists are most easily found in the Northeast. What about Rinzai Zen Buddhists? Or Cambodian American Theravadins? Or romantic-type Buddhist converts? And why are they represented in these areas and not others? For minority religions such as Buddhism, concentration differences in separate places may cause the entire Buddhism of the region to take on a different character. Studies of American Buddhism have always been hampered by the inability to obtain accurate figures about the number of Buddhists in the country. But if the national numbers have proven elusive, perhaps a series of more regional studies will make it possible to produce a more accurate and exhaustive catalog of the numbers and affiliations of American Buddhists.

We need to know not only what groups are located in which areas and why but also why they do not appear in other areas. This form of interpretation can be applied in an almost infinite number of ways, but several immediately suggest themselves. First, we can pay greater attention to the distribution patterns of particular Buddhist ethnic groups. For example, Kalmykian American Buddhists have mainly been found in the narrow corridor between New York City and Washington, DC. This area of early immigration by ethnically Mongolian Kalmyks, dating back to the era following World War II, resulted in the founding of the country's first Tibetan-type Vajrayana Buddhist temple, the Lamaist Buddhist Monastery of America in Howell County, New Jersey.[25] Taiwanese American Buddhists, by contrast, are far more widely distributed throughout the United States, but their single greatest concentration is in the San Gabriel Valley outside Los Angeles. Compared to the Kalmyks, they entered the United States in much larger numbers, with a greater degree of technical and educational expertise, and largely during the period after immigration reform and rising racial tolerance of the 1960s.[26] And, while the Kalmyks came from the eastern reaches of Europe and settled on the American East Coast, the Taiwanese arrived from Asia to the West Coast.

Additionally, we can look at different traditions, denominations, or types of Buddhism. Zen is strongest in the West, but it is noticeably underrepresented on the Plains and (especially when compared to population size and density) in the South.[27] Meanwhile the institutional presence of the peace-activist Nipponzan Myohoji sect of Nichiren Buddhism is mostly eastern, with the largest single concentration in the Southeast.[28] The intermontane West has a relatively high concentration of Tibetan practitioners, but it is one of the only major regions with no Nichiren Shoshu institutional presence.[29] We can break these denominational assessments down into further attention to specific lineages, examining for example where the influential Maezumi lineage of Soto Zen flourishes versus where the Rinzai-influenced lineage of Philip Kapleau plays the predominant local role. And we can combine the two categories of ethnicity or race and tradition or denomination, looking to see if there are particular regional clusters of white Soka Gakkai chanters or African American Gelugpas.

A second approach to use in regional studies of American Buddhism is to examine how different American regions affect the Buddhisms found within them. Buddhism not only differs in concentration and diversity of sectarian affiliation between, for example, the West Coast and the South, but the *experience* of Buddhists also is different in these separate regions, and therefore the practice and philosophy of Buddhists may tend to diverge in these separate places as well. We may object that regional subcultures are not as strong as they once were in the United States. After all, the effects

of interstate highways, easy air travel, ubiquitous television, major advertising campaigns, national commercial franchises and chain stores, economic forces pushing migration, and—perhaps especially—the Internet
have combined to erode some of the regional American subcultures that
existed in earlier periods. True enough, but that also suggests that our historical studies of American Buddhism (which has a presence in the United
States of over 150 years) should pay attention to different regions that may
have been stronger factors in previous eras. And I argue that while modern
transportation, communication, and economic realities have contributed
to greater overall homogenization of American culture, there is still considerable variation that persists between separate parts of the country. Person A in Los Angeles and Person B in Richmond, Virginia, can both shop at
Walmart, watch CBS, use Wikipedia, and travel to visit each other with relative ease, but anyone who has lived in both places can tell you that they are
decidedly *not* the same. Perhaps more important, many of the Buddhists I
have spoken to in both places perceived regional differences between these
two locations. This felt difference, perhaps even more than any actual measurable one, impacts the experience of Buddhism in each place.

We can look to a number of factors in our analyses of regional impacts
on Buddhism. One is climate and terrain. Theravada monks in the northern
states cannot go about with bare feet and head, one shoulder uncovered,
and just the traditional thin robes as they often might in Southeast Asia.
They must develop new costumes that enact creative new interpretations
of the Vinaya (monastic code) in order to survive in these areas, such as
admitting the use of sweaters, hats, and socks dyed to match the acceptable
colors of Buddhist robes now in use at Wat Dhammaran in Chicago.[30] This
is a process of adaptation that monks in Florida do not have to undergo.
When Tibetan Buddhist practitioners sought to erect a massive stupa to
honor their late leader Chögyam Trungpa, they had to take the harsh winter conditions and high altitude of northern Colorado into account. The resulting project—the 108-foot-tall Great Stupa of Dharmakaya—took over
a dozen years to complete and was designed to last on the landscape for
one thousand years.[31] This contrasts with the first stupa built in America,
which enshrines relics of Shakyamuni Buddha and his two major disciples.
The designers who constructed it in 1937 atop the Buddhist Church of San
Francisco had a much milder climate to contend with, but they did have to
keep the possibility of earthquake damage in mind.[32]

We can also look to economics among different areas and how they impact Buddhists: West Coast housing prices and costs of living put a high

burden on newer religious groups, affecting their choices of what sort of practice centers to build, how to construct them, and where to locate them; these considerations especially affect groups in the urban areas where many Buddhists tend to congregate. Another factor is professional opportunities. Buddhist immigration over the past few decades has included significant percentages of white-collar professionals, many of them active in the computer and tech industries. They tend to be drawn to regions where such jobs are concentrated—for example, Silicon Valley in California has attracted Buddhist immigrants able to work in the high-tech computer and communications fields, and these highly educated, highly paid, and often highly stressed Buddhists have supported local temples and meditation groups. A noteworthy further observation is that many Asian immigrants arrive as only nominal Buddhists or are not affiliated with any religion at all, and in these situations of high work pressure and cultural displacement they discover Buddhism as a resource for managing their identities, stress levels, and sense of meaning. Thus Silicon Valley not only imports Buddhists but also produces them.

And of course regional culture cannot be ignored. There is a perception that the South is more conservative, traditional, Christian, and, frankly, prejudiced, than many other parts of the country. While this can very easily be overstated, these perceptions are not completely groundless, and even if they were, the stereotype itself has clear effect. My research suggests that southern culture (including the dominant religion) makes it harder to be a religious minority, decreases the chances of attracting resident teachers to new meditation groups, and puts significantly more pressure on locals enmeshed in conservative family and social networks not to convert to Buddhism (I will have more to say about this in chapter 5). Religious discussion is part of the everyday public culture of the South in a way that it decidedly is *not* part of New England or West Coast culture. But Buddhists are much less likely to be forthcoming about their own religious practices and beliefs in the South than they are in these other regions, especially in work and family situations.

Thus we can combine these various factors to describe general differences between separate parts of the country: Buddhists today on the West Coast (for example, in San Francisco) have access to large numbers of other Buddhists, a wide range of choices of Buddhist denominations, a moderate climate, a relatively liberal and tolerant surrounding atmosphere, a long history of absorption of Asian culture, a high cost of property values to deal with, and other particular local forces to account for. Buddhists in the

Monk at a Laotian temple in Charlotte; lunch offerings from the laity include rice, tropical fruits, and a soda from Hardee's (a regional fast-food chain founded in North Carolina and still based in the South).

South (such as in Charlotte), meanwhile, practice in a region with far fewer Buddhist adherents, more constricted sectarian choices, a relatively more conservative and exclusively Christian dominant public culture, sweltering temperatures, lower historic Asian immigration, lower cost of living, and other circumstances. These regional differences will have specific impacts on the Buddhist groups and individuals that seek to dwell in these separate regions, and these Buddhists need to resort to different types of adapting practices as they navigate their local cultural terrain. And surely there are yet finer, more detailed subregional distinctions within these sorts of regional American Buddhisms that can be profitably mined. Places like "the South" are so large and contain such a diversity of local subcultures and economic situations that we may well be able to discern differences within these broad regions that affect Buddhism in alternate ways.

Beyond distribution patterns and regional influences, a third potential area for study is how Buddhists themselves are affecting the different regions in which they are found. The documentary film *Blue Collar and Buddha* (1987) depicts how the influx of Laotian Theravada Buddhists into Rockford, Illinois, altered the region. In this previously binary black-white area, local attitudes had to be recalibrated to deal with a new tripartite racial reality (Vietnam War veterans and underemployed people concerned about the new competition for jobs seem to have an especially difficult adjustment), and the sudden appearance of Buddhism for the first time as a significant force in the previously Christian community also had to be grappled with. Christians found that they had to decide how to treat their new neighbors, and fault lines emerged between those who wanted to evangelize the Buddhists, those who wanted to help them retain their Buddhist religion in order to mitigate the strain of exile, those who were curious about exploring Buddhism, and those who wanted to exclude the Buddhists from their neighborhoods.[33] Thus not only do Buddhists change when they enter a new region, but also the region's other religions are altered by the introduction of Buddhists. The growth of Buddhism in New York City has led to an expanded concept of ecumenicism in local interfaith organizations that have had to adjust to religious dialogue beyond the classic triumvirate of Protestant-Catholic-and-Jew to include the nontheistic Buddhists as well. This takes place in part because the Buddhists have created pansectarian organizations like the Buddhist Council of New York that then seek to represent their interests to their religious neighbors and the wider urban community. Region-specific sites become places of contact and pressure by the Buddhists for greater inclusion, such as the regular Buddhist participation in annual 9/11 memorial observances at Ground Zero in lower Manhattan.[34]

The fourth aspect of regionalism that I believe merits study is differences within specific Buddhist denominations or lineages themselves. I think this is one of the most potentially interesting and productive avenues for research. Currently, we act like Shambhala Buddhism is entirely the same in Vermont as it is in Colorado, two places that not only are different in region but also have separate institutional histories and are staffed by different practitioners and leaders. Is Suzuki Zen the same in San Francisco as it is in Richmond, Virginia? I doubt it. In the San Francisco Bay area there are many practitioners and centers in this lineage, and people interested in pursuing a formal meditation practice can easily locate instructors. In the Southeast, on the other hand, this lineage is far less represented, and indeed Zen on the whole does not have a strong presence in the South, with the groups that do exist tending toward smaller membership and more modest facilities. Due to the lack of local ordained leadership, southern practitioners who identify with the Suzuki lineage are less likely to stress the need for close study with a trained meditation master, emphasizing instead more of a private, individualistic approach to Zen. They are also more likely to display eclecticism in their understanding of Zen, as they often have to rely on whatever books and resources from various lineages they can get hold of, rather than working directly with and mirroring the approach of sanctioned teachers of this San Francisco Zen Center–based movement.[35] People in San Francisco and in Virginia may be part of the same network, but we deceive ourselves if we imagine networks merely as Indra's Nets, the ancient Buddhist metaphor for the cosmos wherein every jewel in a gigantic web made of gemstones equally reflects every other jewel. Where you are specifically placed in a real world network matters. It is one thing to practice at the mother temple, and another thing to practice at the end of a far-flung network.

A fifth and final major area for regional analysis moves away from looking at separate swathes of the country and considers instead differences as ingrained within varying types of built environments. Here the "regions" being imagined and investigated are not contiguous geographic locations laid out horizontally on a flat map of the nation; instead we might think of them as different layers in a three-dimensional map where the topography is determined not by landform but by population density and urbanization.

Buddhism in Asia can be found in all areas and historically has often been a rural phenomenon. In contrast, Buddhism in America can be found in many environments but is especially an urban phenomenon. It is large metropolitan areas that attract the majority of Asian Buddhist immigrants: large cities more often offer job prospects, opportunities for air travel back to their countries of origin, a critical mass of others from their home countries, and a diverse and relatively cosmopolitan atmosphere that allows minority ethnic and religious groups to find a niche. Furthermore, cities function as important engines for the growth of Buddhism through conversion—the presence of Asian immigrants, established international transportation routes, libraries and museums with Buddhist artifacts and texts, and the cosmopolitan atmosphere of exploration and tolerance all contribute to the healthy growth of Buddhism among various American racial and ethnic groups, including Asian Americans with weak or no personal ancestral connection to Buddhism. And of course there is the common phenomenon of younger persons moving to "the big city" specifically to explore new and allegedly exotic ways of living. Given the relative ease of finding Buddhists in America's major population centers, perhaps it is no surprise that American Buddhist ethnographies almost invariably take place in large cities, whether in the West or East.

But we need to be careful about allowing a handful of the largest metropolitan areas in North America to stand in for the totality of the Buddhist experience. Different forces operate on Buddhists in small cities as opposed to large ones. Both are urban environments with high population density, relatively less green space, and other aspects of city life, but smaller cities may not have the same ethnic diversity as larger ones or may offer less anonymity for newer religious groups anxious not to make waves with their non-Buddhist neighbors. There is a generally observable trend that the larger the city, the greater the variety of Buddhist options available to the seeker—thus big cities offer the opportunity to find just the right "fit," while Buddhists in smaller cities may need to network with one another for support and sufficient critical mass to hold certain events.

We also need projects that examine American urban Buddhism versus American suburban Buddhism (as well as their interactions). American suburbs tend to be middle-class bastions, and some foster relative racial and ethnic homogeneity, qualities that may prove more fertile missionary grounds for different types of Buddhism. For example, Thich Nhat Hanh's Community of Mindful Living has more than three hundred affiliated practice groups in the United States, with locations in every type of area from megalopolis to sparsely inhabited countryside. But a look at precisely where each group meets for its regular meditation sessions suggests that a high percentage of such groups are in fact solidly suburban and tend to draw their ranks from suburbanites. Many of these groups have been founded by individuals who first encountered Thich Nhat Hanh not through a direct teacher-student relationship but through finding one of his many books at a suburban chain bookstore such as Barnes and Noble, and subsequently deciding to start a small local meditation group in his lineage out of their own homes or perhaps in nearby liberal church spaces.[36] This may be a general trend for at least a certain type of suburban American Buddhism: that it spreads especially through individual contacts with print and virtual networks rather than immigration patterns or active missions planted in urban areas by leaders sent out from headquarters to establish Buddhist groups.

Together, I think these five areas offer useful ways to begin theorizing and researching American Buddhist regionalism. Of course, beyond the identification of different types of regionalism, there is the necessity to account for the production of these regions. I have hinted at some specific factors, but let me take a moment to look at this more systematically. As I have already noted, the most obvious influence is differing immigration patterns to the United States and internal migration patterns among more established Buddhist populations. There are more Vietnamese along the

Gulf Coast than in the landlocked western states; more Japanese on the Pacific coast than on the Atlantic; more Thai in the South than the North. Thus the Buddhisms that these groups practice show definite regional patterns of distribution, and, conversely, there are regions whose local Buddhism totally lacks groups or trends common in other places.

We can further analyze the reasons behind these various immigration patterns. One is basic chance: a family from Cambodia moves to an area and soon many others follow simply because they know there are Cambodians there. Or perhaps a church or other organization sponsors refugees from an Asian Buddhist nation, resulting in the accumulation of immigrants from that area. A second reason is proximity to the Old World: the Chinese played a major role in nineteenth-century western American life because they arrived via transpacific ships, disembarking on the Pacific Coast and finding eastward dissemination slow due to difficult travel conditions and dangerous racism. Thus dozens of small temples and shrines appeared in the westernmost regions of America, while such structures were almost totally lacking further east. And a third reason results from actually choosing certain regions because of their specific characteristics: as I note in the Vietnamese case, the Gulf Coast provides tropical environmental conditions familiar to immigrants from Vietnam, as well as substantial fishing opportunities for arrivals from a coastal country with a significant fishing industry. This is one reason why Vietnamese Buddhists have settled more densely in coastal Texas, Louisiana, and Florida than in Idaho or Montana.

A second factor to pay attention to is missionary patterns. Buddhism follows in the wake of missionary efforts by both Asian missionaries and Americans who have encountered Buddhism in Asia or discovered it through reading and seek to propagate it to others. In either case, the presence of a dedicated missionary in a region can substantially influence the amount and type of Buddhism that one encounters in that location. For instance, when Philip Kapleau moved to Rochester—a region to which he had no personal ties—in order to found the Rochester Zen Center, he set in motion a series of events that would create one of the most important new Buddhist lineages. As Rochester Zen Center grew, it became the dominant Buddhist institution in upstate New York and drew adherents especially from other geographically and culturally similar cities in the Great Lakes region on both sides of the American-Canadian border. While Kapleau occasionally valorized the unfriendly climate of Rochester as conducive to inner-directed meditation practice, essentially his landing there was a chance occurrence sparked by the presence of some people who had read his book *The Three Pillars of Zen* (1966) and invited him to be their teacher. Likewise, Korean Son Buddhist teacher Seung Sahn arrived in Rhode Island because of the possibility of finding a job; decades later, the Providence Zen Center is a major source for Buddhism in southern New England. The presence of the Bön master Tenzin Wangyal in Virginia makes it the preeminent American site to study this quasi-Buddhist Tibetan religion; meanwhile, the failure of Geshe Kelsang Gyatso's New Kadampa Tradition to recruit dharma teachers from the Plains states makes it one of the only American regions his transnational network of highly sectarian Buddhist groups have not managed to penetrate.

And of course I have already alluded to a third factor in the production of American Buddhist regions: American cultural regionalism. The existence of subcultures within America is itself a productive element in the creation of American Buddhist regionalism. California is not just the shore closest to Buddhist Asia, it is also a state famous for nurturing new and nonmainstream groups. Likewise, Buddhism's relative success in places like New York and Boston comes not only from their characteristics as large cities with significant trade with Asia, but it is also due in part to their reputation as relative centers of learning, acceptance, and diversity. In contrast, the perception of the South as overwhelmingly Christian and relatively intolerant is a factor in the decision of whether to attempt missionization there at all. The Richmond Zen Group, for example, has had no luck in wooing a permanent teacher from the San Francisco Bay Area, despite courting many prospective resident priests. They simply are unable to attract a Zen person from the liberal, highly Buddhist San Francisco Bay Area to conservative, sparsely Buddhist Virginia.

Taking a regional cultural perspective can help to explain the apparent differences between the sites we study. For example, Caroline Kingsbury in her M.A. thesis was puzzled that her survey results differed so markedly from James Coleman's work: his study of seven American Buddhist groups found that only 8.6 percent of Buddhist converts lacked a religious upbringing, while 26 percent of her Buddhist respondents were raised in a nonreligious household. This wide disparity led her to remark that "the practitioners in Bellingham come from a *uniquely* high percentage of homes with a nonreligious background."[37] But in fact there is nothing unique here at all—rather, what we have is regionalism at work. Coleman's study drew from sites throughout the United States, whereas Kingsbury's work was specifically carried out in Bellingham, Washington. The Pacific Northwest is the region with the lowest religious adherence in the United States—indeed, so marked is the difference that Patricia O'Connell Killen and Mark Silk refer to it as "the None Zone," making the relative lack of religious activity a defining trait of this region. As they explain, 62.8 percent of the Pacific Northwest population does not belong to a specific religious institution—the national average is a far lower, 40.6 percent. And the "Nones"—those who say they have no religious identification at all—are 25 percent, as opposed to the 14.1 percent who claim no religious identity nationally.[38] Thus it is not that the Bellingham Buddhists are unique but merely that they are representative of their region's particular demographics.

Another impact from American cultural regionalism may be apparent in distinctive traits that groups display. The Pacific Northwest (including Northern California) can be used as an example here again. This region is often characterized as highly committed to environmentalism, such that some commentators even suggest that ecological awareness has quasi-religious aspects for inhabitants of this region. This is part of Joel Garreau's Ecotopia region, and Killen and Silk's *Religion and Public Life in the Pacific Northwest* (2004) makes much of the environmental movement.[39] Here one finds a particular concentration of "enviro-Buddhists," whether in the bioregional musings of poet Gary Snyder or in the EcoSangha founded by Buddhist Churches of America minister Donald Castro in Seattle.

American Buddhist Regions

What are the regions within Buddhist America? As we have seen in our survey of general approaches to analyzing American religious regions, there are many possible ways to map this landscape, and the task can be so daunting that some scholars simply throw up their hands and refuse to do so even as they note religious variations in different parts of the country. In the long run it will probably be best to develop various maps that chart different regions according to varying concerns of the researcher. But the project of applying a regional focus to American Buddhism has to begin somewhere. Therefore, I suggest beginning with eight major geographical areas: the West Coast, the Mountains, the Southwest, the Plains, the Midwest, the Northeast, the South, and Hawaii. These designations are quite broad, and they emerge from hybrid considerations—some are topographical, some are cultural, some are based on areas of immigration concentration—but I believe they are useful starting points. Buddhism in each of these regions seems to differ in discernable ways from that in the other regions. As future research is conducted we may find some of these categories are less helpful than others, and hopefully this will lead to better and more fine-tuned regional perspectives on Buddhism in America.

The West Coast is the classic homeland for American Buddhism. Los Angeles alone is said to house virtually every type of Buddhism present on the planet. Chinese Buddhist immigration began here in the late 1840s and even through wars and periods of racist exclusion acts the West Coast has been the major entry point for Asian Buddhists of a staggering variety of cultures. In later decades it was the epicenter for the counterculture, and today it boasts a reputation for religious variety and tolerance. The headquarters for most of America's major Buddhist lineages can be found in this area, including the Buddhist Churches of America, the Buddhist Peace Fellowship, Soka Gakkai USA, Branching Streams (the Shunryu Suzuki lineage of Soto Zen), the Community of Mindful Living, the Foundation for the Preservation of the Mahayana Tradition, the New Kadampa Tradition, Foguangshan, and the Amitabha Buddhist Society of America. With the largest number of Buddhist groups of any region and the most diverse Asian American Buddhist population, the West Coast is an obvious region that will continue to be a primary site for studies of American Buddhism. The West Coast can also be broken into (at least) two subregions for further analysis, with the dividing line going approximately through Santa Cruz, California. The southern West Coast is a geographic area beset by issues arising from water scarcity, contains the second-largest urbanized area in America, and is arguably the entertainment capital of the world. The Pacific Northwest, meanwhile, has a milder, much wetter climate, and is distinctive both for its low rates of religious adherence (even for the American West) and a pervasive environmentalist strain that at times takes on a spiritual dimension.

The second region I propose, the Mountains, is geographically proximate to the West Coast but displays very different Buddhist phenomena. Composed of Alaska, Idaho, Utah, Wyoming, and most of Nevada, Montana, and Colorado, this region is drier and higher than most of the West Coast, with a smaller population as well as lower population density, and significantly fewer Asian Americans. While as much as 30 percent of Idaho's population was Chinese in the late 1800s, today the Mountains largely remain a new mission field for Buddhism, where it must try to compete in a heavily Mormon and Protestant regional religious culture. The Mountains do boast a major Buddhist center, however, in the Boulder area, where the Shambhala Mountain Center and Naropa University have become a mecca for Americans interested in Tibetan Buddhism, especially as embodied by the flamboyant late teacher Chögyam Trungpa.

The Southwest also abuts the West Coast, but it seems different enough from both the coast and the Mountains that it forms its own region, composed of southern Nevada, Arizona, New Mexico, and western Texas. This is another area of relatively low population density, although recent years have seen an explosion of urban centers, especially Phoenix, now the fifth-largest city in the country. While still high in altitude, the warmer temperatures and dramatic wind- and water-shaped landscape have drawn many New Age practitioners who consider locations like Sedona, Arizona, to be "power places." The result is a mixed Catholic, Protestant, and Mormon area with significant pockets of alternative spiritual communities. This eclectic spiritual atmosphere has also attracted Buddhists, particularly adult practitioners from non-Buddhist backgrounds. The Southwest is dotted with Buddhist groups committed to living close to the land, including many retreat centers that take advantage of the low population density for purposes of seclusion and temporary or permanent renunciation of mainstream American life. This is also the region of the most significant encounters between Native American spirituality and Buddhism, both through the dabbling of local spiritual seekers from neither a Native nor a Buddhist background, and from direct encounters initiated by such emissaries as the Nipponzan Myohoji monk Shigeki Minematsu.[40] Important institutions in this area include Upaya Zen Center in Sante Fe, New Mexico, and Diamond Mountain near Bowie, Arizona.

The Plains are the least Buddhist of all our regions. Encompassing eastern Montana and eastern Colorado, as well as North Dakota, South Dakota, Nebraska, Iowa, Kansas, and Oklahoma, the American Heartland is relatively flat, spacious, and heavily Protestant. The Plains have few Buddhist groups; those that exist here are on the average smaller than in most other regions, and there is less denominational and sectarian diversity among them. Buddhism is almost entirely an urban phenomenon on the Plains and in nearly every case Buddhist groups are small affiliates of larger networks that are based and much more active in other parts of the country. Many groups are too small or too disorganized to have their own dedicated spaces and so meet in the buildings of local liberal congregations, such as Unitarian Universalist churches in the larger cities. Japanese-based Buddhism is noticeably less prevalent here than in other areas — even the mission-oriented Soka Gakkai organization has had scant success here, and this is also the weakest region for its parent (and now rival) organization, Nichiren Shoshu. Many other lineages common in the United States are completely unrepresented here: there is no institutional presence of Shambhala here whatsoever, for example, even though it is amply represented to the west in the Mountains and to the east in the Midwest. This region tends to differ on a north-south basis, with Oklahoma City having by far the largest and most diverse Buddhist community, while numbers drop off significantly as one moves toward the Canadian border.[41]

The Midwest, by contrast, has a long history of Buddhist activity and boasts many groups and types of Buddhists. The big cities, such as Chicago, are especially rich places for the study and practice of Buddhism, but many smaller cities and even more modest towns have developed some Buddhist presence in the last twenty-five years. For our purposes, this area is made up of Minnesota, Wisconsin, Michigan, Illinois, Indiana, and Ohio. There are enough Buddhists here to support a large pansectarian organization, the Buddhist Council of the Midwest, with approximately 150 member groups and temples in Wisconsin, Michigan, Illinois, and Indiana. Many types of Buddhism with little representation elsewhere in America, such as Jodo Shu, Shinnyoen, and Sarvodaya, have some presence in this region alongside nearly all the more common forms. Besides hosting major branches of nationwide networks—such as the Chicago Zen Center (in the Philip Kapleau lineage of Zen)—the Midwest is the base for a number of organizations, such as Jewel Heart, founded in Ann Arbor, Michigan, in the late 1980s.[42] Chicago looms large in the historiography of American Buddhism due to the Buddhist presence at the 1893 World's Parliament of Religions and the fin-de-siècle activities of early interpreters Paul Carus and D. T. Suzuki.

The Northeast is both a solidly comfortable area for Buddhism and a far frontier. This region includes the six New England states (Connecticut, Massachusetts, Rhode Island, Vermont, New Hampshire, and Maine) and the mid-Atlantic states of New York, New Jersey, Pennsylvania, Delaware, and Maryland; although arguable, I also feel it should probably include the District of Columbia and its Northern Virginia suburbs. This region has been dominated by waves of immigration from many parts of Europe, as well as significant cross-border migrations to and from Canada. Asian immigration in the greater New York City area has been very significant but has tended to be lower in the more northerly areas. Chinese Buddhism in New York City goes back to the later nineteenth century, and the Transcendentalists and Unitarians of the Boston Bay area were tentatively exploring Asian religions even earlier, but most of this region's rapid increase in

Buddhist groups can be safely placed in the last fifty years. A good number of American Buddhist lineages have their home bases here, including the Insight Meditation Center in Massachusetts, the Kwan Um lineage based in Providence, Namgyal Monastery in Ithaca, New York (the official North American seat of the Dalai Lama), Kagyu Thubten Chöling in Wappingers Falls, New York, and the Rochester Zen Center. At the same time, from the perspective of the American Buddhist majority in Hawaii and the West Coast, the Northeast seems to be at the end of many national networks, and developments on one or the other coast tend to have less effect on sites at the opposite end of the country. This is a liberal area overall where religion plays a relatively lesser public role than in some other places, making it easier for Buddhists to nestle into the landscape and go about their business without disturbing the neighbors — this does not at all mean, however, that conflict never arises and discrimination never occurs. The New England and mid-Atlantic states are grouped here because while they have enough differences (especially historical ones) that in other contexts they are often separated, from the point of view of Buddhists in these regions there seems little to especially differentiate them.

And what of the South? Few people associate the South with Buddhism, perhaps with good reason. While Buddhist groups are more common in the South than they used to be, Buddhism has been very slow to grow in this part of the country, which is characterized by a strong evangelical Protestant public culture (though increasingly challenged by Catholic growth, especially from Latin American migration), a particularly thorny racial history, and a long initial period as a primarily rural region. While Buddhism is indeed on the rise here, it is significantly underrepresented compared to the size of the total population, and for the number of Buddhist groups that can be found there are relatively few trained teachers. The strong Christian presence in the public life of this area discourages many Buddhists from discussing their religion with non-Buddhists; both Asian American and non-Asian based groups can come to have an enclave mentality, and many keep a low profile. In many cases the members of southern Buddhist groups are transplants from other parts of the country, often having brought their Buddhist interest with them rather than discovering it in the South.

The South has one of the strongest regional self-identities in the United States, but it can also be profitably split into two subregions. The first is the Coastal South, stretching from the eastern edge of the Appalachians to the Atlantic (i.e., central and eastern Virginia, most of North Carolina, South Carolina, and Georgia, and all of Florida), and the Gulf coastal parts of Alabama, Mississippi, Louisiana, and Texas. The second southern subregion is the Inner South, composed of the western portions of Virginia, North Carolina, and South Carolina; all of West Virginia, Kentucky, Tennessee, Missouri, and Arkansas; northern Georgia; and the northern and central portions of Alabama, Mississippi, Louisiana, and Texas.

The Coastal South has experienced notable Asian American immigration and migration in the past forty-five years, especially since the end of the Vietnam War. This area has sizable concentrations of Vietnamese American and Thai American Buddhists in both urban and some more rural areas, as well as Chinese Americans, Korean Americans, Burmese Americans, and others who are more likely to be found in city environments. The small cities of this region can sometimes support several Buddhist groups, especially if there is a sizable university nearby, while large cities like Atlanta, Charlotte, and Houston have a comfortable diversity of Buddhist communities, even if they do not match large northern and western cities such as New York, Chicago, or Los Angeles. The Inner South, by comparison, has lower total Asian American Buddhist populace and fewer Buddhists, period. But somewhat similar to the Southwest, the Inner South has many more retreat centers than might be expected, including the Bhavana Society in West Virginia, the Southern Dharma Retreat Center in the mountains west of Asheville, and the Furnace Mountain Zen Retreat Center in Kentucky.

For the most part the South, both coastal and inner, is at the end of Buddhist networks that originate in the North or on the West Coast, rather than being a significant base for lineages that stretch outward into other areas. There are, however, a number of small regional networks that are mostly confined to the South, such as the Zen temples in the Matsuoka lineage originating from his disciple Michael Elliston at the Atlanta Soto Zen Center, and those in the Deshimaru lineage that spring from his disciple Robert Livingston at the New Orleans Zen Temple. Both the Matsuoka and Deshimaru lineages are not particularly prevalent in other parts of the country. Their location in the South points out how this area has been undercolonized by the groups that tend to dominate American Buddhism; for this reason the South also has a tendency to support unusual Buddhist phenomena rarely found anywhere else in America, such as the multidenominational temple in Richmond, Virginia, and a Sri Lankan–based Theravada temple in Greenville, South Carolina, run by a white ordained Buddhist nun.

The final region to account for is Hawaii. Geographically isolated from the rest of the United States, the Hawaiian Islands have a very distinct

The Carolina Buddhist Vihara in Greenville, South Carolina, is supported by Sri Lankan American laypeople in the neighborhood and led by a white, fully ordained Theravada nun.

Asian melting pot, with a heavy Buddhist presence. In fact, with its relative proximity to Asia this is the only state in America where Buddhists are the second-largest religious group, behind Christians. Hawaii shows far more diversity of Japanese forms of Buddhism than most other regions, and it is one of the only places where one can easily find Japanese Buddhist material culture often absent from mainland American Buddhism, such as temples with large graveyards holding Buddhist statuary carved from volcanic rock a century ago, proxy sites for miniaturized pilgrimage to the eighty-eight sacred temples of Shikoku, and Zen temples selling protective amulets.

Caveats and Other Possible Buddhist Regions

Collectively, these eight regions encompass the entirety of the United States of America, and they provide a jumping-off point for explorations of American Buddhist regional phenomena. But while hoping they will prove useful to other researchers, we should remain aware that the regions we "discover" are in fact partially a product of the observer's particular interests. We can find different Buddhist regions if our concerns are specifically political or cultural or meteorological or geographical, and so on—thus it sometimes makes sense to include suburbs of Washington, DC, in Vir-

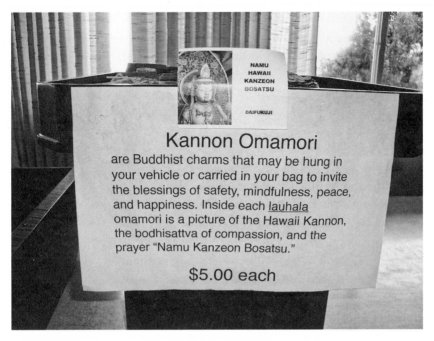

NAMU
HAWAII
KANZEON
BOSATSU

DAIFUKUJI

Kannon Omamori

are Buddhist charms that may be hung in
your vehicle or carried in your bag to invite
the blessings of safety, mindfulness, peace,
and happiness. Inside each <u>lauhala</u>
omamori is a picture of the *Hawaii Kannon*,
the bodhisattva of compassion, and the
prayer "Namu Kanzeon Bosatsu."

$5.00 each

Protective amulets for sale at a Soto Zen temple in Hawaii.

ginia, Maryland, and Delaware as part of "the Buddhist Northeast" and
sometimes as part of "the Buddhist South," for example. Furthermore, these
general regions may apply for some types of Buddhism, while being nearly
useless for the interpretation of certain other denominations or groups,
which require attention to what unique regions manifest in their particular networks. As I discuss in the conclusion, from the point of view of the
Buddhist Churches of America, there are really only two regions: the West
Coast and Everywhere Else. An argument could be made for separating the
country into three large zones: the West, inclusive of everything between
Hawaii and the eastern edge of the Rockies; the East, more or less bounded
by an imaginary line drawn between Chicago and Houston; and the Center,
encompassing the rest of the middle part of America. The West and the East
both have relatively large concentrations of Buddhists and tend to somewhat different mixes of specific Buddhist lineages that have succeeded in
each area, while the Center has fewer Buddhists and few significant Buddhist networks of its own.

Yet another way of mapping Buddhist America might be to mostly retain
the eight regions laid out above but to divide them somewhat differently. A
Lakes region including eastern Minnesota, Wisconsin, Michigan, northern

Illinois, northern Indiana, northeastern Pennsylvania, western and north-ern New York, and northern Vermont could be argued for. This would leave the remaining parts of the Northeast to become a new region called the Coastal North, and would blend the remaining parts of the Plains and the Midwest with the Inner South to become a region called the Center. This could make sense because the Lakes region shares some notable Buddhist networks, the areas within one hundred miles of the Atlantic coast in the Northeast are demographically distinct from those further inland, and the Center has the lowest Buddhist population.

Another point to keep in mind is that the regions we identify are not static. Regionalism may appear at certain times and disappear at others. For example, regionalism, religion, and assimilation issues sometimes made for a volatile mix in Japanese American World War II military units. Hawai-ian and mainland Buddhists in the military clashed because of cultural styles that developed in these different regions. The mainlanders called the Hawaiians "Buddha-heads" while the Hawaiians called the mainlanders "Katonks," neither of which was meant affectionately at first. Yet that very contact during the 1940s led to greater cooperation and understanding after the war. Nor does regional Buddhism remain the same over time. To be a southern Buddhist meant one thing in the 1950s, when Jack Kerouac medi-tated behind his mother's house in Rocky Mount, North Carolina; it means something else today. Because of the mercurial nature of regions and the way our own positionality helps to produce them in the first place, I deploy alternate regional boundaries at various points throughout this book. For example, while I argue that overall Springfield and Fairfax Station, Virginia, can be seen as the southernmost tips of the Northeast, I will also often speak of them at times in this book as being part of the South. Borderlands are particularly difficult to classify as belonging squarely to one region or another; not coincidentally, they are often among the most interesting sites to explore.

Regionalism as an interpretative approach can also be applied to smaller and larger frames of reference. First, I want to suggest the importance of looking at not just regionalism but microregionalism as well. For example, the San Francisco Bay Area has been one of the most heavily studied areas of Buddhism in America, and yet without attention to its unique proper-ties, even within California, it may be one of the worst sites for research on American Buddhism. Why do I make such an outrageous claim? Simply be-cause the Bay Area in its fascinating diversity is so completely unrepresen-tative of Buddhist America. For instance, this is the only place in the world other than Japan where the obscure esoteric mountain asceticism of Shugendo has been practiced.[43] If we make the Bay Area stand in for America as a whole, we distort the picture of Buddhism in the United States. But if, in contrast, we recognize it as a unique microregion, we can explore it fruitfully. For example, as I have already mentioned, there is a particular clustering of Zen groups and teachers in this microregion that have been produced by the San Francisco Zen Center and, in many cases, have been reluctant to leave the comfort of the Bay Area for thankless missionary work in the hinterlands (i.e., the rest of the nation). In March 2010 there were more than fifty teachers or practice leaders from this lineage active in the Bay Area alone; meanwhile, there were no teachers from this lineage teaching publicly anywhere in Virginia, Alaska, Hawaii, Nevada, Utah, Wyoming, North Dakota, South Dakota, Kansas, Iowa, Missouri, Oklahoma, Arkansas, Louisiana, Wisconsin, Alabama, Georgia, Tennessee, Kentucky, South Carolina, Maine, Massachusetts, Rhode Island, Vermont, New Hampshire, Michigan, Indiana, West Virginia, Ohio, Nebraska, Idaho, or Arizona.[44] This leads to the possibility of Zen overcrowding in the San Francisco area, which may itself be productive of new developments in American Buddhism that then subsequently get exported to other regions.

And while we can zero in on microregions, another approach likely to prove fruitful is to explore what this turn toward regional studies in American Buddhism can offer for research on Buddhism in other Western countries. Identifying the influence of regionalism in the United States can help us to look for regionalism in Canada, for instance. Some Tibetan Buddhists in Atlantic Canada practice the compassionate releasing of lobsters back into the ocean. This practice brings Buddhists into contact and dialogue with the fishing industry, impacting both. And it is a practice confined to that region — if a monk passionately dedicated to the salvation of lobsters moves to Edmonton, well, he is going to have to find other practices to devote himself to. Just as there is no one American Buddhism, it seems hardly likely that there is a single Canadian Buddhism, nor a solitary British Buddhism, and so on. As these countries have all the marks of the sorts of regionalisms listed previously for the United States, they probably also have regional Buddhisms that could be productively studied. And we may find that there are transnational regions in North American Buddhism. Certainly there is some logic to grouping southern British Columbia with the West Coast region (or at least the Pacific Northwest subregion) of America, putting Alberta and Saskatchewan in with the Plains, or greater Toronto with the Midwest or perhaps the Northeast (or, especially, a Lakes region).

Bringing regionalism to our awareness can benefit the study of Buddhism in America in many ways. In particular, it can serve, first, to prevent us from mistaking local phenomena as representative of American Buddhism generally. Second, it can stimulate new studies that look at regionalism specifically as an interpretive lens. And, finally, it can add depth to studies that are not about regionalism specifically. Just as we have learned the value of paying attention to gender, race, and class, even when they are not the primary subjects of our research, so too we may find that keeping regional specificity in view as we conduct our projects will make them richer, more accurate portraits of whatever group or topic we are studying. And for scholars of American religion working on regional perspectives already, incorporating attention to Buddhism may add further insights.

Sure enough, it must be admitted that there is religious diversity in the South.

—David Edwin Harrell Jr., "Religious Pluralism: Catholics, Jews, and Sectarians,"
   Religion in the South, 1985

Chapter Two

THE GIFT OF LIGHT

Buddhist Circuit Riders and New Religious
Developments in Richmond, Virginia

Many of the houses along Grove Avenue fly flags—the star-spangled banner, the Virginia state flag, banners with animals or floral designs, as well as the occasional Confederate battle flag. So the five-colored flag sometimes flown outside Ekoji Buddhist Sangha of Richmond does not seem to attract much attention from passersby. But this is not simply a variation on the rainbow motif—the stripes of blue, yellow, red, white, and orange form the pattern of the so-called Buddhist Flag, a design originating in the Buddhist revival of nineteenth-century Ceylon and now used by a wide variety of Buddhist groups.[1] To the uninitiated it is simply colorful, but to insiders, it is a clue that something special goes on inside.

Ekoji, the case study that I use for exploring the idea of American Buddhist regionalism in this book, shares much in common with Buddhist centers in other parts of the United States, and yet we will also see that regional considerations and impacts are far from incidental. This chapter recounts Ekoji's founding, and briefly describes the convoluted history of the different groups that have used the space. I then provide a general description of the temple's layout, background material that serves as the launching point for chapter 3, where I focus on the five established groups currently sharing Ekoji, and consider the particular uses each makes of the space. A further concern of this chapter is to introduce Reverend Takashi Kenryu Tsuji, the founder of Ekoji.[2] The work he did to establish a temple in Richmond exemplifies how Buddhism attempts to enter the South. And he is a fascinating figure emblematic of an important type of American Buddhist who has been largely left out of the mainstream narratives of the field: the modernist Shin priest.[3] I present additional information about Richmond and Buddhism in the South in chapter 5, as part of my specifically regional analysis.

History of Ekoji

The story of Ekoji begins in 1981, when the Reverend Takashi Kenryu Tsuji, recently retired bishop of the Buddhist Churches of America (BCA), moved to Virginia to spread Jodo Shinshu Buddhism in the Southeast.[4] The Buddhist Churches of America is the oldest Buddhist organization in the United States—it was founded in San Francisco in 1899 and until World War II was known as the Buddhist Mission of North America. While individual whites and African Americans have played important roles in the BCA's history, the denomination's base has always come from Japanese immigrants who began arriving on the West Coast in the late nineteenth century and their descendents.

Despite its status as the largest Buddhist denomination in Japan, the oldest form of organized Buddhism in the United States, and one of the largest forms of Buddhism in America, Jodo Shinshu (Shin Buddhism) is poorly represented on the East Coast, where Japanese immigration has been relatively minimal.[5] After establishing a temple (also named Ekoji) in Northern Virginia, Tsuji was persuaded by several people in Richmond to start a second temple.[6] Beginning in 1984 he made trips to Richmond, conducting services in people's homes or at the Richmond Friends Meeting-house.[7] In June 1985 a house in western Richmond at 3411 Grove Avenue was purchased through the assistance of the Numata Center for Buddhist Translation.[8] By September the temple had been accepted as an affiliate member of the BCA, although it had not yet opened for regular services.[9]

The official dedication of the temple took place on May 17, 1986, at a ceremony presided over by the then-current bishop of the BCA, the Reverend Seigen H. Yamaoka.[10] Ekoji's first president, Mark Jacinto, made a speech reminding listeners that "Buddhism is universal and maintains no discriminatory boundaries."[11] While the ceremony itself was brief, the import of the event impressed itself on many. As one observer noted, "You know that you are the *first* non-Japanese, totally American, Shinshu temple in the U.S. This is more than a statistic — you all can determine the future of Buddhism in the U.S. One Hell of a responsibility."[12] Tsuji's experiment of a temple that did not have an ethnic Japanese American base met with only limited success. Temple growth was slow, and the average participation was perhaps a half-dozen participants, plus Tsuji and sometimes his wife or a member or two of the Northern Virginia Ekoji whom he brought along with him.[13] Within the first several years the most important early members had resigned, including the president, most of the trustees, and the member largely responsible for the renovation of the house into a temple. Documents in the temple archives and interviews with current members who overlapped with or otherwise knew these founding fathers suggest that these men were interested not so much in Jodo Shinshu, but in Buddhism generally, especially as a philosophy. In at least one case conflict originating in divergent managerial styles between off-site Japanese American BCA leaders and the local university-based white lay members seems to have been a source of tension.

The small size of the congregation can be traced to several factors. First, because Tsuji had to serve the needs of Buddhists throughout the South, he could only come to Richmond once a month; even later on he still only came every other week. Second, the Japanese American Buddhist population of Richmond (the natural constituency for the temple) was extremely small. During the temple's initial years there was only a single local Japanese American regular attendee — a retired Shin minister who was already in her seventies. Third, the Jodo Shinshu sect, despite its historical importance for Buddhism in America, is little known in the wider American Buddhist community. Jodo Shinshu is a form of Pure Land Buddhism, focusing on the power of a primordial Buddha to liberate all beings in a nirvanic realm known as the Pure Land. While the tradition contains sophisticated symbolic interpretations of this founding myth, the superficial resemblance to Christianity and Jodo Shinshu's historic indifference to formal silent meditation practices have blunted its appeal to many potential converts, who are often seeking a radically different alternative to the Christianity they were raised with and who typically associate Buddhism with individualistic meditation, not devotional activity. Information about Jodo Shinshu would have been hard to come by: in the mid-1980s, prior to the rise of the Internet, not a single English-language book about Jodo Shinshu would have been available on regular bookstore shelves in the Richmond area. Finally, Tsuji and Ekoji appear not to have made any appreciable efforts to recruit new members from the neighborhood, adopting a low profile as a new, unfamiliar, and non-Christian religion on the scene.

Tsuji was brought up short by the departure of so many initial members and began to reevaluate the value of teaching mainstream Jodo Shinshu to non-Japanese in the South. As a result, he shifted his teaching style. Thereafter, while the forms remained primarily Shin, he often supplemented the Pure Land material in his sermons with ideas and examples drawn from Theravada, Zen, and Tibetan Buddhism, and he deemphasized traditional sectarian Jodo Shinshu concepts in favor of teaching through example and story. Turning to outside forms of Buddhism as a way of making the dharma appealing to non-Japanese proved to be a winning strategy in the long run, as he eventually attracted sufficient numbers of whites and Chinese Americans to keep the temple afloat. While Tsuji had to make course corrections midstream as he nurtured the new temple, adaptation was by no means a new experience for him. As a modernist teacher who taught in many different environments (as we will see), Tsuji had always had to adjust his message to new audiences, and he already had a familiarity with non-Shin forms of Buddhism that he could marshal to serve the needs of his newest congregation.

This movement away from Jodo Shinshu particularism took a dramatic turn in the following year, marking an important shift in the conception of Ekoji's mission in Richmond. By 1987, the local Vietnamese population was on the rise. Arriving in the United States in the wake of the warfare in their homeland, Vietnamese immigrants, including large numbers of Buddhists, settled in many parts of the country. Occasionally a monk would come through Richmond, but the community—made up primarily of first-generation immigrants who had once been refugees—lacked adequate means to establish their own temple. In 1987 Tsuji was approached by leaders of Richmond's nascent Vietnamese Buddhist community about their plight. Tsuji was willing to share his mostly empty temple with other Buddhists who needed a home, and he allowed these new neighbors to occupy most of the upstairs floor. The new arrivals alternately called themselves Chua Hue Quang (Vietnamese for "Ekoji") and the Richmond Buddhist Association, and they began to hold their own services in Vietnamese at 4:00 P.M. on Sundays.[14] Ekoji was now a multidenominational temple.

While the addition of a second, larger denomination to the temple seems to have occurred with little fuss, this also created a temple with little precedent in Asian Buddhist history. Few temples in Asia are occupied by more than a single sect, although Mahayana and non-Mahayana monks sometimes shared monasteries and universities in premodern India. And while some American temples, mostly Jodo Shinshu–affiliated ones, had hosted groups of new Buddhists or non-Japanese immigrants practicing another form of Buddhism (in particular, Shin temples often allowed displaced Vietnamese groups to get a start by meeting in their space), these groups were smaller and would move out when they gained sufficient strength to support their own temple. This is what happened with the Richmond Buddhist Association, but, as we will shortly see, the addition of the Vietnamese to Ekoji set in motion events without any precedent. Rather than becoming the temporary shelter of wayward Buddhist groups, Ekoji became permanently multidenominational. The addition of the Vietnamese also brought the temple into direct conflict with city authorities, and eventually resulted in attempts to shut it down, as I discuss in chapter 5.

The temple grew again in 1990 with the addition of a Zen group. As Allen Galloway, the founder of the group, recounts in the temple's newsletter: "Several years ago I met Reverend Tsuji for the first time. He didn't know me at all but this did not deter him from being open and friendly. I mentioned that I was very much interested in Buddhism but that my inclination was toward a zen approach. Reverend Tsuji smiled that smile of his that can be so infectious. It wasn't long before he reached into his pocket and handed me a key to the building. He said something to the effect, 'Now there is a zen group at Ekoji.' He smiled again. I probably stood there with my mouth wide open as if I'd been struck by a large vehicle. Perhaps I was struck by a large vehicle: 'mahayana.'"[15] This new addition, calling itself the Chimborazo Zen Group, began to hold regular services at Ekoji at 8:00 A.M. on November 6, 1990. Like the Shin group, its growth was slow, averaging four or five attendees for the first several years.[16] Then in October 1993 members of the small Richmond Zen Group, who had been meeting at a local New Age bookshop, merged with Chimborazo. The resulting amalgamation restyled itself as the Ekoji Zen Group.[17]

The next group to appear was Kagyu (a school of Tibetan Buddhism). It was started on January 19, 1993, by several members of the temple.[18] This group met at 7:30 P.M. on Tuesday nights. Ekoji was now serving four different lineages: Jodo Shinshu, Zen, Vietnamese Mahayana, and Kagyu. The growing diversity of the temple was recognized in the *Dharma Wheel*, the temple's newsletter, which in 1994 began to print an unofficial motto on the front of each issue: "Just as all oceans have the same taste, so all true Dharmas have one taste: the taste of liberation."[19]

Things shifted once again in early 1995. Eight years after joining Ekoji,

Chua Hue Quang, the temple built by the Vietnamese American Buddhists when they moved out of Ekoji.

the expanding Vietnamese group left to establish its own temple, which is physically much larger than Ekoji itself.[20] Within a matter of weeks, however, two new groups had filled the vacuum left by the departure of the Richmond Buddhist Association: on March 3 a Vipassana meditation group held its first meeting at Ekoji, and the following day a Chinese sutra study group was created.[21] In December the Vipassana group disbanded, but it was immediately replaced by a second Vipassana group that continues today.[22] And in early 1996 the Chinese sutra study group combined with the Jodo Shinshu services to create a nonsectarian Pure Land group—on weeks when Tsuji came they practiced in Shin style, but on alternate weeks they performed a modified service that incorporated significant amounts of Chinese chanting.[23]

The most recent innovation at the temple is the creation of a Meditative Inquiry group. This lineage has roots in Zen Buddhism but has moved beyond them to become a less traditional form of quasi-Buddhist meditation. Its founder, Toni Packer, studied for years with Philip Kapleau at the Rochester Zen Center and was designated as his heir in that tradition. But Packer came to feel constrained by the formality and other aspects of the Zen she had been taught and left with about half the Rochester Zen Center's membership to form the Genesee Valley Zen Center. This was not the final destination on her trajectory away from Zen, however, as one of her books explains:

> In time, the Genesee Valley Zen Center became Springwater Center. The word Zen was dropped, Toni no longer called herself a teacher, the traditional Zen emphasis on posture and form fell away, people stopped wearing Zen robes and began sitting more frequently in chairs as well as on cushions on the floor, and sitting in an armchair became as acceptable as the lotus position. Toni stopped using koans (Zen riddles) and formal inquiries in working with people, group meetings were introduced into retreats in addition to the private individual meetings with Toni, untimed sittings were experimented with, things got simpler and more open. There has been a steady movement away from the rigidity and athletic qualities of traditional Zen practice, a movement toward shorter sittings, more comfortable postures. But through all these shifts in style, the essence of Toni's work and the acuity of her vision has remained very much the same.[24]

Today the Springwater Center for Meditative Inquiry is described by scholar Marilyn Ivy as "post-Buddhist." It is certainly closer to Buddhism than to any other religion, and Packer and the teachers there read works in the Buddhist tradition and reference Buddhism in their talks, but the center eschews any formal Buddhist content, and other influences are also counted as important sources, such as the non-Buddhist Indian teachers Krishnamurti and Ni Srigidatta Maharaj.

Beginning in the later 1990s, one of the most heavily involved Zen practitioners at Ekoji became interested in Packer. He began attending sessions at the Springwater Center in upstate New York as his schedule allowed, and over time the looser style of the center appealed to him. When another person interested in the Springwater form of Meditative Inquiry moved to Richmond in 2005, they met and decided to start a new group at Ekoji. It took a bit of convincing to get permission from the Ekoji board of directors (as I describe in chapter 4), but ultimately the board unanimously allowed the creation of a Meditative Inquiry group at Ekoji. Beginning in late 2005, the group became the fifth congregation at Ekoji. They meet on Sunday evenings at 7:00 P.M.

Other, shorter-lived, groups have used the space as well. These include a second Vietnamese group that met at Ekoji in the later 1990s before merging with the Richmond Buddhist Association, and a Unitarian Universalist Buddhist group that formed at Ekoji in 2001 and moved to the First Unitarian Church of Richmond later that year. In 2003, just after the war began in Iraq, a Richmond-area Buddhist Peace Fellowship was organized, and it typically held organizational meetings at Ekoji, though most public events were held elsewhere.[25] It was under the banner of this group that the slave trade meditation vigil discussed in chapter 6 was organized.

The net result of all this coming and going was that Ekoji's identity shifted fundamentally from a monolineal, Jodo Shinshu temple to a multidenominational one especially informed at present by Japanese, Chinese, Tibetan, Burmese, and American lineages. It is the only site in the United States used on a weekly basis by five completely separate but closely cooperating forms of Buddhism (or, in the case of Meditative Inquiry, Buddhist-influenced practice).

The Layout of Ekoji

The brick and wood building at 3411 Grove Avenue that is now Ekoji was once a two-story house built in 1929, during the first decades of the twentieth century that gave birth to what has come to be known as the Museum District.[26] In what is today a majority-black city, the residential section where Ekoji lies has always been dominated by whites. Even as other neighborhoods, especially to the east, experienced in-migration of African Americans and white flight to the suburbs during the middle and late twentieth century, the corridor between West Broad and West Cary Streets remained stubbornly white in complexion. The area has not been entirely without diversity, however, as it and points west also housed the largest concentration of foreign-born white ethnics, as well as one of the city's primary Jewish populations.[27]

By the 1980s, when Ekoji came into being, this western side of Richmond was one of the most affluent parts of the South, while some of the African American areas in the eastern part of Richmond were among the South's very poorest urban pockets.[28] The original trustees of Ekoji and some of its first key members were all white, and most came from respectable, indeed quite high-status Richmond families of the city's elite. Since they were no longer available for consultation by the time I began my research into this part of the temple's past, I can only offer speculations. But it is quite interesting that—even though they were not primarily using their own money, but instead relying on the Numata Foundation to purchase the property—this elite white group located a house for sale in one of the city's whitest, richest, and most exclusive neighborhoods of the time. Prop-

Ekoji Buddhist Sangha of Richmond, on Grove Avenue.

erties in the eastern end of Richmond would have afforded far more space for the money spent ($69,500), but there is no evidence that such locations were considered.[29] This is worth noting in relation to a number of issues I discuss later in this book, such as the complaints over Ekoji's cramped quarters by members of the Zen group (discussed in the next chapter), the problems with the city over taxation (especially in relation to the allegations that the Vietnamese presence at the temple caused neighbors to ask the city tax assessor to investigate the property, discussed in chapter 5), and the temple's extremely low African American attendance (discussed in chapter 6). The house was sold to the trustees by an out-of-town owner: it had been purchased to house a medical student from Los Angeles while he attended school in Richmond, and when he graduated his father sought to offload it.[30] The seller thus was not a part of the neighborhood and was unconcerned with whether a Buddhist group would be appropriate in that location.

The exterior of the house that became Ekoji has not been significantly modified by the Buddhists, and it does not immediately stand out as a temple. But on closer investigation, an informed pedestrian might notice some distinctive features. Besides the Buddhist flag that Ekoji occasionally flies, a second noteworthy feature is the dry garden on the temple's front lawn. Built of pebbles, several strategically placed boulders, and a few closely manicured bushes and trees, this garden is informed by Japanese aesthetics, such as the famous gardens found at the Zen temples of Ryoanji and Daisenin.[31] Like the flag, there is nothing obviously Buddhist about this landscape to the untrained observer. Finally, there is a small plaque by the door that says "Ekoji Buddhist Sangha of Richmond" and a sign in the window with the meeting times of the various groups, neither of which is easily noticeable from the sidewalk. Through such subtle details the members have attempted to designate this building as a Buddhist temple and perhaps catch the eye of informed pedestrians, while remaining well within the standards set by the other houses in the neighborhood. Still a very small minority in this southern city, the Buddhists have done little to announce themselves.[32]

The temple has two floors, with an entrance on the street and another in the rear, where parking is available. Opening the front door, one enters what was once the living room. A folding white screen blocks off an area where attendees leave their shoes. Also in this area are boxes for donations, free books donated by various Buddhist organizations, a bulletin board for announcements of temple and wider-community events, and a rack with

Facing the front door in Ekoji's hondo (main worship and practice room).

pamphlets by each of the five Ekoji groups. The screen partially hides an un-used fireplace on whose mantle sit framed photographs of Reverend Tsuji; Josho Pat Phelan, the abbess of the Chapel Hill Zen Center, who comes from North Carolina to counsel the Zen group that meets at Ekoji; and Lama Norhla, a teacher in upstate New York who is the leader of the Ekoji Tibetan group's lineage and who also visits Ekoji approximately once a year. Sometimes a Buddha statue or a flower will be placed on this mantle, but only the three photographs seem to have a permanent home here.

On the other side of the screen is the main part of the room, which once comprised the dining and living rooms of the house (a wall was removed to make this space larger). A sign indicates that this area is known as the hondo, a Japanese term for a Buddhist worship hall. The room is approxi-mately twenty-five feet long by twelve feet across, carpeted and with several doors leading to the kitchen, stairs, bathroom, and storage room. At the end of the room is the altar, the focal point of this space, where a one-foot-tall statue of Amitabha Buddha — the principle devotional focus of Pure Land Buddhism — is enshrined.[33]

Amitabha stands on a simple platform built of unpainted wood. A sec-ond Buddha, approximately four inches tall, sits to Amitabha's left, his right hand stretching down in the "earth-touching" gesture.[34] To the right is a thick white candle, and to the left is a vase for flowers, which are collected from the garden outside when the season permits. An embroidered brocade cloth hangs down between them, while a bronze incense burner squats in the center.[35] A small black dish holds powdered incense, and slips of folded paper display names and concerns: "Raymond—cancer." This altar is much less ornate than in other Jodo Shinshu–associated temples in America.[36] Furthermore, the altar area—known as the naijin in Japanese—is typically separated from the congregation and considered sacred: laypeople at other temples usually do not enter it and typically shoes are not worn in a temple's naijin. Rather, laypeople sit in the area known as the gejin, which is typically separated from the naijin by a fence, a difference in height, or some other immediately apparent physical means. In Japanese American temples—regardless of denomination—the gejin contains pews, or sometimes chairs for the laity. At Ekoji, however, there is no naijin or gejin, nor are there any pews or permanent chairs.

The rest of the room is even less flashy. The walls and ceiling are a light green. In one corner black mats known as zabutons are stacked, along with round black cushions: zafus filled with kapok. Seven framed drawings depicting dramatic moments in the Buddha's life are displayed along the right-hand wall, while the left-hand wall sports a five-foot-long Japanese calligraphy scroll. Tsuji bought the pictures during a pilgrimage to India at the Japanese temple at Bodh Gaya, the place of the Buddha's enlightenment; the calligraphy was done for Ekoji by Fukashima Roshi, a Rinzai Zen teacher who lectures yearly at the University of Richmond and gives occasional programs at Ekoji.[37] Next to the scroll sits the radiator, which is covered by a wooden shelf that supports a greenish statue of the bodhisattva Guanyin (Avalokiteshvara), the female Chinese embodiment of infinite compassion and an increasingly popular figure across many Buddhist lineages in America. Many of her devotees are from non-Chinese lineages and in some cases even belong to Theravada Buddhist groups, a form of Buddhism widely depicted as not partaking in the cult of the bodhisattvas.[38] The statue was donated by several members of the Zen group to commemorate taking vows in the ceremony known as jukai.

The hondo shares some similarities with Christian churches. There is a general rectangular shape to the space, orienting the viewer toward one end of the room. The life of the Buddha, a common display in American Buddhist temples of various denominations, in some ways replicates the spatial arrangement and pedagogical function of the stations of the cross of Catholic churches. There is a makeshift narthex, the hondo is rather like a nave, and the altar could be seen as occupying a sort of sanctuary area.[39] Yet the

The Tibetan room at Ekoji.

comparison has its limits. There are easily movable cushions, not pews, and most practitioners sit on the floor (a few sit on folding chairs, mainly the elderly). There is no separation between the altar and the rest of the room, and little of the space has been formally set aside. There is no pulpit, nowhere for a choir, and certainly no baptismal font.

Most of the other rooms require less elaboration. Immediately to the left of the hondo is the kitchen, a long, narrow room whose only discernable Buddhist element is a small Buddha statue seated on an upper shelf, and a little ceramic bodhisattva Guanyin guarding the microwave oven. At the back of the hondo is a small room used for storage of service books, service book benches, and other ritual implements. The bathroom is also back here, through a door to the left.

The staircase leads to the second floor, which has four rooms and a bathroom with a tub and shower. The first room is perhaps the most significant, as it is exclusively used by the Tibetan group to hold its services. This room is the most highly decorated in the temple. The walls are yellow, and the two altars are red. A huge drum stands in one corner, while the walls host images of various multiarmed deities and Buddhas. The altars have four tiers, in keeping with Tibetan style, and are covered with numerous pictures of divine beings and gurus in the group's lineage. Specifically Tibetan altar adornments — such as peacock feathers; white kata cloths; little cups with

ghee, water, and other offerings in them; and eye-shaped decorations—
crowd the altars. Large wall hangings with Tibetan endless knots and Buddhist wheel symbols hide corners where cushions are stored. The hardwood
floor has been kept exposed, unlike the carpeting in the hondo downstairs.
A sign admonishes visitors to be quiet while in the practice room.

The next room, sharing a wall with the Tibetan one, is known as the
Zen room. The walls and ceiling are stark white; a tan rug with some abstract gray swirls covers part of the wood floor. A graceful wooden cabinet
serves as a makeshift altar, where a seated Buddha carved from lava sits,
surrounded by a candle, a vase, and an incense burner. Two zafus and zabutons are often placed facing each other on the floor. On the wall is a family
tree charting the many previous generations of Zen adepts. This room is
used by the Zen group to hold private meetings with visiting teachers, as
well as for overflow when too many people show up for the hondo to hold.
The difference between these two rooms has been noted by both temple
members and outsiders. An annual Mother's Day walking tour of the neighborhood sponsored by the Museum District Association included Ekoji in
2002. The temple received more than six hundred visitors, many of whom
had been unaware of the Buddhists in their midst. As the association noted
in its newsletter, "The front room upstairs is used by the Tibetan group for
meditation, chanting, and study and is in the theatrical (to American eyes)
Tibetan style, with a stepped altar. . . . In severe contrast to the Tibetan
room is the Zen meditation room (also called a 'Zendo') in the next room
to the right. The minimal decoration and spare iconography show the amaz-
ing variety within the Buddhist community—sort of like entering a Quaker
meeting house after leaving a Spanish cathedral."[40]

At the end of the hall is the office, an open space with a desk and equip-
ment: computer, fax machine, and copier donated by Temple Beth-el, the
Jewish synagogue one block from Ekoji, so that Ekoji could produce its
own newsletter.[41] Buddhist statues and paintings haphazardly adorn some
of the shelves and walls, including a fat laughing Buddha similar to the one
familiar to patrons of Chinese restaurants in America.[42] The office opens
out into the library, a small room with several hundred books on Buddhism
arranged into various categories. Temple members are allowed to sign out
books, most of which are in English.

Converting the house at Grove Avenue into a temple required a number
of structural alterations, but almost all of them were prompted by secular,
not religious, concerns—primarily to meet local laws related to safety and
access in public buildings. A ramp for wheelchairs was added in the back,

the bathroom was made handicapped-accessible, panic bars were added to the doors, blacktop was poured over much of the backyard to make a parking lot, and some modifications were made to the kitchen.[43] Further work, such as building more fencing in back, was prompted by security and privacy concerns.[44] The only real modifications specifically made in order to create a temple, as opposed to any other sort of public building, were knocking down a wall that originally divided what is now the hondo into two rooms, and adding the small Japanese garden in front.[45]

With this overview complete, it is now possible to make a general statement about the ways in which this former house has been reconfigured as a Buddhist temple. Since only a few voluntary structural alterations have been made, the primary method has been to remove the furniture related to living quarters (beds, sofas, televisions) and fill it with Buddhist "stuff." Walls that once would have held art prints or family photos now sport paintings of bodhisattvas and photos of Buddhist teachers. Buddha statues have replaced other knickknacks and works of art. The kitchen now has a superabundance of tea.[46] The family library is now stocked exclusively with dharma books. More significant, Buddhist altars have been set up in several rooms. Nonetheless, it would only take a few hours to remove all of the temple trappings and revert the building to a livable residence.

A temple in Asia would likely have been built specifically to serve as a religious gathering place, and it would proclaim its purpose much more permanently. But in America Buddhists often must make do with the structures they find already in place, except for the relatively small number of groups with sufficient size, wealth, organization, and social capital to build new structures. While Ekoji is unusual in that it has five separate groups meeting under one roof, the pattern of Buddha-cizing preexisting spaces by simply bringing in Buddhist images and ritual implements is repeated across the country, in houses as well as apartments, storefronts, garages, and even barns.[47] Part of this demonstrates a pragmatic approach that makes use of whatever is at hand and tends not to place importance on the sacred nature of spaces as such: "It's just a house that's been converted into a temple," says Martin Boyd, a member of Ekoji since 1989.[48] This observation is supported by the dedication ceremony held when Ekoji was officially opened. The order of service indicates that this event was a celebration, not a sanctification. No steps were taken to make this a specifically sacred space, set off in some metaphysical way from the "profane" space outside the temple.[49] But I argue that perhaps a greater factor in the adaptability of Buddhists to various secular spaces and the seemingly minimal requirements for a Buddhist temple in America are also rooted in a sense of what makes a space fittingly religious: that is, the use to which the spaces are put during the services themselves. It is also here that the boundaries between sects are distinguished, as each group utilizes the same space and ritual elements to evoke its own understanding of proper Buddhist practice and worldview. The next chapter details these alternate configurations.

Buddhist Circuit Riders

Ekoji Buddhist Sangha of Richmond is the product of multiple sources and the efforts of many people. But there is one person of whom it is fair to say that Ekoji would not exist had it not been for his work, and that he contributed more to the founding and early development of the temple than anyone else: Reverend Takashi Kenryu Tsuji. It behooves us, therefore, to examine the life of this itinerant Buddhist priest in order to discover what brought him to establish the first Jodo Shinshu temples in the South.

Takashi Tsuji was born on March 14, 1919, on a poor farm in Mission City, British Columbia, about forty miles from Vancouver. His parents, Kamejiro and Suya Tsuji, were immigrants from Shiga prefecture in central Japan. Like many people in Shiga and most of the Japanese immigrants during this time period, the Tsujis belonged to the Jodo Shinshu Honganji-ha (also known as Nishi Honganji) sect of Pure Land Buddhism. Takashi Tsuji had three older brothers and an older sister. Despite the hardships imposed on Asian immigrants in British Columbia, he was able to complete elementary and high school and attend a year at the University of British Columbia.

In 1938 Tsuji was awarded a scholarship to attend Ryukoku University in Kyoto. Located next to the head temple of the Honganji-ha, Ryukoku served as a seminary as well as providing courses in secular education. Tsuji entered the ministerial track as the first Canadian and one of the first persons from outside Japan to pursue ordination in Jodo Shinshu. He was also hampered by the fact that he possessed only the most rudimentary knowledge of the Japanese language and often could not understand the advanced technical Buddhist terms being discussed in Japanese in his classes. Luckily, he acquired friends who helped him to study, and with intensive effort he was eventually able to master Japanese and come to understand most of his coursework.

The world situation, meanwhile, was deteriorating. Japan's aggressive overseas military advancement had brought it into conflict with many na-

Reverend Takashi Kenryu Tsuji. Photograph by Evan Cantwell, used with permission.

tions, including the United Kingdom and its former colonies, and it became clear that war between Japan and Canada was coming. Tsuji was advised to leave Japan quickly before war broke out since as a young man he was likely to be conscripted into the Japanese army despite his Canadian citizenship. After three years of study he had been ordained (receiving the Buddhist name Kenryu) and had acquired significant knowledge of Buddhist theory and ritual, but his intention had been to complete a full six-year training regimen. It was with some reservations that he left Japan in October 1941, on what would prove to be the final ship to leave Japan for Canada.

Tsuji arrived in Vancouver the next month and was appointed assistant minister of the Honpa Buddhist Temple. The following month Japan attacked Pearl Harbor, and Canada, already fighting in Europe since 1939, was drawn into the Pacific theater of World War II. Immediately, Canadian agencies began to move against the Japanese and Japanese Canadian population in the country. Five of the seven foreign-born ministers were interned (some were sent to labor camps), and movement began on a plan to force all people of Japanese descent (including natural-born Canadian citizens) to leave the West Coast. Tsuji, as the only natural-born Canadian minister, was temporarily allowed to remain in Vancouver; the government needed him (as a speaker of both English and Japanese and a local authority figure) to coordinate the removal of so many people to camps further inland, and his youth and low rank in the Canadian Buddhist administration must have made him seem relatively harmless. Thus in January 1942, at age twenty-two, Reverend Takashi Kenryu Tsuji became head minister of the Honpa Buddhist Temple and de facto leader of the Buddhists of Canada.[50]

Throughout 1942 Tsuji assisted in moving the Japanese and Japanese Canadian population to internment camps away from the Pacific Coast. He traveled to sites selected by the government and surveyed them so that he could help evacuees coordinate, he raised money for the evacuation, and he managed the transference of property from the evacuees to legal guardians. Most of all, he provided spiritual and moral support to the displaced community as its members were forced out of their homes and away from their businesses (most of which they would never be allowed to reclaim). Finally, in October 1942, Tsuji took the last train from Vancouver with the final evacuees, bound for the frozen mountain ghost town of Sandon, five hundred miles away in the Slocan Valley, on the border with Alberta.

Immediately after arriving at the concentration camps Tsuji organized a new temple, the Slocan Buddhist Temple. Besides his religious and community leadership duties, he also became principal of the Bay Farm Elementary School (in the nearby Bay Farm camp, where he also led the Bay Farm Buddhist congregation). It was at the school that he met Sakaye Kawabata, who would become his wife. Conditions were harsh in the Slocan Valley camps, which received only a few hours of daily sunlight. Almost all possessions had been left behind in the hands of the Custodian of Alien Property, from whence they were eventually sold for a pittance to non-Japanese and passed permanently out of the community's hands.

After two years of working and ministering to the Slocan internees, Tsuji began to think about the postwar situation. It was clear that the Japanese and Japanese Canadians would not be allowed to return to the West Coast or to reclaim their property, and that therefore when they were released from the camps they would have only two choices: move to Japan or migrate further eastward into areas of Canada without historic Japanese immigrant populations. Tsuji realized the east, which had been completely unserved by the Buddhists, would be the next great mission field for Jodo Shinshu. He reasoned that Toronto was where the largest number of migrants was likely to congregate, and he thus laid plans to move there and assist them in their resettlement. In mid-1945 he left the Slocan area and relocated to Port Credit, near Toronto. As a newcomer and a Japanese Canadian, he found work difficult to come by and performed a succession of menial jobs, such as mushroom farm worker, dishwasher, and laborer in a chemical factory. He finally managed to enroll as a student at the University of Toronto, permitting him to transfer into the heart of the city (though not universally applied, Toronto's policy at the time was that students were the only former internees allowed to live in the city) and move about more freely in the growing Japanese Canadian community. As the only minister in the province, he organized the Toronto Buddhist Church; he also organized temples in Hamilton and Thunder Bay, Ontario, and Montreal, Quebec. Eventually more ministers would join him, but he spent much time traveling between these various places to nurture their congregations.

Tsuji shepherded the eastern Canadian churches for years: in the process he developed many rituals and programs that would be used not only throughout Canada but also in the United States, including Sunday school curricula, Buddhist wedding ceremonies, dedication rituals for infants and affirmation ceremonies for adults, and various programs for adult religious education. His perambulations were not restricted to Canada, however. His excellent public speaking skills (including his fluent English), progressive views on modern Buddhism, and willingness to travel in order to spread Buddhism soon came to the attention of the much larger Buddhist community in the United States. During the summer of 1948 Tsuji was chosen to be the first traveling minister of the Eastern Young Buddhist League. That October Tsuji, not yet thirty years old, embarked on a two-month-long speaking tour in the United States that took him to Minneapolis; St. Louis; Chicago; Cleveland; New York; Philadelphia; and Seabrook, New Jersey. In all of these cities, he not only spoke to Buddhists but also made presentations to numerous university groups, civic organizations, and Christian churches and did radio broadcasts. He thus reinforced local Buddhist communities and disseminated information on Buddhism to the wider public. He also came into contact with many hundreds of non-Buddhists and became aware of some of the gross distortions of Buddhism that were present in North America. From this time he would continuously seek to not only nurture the Buddhists in Canada and America but also bring non-Japanese into Buddhism and educate all North Americans about the Buddhist religion. He continued as a popular speaker on both sides of the international border, serving, for example, as a speaker in 1952 at the first session of what would become the important Pacific Seminars (annual California lectures to the public on Buddhist themes).

A major shift in Tsuji's life occurred in 1959. He was invited to fill the newly created position of director of the Bureau of Buddhist Education at the San Francisco headquarters of the Buddhist Churches of America. The BCA is the mainland American branch of the Honganji-ha sect (the Hawaiian temples are organized separately) and significantly larger than its Canadian counterpart. Tsuji and his family (he and his wife then had three daughters; a fourth was subsequently born in the United States) moved to California, ending his time at the Toronto Buddhist Church. Still not quite forty years old when his term began on February 3, 1959, Tsuji was effectively in charge of Buddhist educational activities throughout all of North America. He undertook a tour of all temples in the BCA (approximately fifty), organized the country's first Buddhist bookstore, and coordinated the creation of seminars and conferences for each of the BCA districts. He and his department also authored numerous books, pamphlets, and other resources for temple use, and he created an audiovisual division with educational slideshows in order to expand Buddhist education into newer media. In 1964 he was also appointed director of ministerial applications, increasing his importance at the headquarters of American Jodo Shinshu. That year he also became a U.S. citizen.

Further changes for Tsuji and the BCA came in 1969, when he was elected bishop (the head of the organization). Tsuji's election was unprecedented in many different ways. Fifty years old, he was the youngest person ever elected and the first Nisei (second-generation Japanese North American). Both laypeople and ministers were involved in his election, a new development. And the election signified a renegotiation of the power relationship with the head temple in Kyoto: the bishop was chosen by Americans and then confirmed by the Honganji-ha rather than being selected by the headquarters in Japan. Tsuji celebrated his election with a three-week speaking and listening tour of the temples in the eastern United States and Canada, followed by a tour of Buddhist sites in Japan and Southeast Asia. He returned to be ordained bishop in San Francisco, the first time the ceremony had occurred outside of Kyoto, on June 1. In his inauguration speech—delivered first in Japanese and then English—he proclaimed that while the accomplishments of the previous generation had to be recognized and honored, the BCA still had much work ahead. His intention was to adapt Buddhism to America and to expand Buddhism beyond the confines of BCA temples into the general public.

Tsuji served as bishop from 1968 to 1981, the second-longest term of any bishop to date, and a good case can be made that he is the most significant single figure in the organization's history. During his three terms (he was reelected in 1971 and 1976) the BCA expanded and formalized, systematically compiling membership statistics, acquiring new headquarters, standardizing ministerial salaries and instituting disability and pension plans, revising election procedures and terms, undertaking membership activities aimed at young Japanese Americans and at non-Japanese Americans, consolidating its newspapers into the bilingual monthly *Wheel of Dharma* (still in publication), dedicating a memorial for all the BCA members who had died in America, and receiving accreditation for its seminary and graduate school (the Institute for Buddhist Studies, of which Tsuji was president). Tsuji created multiple educational Buddhist films while on pilgrimage in Sri Lanka and India, and he represented the BCA at Buddhist functions worldwide, as well as at interfaith gatherings in Washington, DC; New York City; and elsewhere. He traveled frequently to speak at temples, focusing especially on underserved areas such as the Eastern District and Mexico, the latter in a missionary tour in 1972. Tsuji cultivated lay leaders for the BCA and recruited new ministers and seminarians, and he continued to produce new educational pamphlets and other materials. He also encouraged the development of Boy and Cub Scout and Campfire Girl activities at Buddhist temples. One of the more noteworthy changes during his tenure was a clear drive toward greater engagement with American society and activist interaction with the political scene. Under Tsuji's leadership, the BCA publicly opposed prayer in public schools, objected to inaccurate portrayals of Buddhism and to the inclusion of creationism in California textbooks, and issued public statements on important social issues such as abortion.

All of this is, from a certain perspective, prelude to Tsuji's importance in this book. It was in 1981, when he retired from the position of bishop, that he began to directly make his mark felt in the South. Tsuji had visited Washington, DC, numerous times as director of Buddhist education and as bishop and had long harbored a desire to see Buddhist temples planted in the Southeast, especially near the nation's capital. In preparation for the seventy-fifth anniversary of the BCA in 1974, Tsuji told the Nisei Buddhist Society that at the one hundredth anniversary in twenty-five years' time there should be "a strong delegation of non-Japanese Shin Buddhists, black, brown, white and red, from the southern States" and elsewhere.[51] He was also advocating for a doubling of ministers within fifteen years and for these to be mission priests who went out and organized new temples in unserved areas, such as the East Coast.[52] This was in some ways merely a continuation of efforts to plant new temples in the East since 1945 and part of the truly national vision he had articulated early during his tenure as director of Buddhist education, when he described his desire to see the BCA include "the cattleman of the great plains" and "the young secretary in the crowded Uptown subway in Manhattan" and claimed that "it is only when we enlarge the field of our Buddhist consciousness, make decisions and follow through with effective actions, institute nation-wide programs to embrace and include all those who recite the Nembutsu in this fair land, that we can say the Buddhist Churches of America has attained national stature. Herein lies our immediate objective and for American Buddhism, a national purpose."[53]

As the final phase of his long ministerial career, Tsuji decided to set the example for mission priests. Soon after retiring as bishop he moved to Washington, DC, and founded the Ekoji Buddhist Temple in nearby Springfield, Virginia, drawing on the membership of the Washington, DC, Sangha, a group of local Shin Buddhists who had gathered informally in 1959. He became head minister of this Ekoji and used it as a base from which to begin ministering to Buddhists throughout the South. It was in this capacity that in 1984 people in Richmond heard of his presence in Virginia and invited him to begin giving talks in Richmond, which eventually led to his founding of Ekoji Buddhist Sangha of Richmond in 1986. This was not the full extent of his activities in the South, however. Tsuji also organized Jodo Shinshu congregations in Morganton, North Carolina; in Augusta and Atlanta, Georgia; and in Dallas, Texas. He itinerated through the South, making periodic circuits from Northern Virginia to Richmond, then to Morganton, on to Augusta and Atlanta, and thence to Dallas before returning to the DC suburbs again. He also made occasional visits to Buddhists in Florida.

Essentially, Tsuji went wherever the possibility of promoting Buddhism offered an opportunity. Typically, such as in Richmond and Morganton, this occurred when individuals interested in Buddhism contacted the Ekoji temple in Northern Virginia. Once he had a contact person in a new town, Tsuji would add it to his list of destinations and pass through on his next regional tour to deliver sermons, lead rituals, and discuss Buddhism with any interested locals. In all of this, he was following in the footsteps (or hoof prints) of a venerable tradition of itinerant preachers and religious organizers who brought religion to scattered communities in the southern United States. Most famous were the Methodists, whose exploits in organizing "class meetings" became legendary in the nineteenth century. My informants in Richmond readily equated these patterns, with many of them referring to Tsuji as a "circuit rider" and praising his efforts to spread Buddhism over such a gigantic territory in the South. It was a model for which in some ways his entire life had prepared him: as a child he was first inspired to pursue the ministry by itinerant Buddhist priests who would stay with his family in British Columbia, and his adult life was characterized by many traveling preaching trips and an ongoing concern to bring non-Buddhists into contact with Buddhism.

As a Buddhist circuit rider, Tsuji had it easier in certain ways than his Methodist predecessors. For one, of course, he was more of a "circuit driver" than a rider, since he could take advantage of a well-established network of highways and even sometimes air travel, rather than the dirt roads or pathless wilderness that the Methodists traveled through. He was often accompanied by his wife on such trips, rather than enduring the lonely bachelor existence that the Methodists experienced. He could telephone ahead to coordinate his visits, or at least take advantage of the faster and more reliable postal service of the late twentieth century. There were, however, certain relative disadvantages as well. The Methodists evangelized a basically Christian (if largely unchurched) population, while most southerners in Tsuji's time had little understanding of or interest in Buddhism. Tsuji's race was probably a disadvantage at times as well, and he was far older than most of the Methodist circuit riders during their time (indeed, older than many of them ever got, since they often died from their exertions at relatively early ages). But perhaps the greatest comparative disadvantage he faced was the difference in ministerial ordination process and congregational organization. The itinerant Methodist circuit rider was empowered to gather classes wherever possible and appoint class leaders. This allowed new congregations to come into being easily and to be led by locals who were of the same stock and station as those they exhorted, at which point the circuit rider could shift his attentions to new flocks. Under the towering figure of the bishop Francis Asbury, the entire force of the denomination's leadership was oriented toward itinerancy, with clearly worked-out procedures and strong moral and theological (if not always financial) support. And this focus on uneducated ministers who came "from the people" included a drive to penetrate ever more regions of the country and to exhort the people publicly, without invitation, in order to gather new flocks in virgin territory.[54]

By contrast, the Honganji-ha process stifled new congregations. Individual ministers could not train or ordain other ministers — all ordinations had to take place in Kyoto — and there were no clearly defined roles for lay preachers or study leaders. Whereas the Methodist minister merely had to have a conversion experience, loyalty to the Methodist church, and a basic knowledge of Christianity, the Jodo Shinshu minister had to be a ritual and doctrinal expert ordained only after a rigorous, years-long process of training, unavailable outside California or Japan, that involved three successive levels of certification (tokudo, kyoshi, and kaikyoshi). The ordination ritual itself was only available in Japan. And prior to the commencement of religious training, the applicant was expected to have acquired a college education. In fact, while outsider characterizations often paint Jodo Shinshu as a Buddhism of faith and assume that this entails a lower respect for reason, science, and learning compared to other forms of Buddhism, Shin ministers as a class are among the most highly educated of Western Buddhist leaders, as their seminary training is longer and more academically rigorous than that of most other leaders (such as Zen teachers, for example), and secular college education is expected on top of religious training (many Buddhist leaders in the West have such education, but it is not required by other denominations). The entire system of Honganji-ha was oriented toward leadership by highly educated and trained settled ministers serving particular established parishes; to the extent that models for missionary activity even existed, they were designed to serve the needs of recognized Shin Buddhist families who had emigrated to non-Japanese locales. And while congregations could gather informally, the certification process for full temples was also complicated and controlled by forces far outside the region, in California and Japan. Thus Tsuji could travel and speak to groups in the South, but he could not cultivate a stable population of Jodo Shinshu ministers or lay leaders to nurture true temples during the times that he was unavailable. As a result, he fell back on creating loose networks of southern Buddhists who gathered to meet locally when he was in town and supported each other through correspondence and private reading when he was away—a model that perhaps suited the overwhelmingly educated nature of the converts who came to Jodo Shinshu but that was inadequate for creating a mass movement on the order of the earlier Methodist missions. This pattern continued from 1981 until Tsuji's final retirement from the ministry, after fifty-eight years of service, in 1999. By that time Tsuji was suffering from Alzheimer's disease and becoming increasingly forgetful. He and Sakaye moved back to California to be near his adult children and grandchildren. He passed away from pneumonia in 2004.

Takashi Kenryu Tsuji's activities in the South point to a type of American Buddhist who has not received sufficient attention in the historical annals of Buddhism in America: the Buddhist circuit rider. Research has tended to focus on two types of subjects—specific Buddhist communities or famous monks and other leaders (especially if they attracted large numbers of white followers and published books about Buddhism). In the case of communities, these naturally are approached as groups in specific locations or with diffusion throughout the country, and thus movement is not an important subject for analysis. As for monks and leaders, most attention has been given to famous teachers who founded specific temples or meditation groups, typically in parts of the country where they could locally attract sufficient members and therefore did not need to travel constantly in order to serve a thin mission field. Examples include Shunryu Suzuki, Robert Aitken, Philip Kapleau, Taizan Maezumi, Jack Kornfield, and other familiar names in American Buddhist historiography.

The Buddhist circuit rider, by contrast, is a solitary figure in constant movement. He or she eschews a fully settled lifestyle in favor of frequent travel in order to bring the dharma to groups without their own local leaders or who do not have any local exposure to Buddhism at all. This is a hard life and often does not reap terrific benefits: of the many places in which Tsuji invested his time and energy, today only Ekoji Buddhist Temple is a Jodo Shinshu temple, while Ekoji Buddhist Sangha of Richmond has a small Pure Land presence among a larger, leaderless collection of Buddhist groups, and the Morganton sangha has evolved into an explicitly nonsectarian lay group with only a slight Jodo Shinshu membership—the other sites no longer have any active Buddhist activity at all derived from Tsuji's efforts. In part because such leaders rarely gather large communities that are able to publish and promote their lineages, and also because they operate in places where there are supposedly few if any Buddhists, they are unseen by many researchers. Another reason is that those Buddhist circuit riders who do establish large congregations may then settle down in one place, and it is often only at this point (as settled ministers) that they begin to attract outside notice. But the circuit riders' activities are an important part of the story of American Buddhism, and their contributions are substantial: most of the Buddhist groups in the Richmond area owe their existence to Tsuji (either as inhabitants of Ekoji, former tenants, or schisms from former groups), not to mention the Ekoji temple in Northern Virginia and pockets of individual practitioners in many parts of the South.[55]

Tsuji was hardly the only such Buddhist circuit rider in the South, although he was one of the first. Due to the low numbers of Buddhist leaders in this region, even monks and priests at established temples are called on to travel widely. Josho Pat Phelan, for example, abbess of Chapel Hill Zen Center in central North Carolina, not only ministers to her own temple but also travels regularly to Richmond to serve the Richmond Zen Group; in addition, at times in the past she has driven to serve groups in Wilmington, North Carolina, as well as in Roanoke and Virginia Beach, although now she has trained an assistant priest who can help with satellite groups as well as teach in Chapel Hill. Chinese American Buddhists in Richmond have been served by itinerant monks and nuns from the Foguangshan temple in Cary, North Carolina, and the Dallas temple of the Amitabha Buddhist Society. And Oliver Akerman, whose story I tell in chapter 5, now travels to serve Buddhist groups in different parts of Virginia. Thus while the numbers of formal Buddhist leaders are low in the South, a closer examination reveals far-flung regional networks of teachers who crisscross the southern states to support Buddhists in areas with few resources.

Kenryu Tsuji: Modernist Shin Buddhist Priest

Besides being a Buddhist circuit rider, Tsuji also represents another type of Buddhist leader who has been mostly overlooked in the general historiography of American Buddhism, though the model is recognized by scholars who work on Japan: the modernist Shin Buddhist priest. In this capacity he made an indelible impression on Buddhism in Richmond. Modernist

Buddhism is a category that has been advanced by several scholars of Buddhism, and especially but not solely of its history in the West, including most recently and in excellent detail by Donald S. Lopez Jr. (*A Modern Buddhist Bible*, 2002) and David L. McMahan (*The Making of Buddhist Modernism*, 2008). Lopez assigns a number of easily recognizable characteristics to modernist ("modern," to use his term) Buddhism: it identifies the present as a standpoint from which to reflect on the history of religion and identify deficiencies; it sees itself as a return to purer religion closer in spirit and practice to original Buddhism; it is oriented toward philosophy and doctrine more than daily practice; it is rational and ethical in nature; it is pluralistic (although this does not prevent Buddhists from claiming that their particular sect is best); it is socially engaged; it values meditation; and it is individualistic. McMahan agrees with these characterizations and also points out the importance of psychological approaches to Buddhism, demythologization, democratic elements, disposal or reinterpretation of traditional images, and opposition to orthodoxy. This modernist Buddhism has been two centuries in the making, a complicated process that has taken place in both Asia and the West, created by people from many countries and with many sectarian affiliations, and with influences not only from Buddhism but also from or in reaction to Christianity, colonialism, the industrial revolution, nationalism, Enlightenment rationalism, Western humanism, Romanticism, and postmodernism. Today, much if not most Buddhism in the West can be classified as modernist to a substantial degree, regardless of the ethnic basis or sectarian orientation of particular groups.

It is clear that Tsuji should be classified as a modernist Buddhist. From early in his teaching career he was noted for stressing that Buddhism was characterized by a "scientific" approach—calling Buddhism the culmination of an instinctive search for truth and stressing the buddha-nature of all individual persons—and for his focus on "Americanizing" Buddhism.[56] One of his early essays, from 1949, stresses the freedom found in nembutsu recitation:

For the pilgrim of the Nembutsu, there is no place in his being for any trace of fear. He lives in the Nembutsu, the holy name—Namu amida Butsu, meaning, "I place my wholehearted trust in Amida Buddha." Since Amida Buddha is Truth, it signifies man's discovery of the heart of Truth. When man identifies himself with Truth, he walks the Path of Freedom. No moral law, no universe, no authority can subjugate him. Socrates was thrown in jail, but his spirit which loved Truth, could never be put in shackles. Honen was banished from the city of Kyoto by imperial proclamation for teaching the Nembutsu, but no edict could inspire fear in his heart.[57]

It is important to note that this address was first delivered to Japanese Canadians, for whom imprisonment and banishment were not abstract concepts. Tsuji's years spent in Canadian concentration camps and his postwar experience ministering to a Buddhist population traumatized by their own government pushed him to emphasize a Pure Land Buddhism that inspired courage and confidence and promised personal freedom rather than stressing conformity, acceptance of authority, or religious passivity. When his mother passed away later in 1949, he memorialized her by stressing how she had lived as a Buddhist rather than focusing on her rebirth in the Pure Land: "My mother could hardly read or write but she spent a life in complete harmony with Buddha. The Nembutsu was always on her lips. In the recitation of Namu Amida Butsu, she found an outward expression of an inward harmony with the Great Compassionate Heart of the Buddha. To her, knowing the life to come did not simply mean the life after death. It signified a life that was fully lived, ever conscious of the moving heart of the universe and greater life, lived in oneness with the spirit of Amida Buddha."[58] And as he explained on another occasion: "'Namu Amida Butsu' signifies harmony with Amida. It is the spirit of universality. It is the Compassionate Heart that identifies itself with the hearts of others, cries when other hearts cry and rejoices when other hearts rejoice. Man can never find his true self until he begins to feel with the universe. . . . 'Namu Amida Butsu' is the discovery of the true 'I' in the light of the Universal Amida."[59] In these quotations we see Tsuji playing with the traditional elements of Jodo Shinshu: nembutsu, Amida Buddha, and birth in the Pure Land, exploring meanings that have greater relevance to the present day than the afterlife and which are both more individualistic and more universal.

In 1954, while ministering to the Toronto Buddhist Church, Tsuji authored a booklet called *An Outline of Buddhism* that was reprinted numerous times over the coming decades and is still available from the Buddhist Churches of America. He devotes three-quarters of the booklet to the history of Buddhism (mostly in India) and to what he calls the "Fundamental Teachings of Buddhism":[60] the Four Noble Truths, the Eightfold Path, and the Twelvefold Chain of Causation. In the final section he describes Jodo Shinshu doctrine in a fairly straightforward way, but with a modernist twist at select moments. For example, "Rebirth in the Pure Land (Ojodo) symbolizes the religious aspiration of man to attain Enlightenment," and "Amida Buddha is a manifestation of the Truth of the Universe in human form."[61] Thus he does not deny the reality of the Pure Land or Amida, but he interprets them in ways that allow for a greater emphasis on personal spirituality and a generic Buddhist quest for awakening, and he suggests there is an underlying universal truth behind the apparent anthropomorphic form of Amida. When discussing memorial services he goes out of his way to criticize the "mistaken notion [that] the chanting itself and the service brings benefits for the deceased."[62] Instead, he insists that the chanting is performed because the sutra describes the laudable virtues of the Pure Land and Amida. This too is orthodox Jodo Shinshu, but it is notable that Tsuji feels a need to insist on an expressive interpretation of sutra chanting ritual that denies merit-making approaches.

If anything, this modernist trend seemed to accelerate once Tsuji moved to the United States. In the leaflet "Reincarnation: My Answer" that Tsuji produced for the BCA as director of the Bureau of Buddhist Education, he spends most of his time refuting the idea that Buddhists believe in past lives and future rebirths as animals or new persons. Instead, he says that Buddhists believe in karma, which is the law of the conservation of moral energy and explains how our actions affect the world and our own experience of life. The ten realms of being (buddha, bodhisattva, solitary buddha, disciple, heavenly being, humans, fighting spirits, animals, hungry ghosts, and hell beings) are not taught as explicit places or realities. "These ten realms are not fixed objective worlds," Tsuji writes. "They are mental and spiritual states, created by men's thoughts, actions and words. In other words, they are psychological states."[63] In 1960 he combined American booster rhetoric with Shin Buddhist motifs to proclaim that "the values inherent in the teaching of Nembutsu—humility and thanksgiving; moral action prompted by contrition and gratitude; justice, liberty and equal opportunity for all founded on Amida's Wisdom and Compassion—cannot be truly preserved and given forceful expression if we remained provincial in our thinking, conscious of only the small circle of our church."[64] Always, Tsuji was concerned not only with his own ethnic community but also with the wider society in which it existed. In 1967 Tsuji published a booklet titled *Three Lectures on the "Tannisho."* The *Tannisho* is an anonymous tract claiming to contain a record of the teachings of Jodo Shinshu's founder, Shinran. Traditionally it was an obscure text whose difficulties led it to be confined to a small circle of clerical elites within Jodo Shinshu. But ever since it was first promoted by the original Shin modernist, Kiyozawa Manshi, in the late nineteenth century, the *Tannisho* has been the most important single text for the promotion of a more contemporary Jodo Shinshu. By 1967 Tsuji had adopted a new way of speaking of Amida that had evolved from his earlier presentation. He speaks of Dharmakara (the bodhisattva who became Amida according to the Larger Pure Land Sutra) as "a mythological figure" and says that "Amida is the personification of the timeless spirit of Buddhahood."[65] It is clear in context that by this he does not mean that Amida is nonexistent. Instead, he means that the story of Amida's enlightenment and creation of the Pure Land has come to be portrayed mainly as a useful teaching device, as a "myth" taking place "in timeless time" rather than as a historical fact.[66] The modernizing trend is clear in his presentation of Shinran as well. Tsuji proclaims "I cannot help but be drawn to Shinran Shonin's humanity. Shinran Shonin was a human being; he never claimed to be a saint."[67] The human Shinran, a role model we can emulate and at the same time a foolish being like us all, is a popular trope of modernist Shin Buddhism and greatly contrasts with the premodern presentation of Shinran as an enlightened, saintly miracle worker equivalent to (or perhaps an incarnation of) Amida Buddha.

By the time Tsuji retired as bishop and relocated to the South, he had perfected a manner of expression that universalized and privatized the encounter with spiritual reality and affirmed the compassionate, dynamic truth that Amida embodied while making it clear that the motifs of Pure Land Buddhism were skillful symbols that should not be treated as idols. Thus he spoke of the "law of the universe" and the "power of infinite wisdom and compassion" that "in my religious consciousness" is "personified and called Amida Buddha."[68] According to Tsuji,

> Shinran Shonin and the teachers before him explained that the Pure Land was situated in the western corners of the universe, zillions of miles away. It was pictured as a very beautiful place, free of suffering, where everyone is happy. Philosophically speaking, however, the Pure Land does not refer to a specific location out there somewhere. Rather, the Pure Land is symbolic; it symbolizes the transcendence of relativity, of all limited qualities, of the finiteness of human life. In this transcendence, there is Compassion-Wisdom, an active moving, spiritual force. The Pure Land ideal is the culmination of the teaching of Wisdom and Compassion.[69]

Amida Buddha was not an objective entity existing somewhere in time and space; he was a reflection of the individual's connection to the inner truth of reality:

> When I experience this Dharma in my kokoro—mind/heart—I call the Dharma "Amida Buddha." When I bow my head, I am bowing before the great Dharma of the Universe. When I put my hands together in gassho, I am physically expressing my inner acceptance of the Dharma. In the humble act of gassho I turn from the philosophic acceptance of the Dharma to the religious experience of Amida Buddha. The Dharma of my cold philosophy and ratiocination is transformed by my religious experience into the Dharma with personal characteristics that is vibrant, warm, breathing, caring, all wise and all compassionate. Thus the Dharma is transformed into Amida Buddha, the Buddha of Infinite Wisdom and Compassion.[70]

Tsuji also promoted silent meditation as a way to deepen and expand awareness, perform self-reflection, and achieve a calm and peaceful mind.[71] Although Tsuji was only one of many to make such suggestions in the BCA, his advocacy of meditation is a significant fact to observe. Silent meditation is not a traditional practice of Jodo Shinshu, which holds that nembutsu recitation is fully sufficient; in some interpretations, silent meditation is even considered pernicious and anti-Shin as it can lead to egoism. Thus while he left silent meditation as a peripheral practice—to be used when appropriate, with nembutsu remaining for him the central practice—that he included it at all was a notable innovation.

In *A Challenge for American Shin Buddhists*, one of his final published essays, Tsuji laid out his clear opposition to inherited dogma. Proclaiming that Shin Buddhist education must not only be the provenance of ordained ministers but must also involve active laypeople (because "in the Shinshu Sangha there is no differentiation between the lay and the ordained"), he warned that if people failed to interpret the concepts of Jodo Shinshu "into a language that the ordinary person can understand, Shinshu cannot offer any fresh insights into the meaning of modern life."[72] Therefore, "the time is now when both ministers and lay members must join forces to extricate ourselves from the dark morass in which we find ourselves."[73] This morass was what Tsuji characterized as "Shinshuology," a dogmatic and insular approach to Jodo Shinshu developed during Japan's feudal era. Because self-cultivation and self-effort are anathema in Shinshuology, they have stifled important adaptations that must take place if Shin Buddhism is to find a place in American society and nurture twentieth-century Americans, who live in a context very different from premodern Japan. Tsuji urged American Buddhists to "remember that both Buddha and Shinran were reformers."[74] He suggested that Jodo Shinshu "must study Zen's approach to inner tranquility and love of nature, Theravadin moral principles, Nichiren and Christian social activism and so on. . . . Because of the universal nature of Amida's cosmic compassion there is no reason why we cannot receive unending inspiration from the sacred writings of all the world's great religions."[75] Tsuji's pluralist agenda could not be any clearer.

One more aspect of Tsuji's approach to Jodo Shinshu should also be emphasized: he was something of a nature mystic. Perhaps this should not be surprising in someone who grew up on a farm. In "I Gassho to Amida," a widely used liturgical piece that Tsuji originally composed for use in Sunday schools, he sings:

> Trees and grasses and flowers
> All grow in His Compassion.
> His Light shines throughout the world.
> I gassho to Amida.
>
> Flowers bloom and flowers fall;
> From the seeds sprout new flowers;
> This is the Truth unchanging.
> I gassho to Amida.
>
> Springtime brings the happy birds,
> Their songs all praise Amida;
> I join them in Nembutsu.
> I gassho to Amida.[76]

The idea that animals and natural phenomena say nembutsu through their cries and sounds occurred often in his essays: "Here in Virginia, in the hot humid evenings the fireflies light up the lawns with their natural glow and the cicadas join the myriad of insects in the recitation of the Nembutsu."[77]

In Tsuji's understanding, nembutsu goes beyond the words "Namu Amida Butsu" to become the essence of reality and enlightenment itself:

> The Nembutsu is the sound of the universe.
> It is the sound of the wind
> as it rustles the leaves;
> It is the roar of the waves

as they rush toward the shore;
It is the song of the robin, the whippoorwill
and the chorus of cicadas on a summer evening.
The Nembutsu is naturalness.[78]

That such nonhuman beings and things can express the nembutsu is a result of the buddha-nature that they share with all things: "Buddha-nature
is not restricted solely to human beings. The fundamental Dharma teaches
us that even 'the mountains, rivers, trees, grass all possess Buddha-nature.'
This means not only human beings but all sentient beings, all things in the
universe, possess the capacity to become a Buddha. Once a scientist asked
me, 'How can a rock become a Buddha?' I replied, 'When you have become
a Buddha.'"[79]

In this nature mysticism we see a very particular approach to the Pure
Land tradition. This is not a Pure Land Buddhism that despises the things
of this world and seeks salvation in the blissful realm of Amida in the afterlife. Rather, it affirms that awakening occurs in this lifetime and in this
world when it is viewed through the mind that has been opened by Amida,
"the Cosmic Compassion of the Universe": [80] "Enlightenment is found in
the earthly realms of suffering, hunger, instinct, conflict, human frailties
and pleasure. For the spiritually awakened person, Enlightenment is here
and now, amidst the trials and tribulations of human existence."[81]

It should be obvious by now that Tsuji's Jodo Shinshu is a form of modernist Buddhism, with the qualities described by Lopez and McMahan. Yet
despite its size and international presence, in their books Jodo Shinshu is
entirely absent, nor does Shin Buddhism appear regularly in other works
on these modern approaches to the Buddhist tradition. Instead, modernist
Buddhism is typically confined to a narrow spectrum of Zen, Tibetan, and
reformist Theravada (especially Vipassana) Buddhism.[82]

Why are figures such as Tsuji left out of this primary narrative for the
transmission and adaptation of Buddhism in the contemporary world and
especially for the West? There appear to be three main reasons. First, despite
being one of the primary locations for the production of modern Buddhism
in Japan and North America, Pure Land Buddhism has received little attention or respect from Western scholars of Buddhist modernism, who most
often have personal affiliations with the Zen, Tibetan, or Vipassana traditions. Pure Land Buddhism is stereotyped erroneously as a more tradition-
alistic or anti-intellectual form of Buddhism by outsiders who have minimal contact with its modern history and manifestations. Second, Pure Land

motifs when only given cursory attention can *appear* to be nonmodern in nature, since they involve cosmic buddhas, heavenly pure lands, less esteem for silent meditation, and a rhetoric of faith. But when these motifs are actually examined, it can be clearly seen that the manner in which they are actually understood, promoted, and used is often fully consonant with the generic modernist Buddhist approach. Third, the overwhelmingly Japanese American nature of the Buddhist Churches of America has led some scholars to interpret it as an ethnic fortress intent on preserving the modes of traditional Japanese religion, rather than to recognize the exhaustive nature of the modifications and new interpretations that have been introduced over generations of active search for an American Buddhism.

Takashi Kenryu Tsuji is a useful figure because he allows us to bring attention back to the Buddhist Churches of America and place this organization squarely in the mainstream of modernist American Buddhism. It would be a mistake to interpret him as somehow an exceptional figure unrepresentative of the BCA. True, he was exceptional in the extent to which he shaped the BCA in the second half of the twentieth century, and his experiences were more varied than most. But he was in no way exceptional in his modernist Shin Buddhism. Indeed, he never could have operated as such an insider—including more than twenty years in key positions at the national headquarters—if he had been an outlier. Rather, Tsuji's modernist approach was and remains mainstream for North American Jodo Shinshu, as reflected in the majority of the hundreds of ministers who have served in the BCA and countless lay members. The modernist Shin priest is in fact a staple figure of BCA history, including such important persons as Hozen Seki, Kanmo Imamura, Alfred Bloom, Newton Ishiura, Taitetsu Unno, Seigen Yamaoka, and the current bishop, Koshin Ogui, men whose histories collectively span the entirety of the twentieth century and the twenty-first century up to the present day. The truth is that in the 1970s, Tsuji was the head of the largest modernist Buddhist organization that has ever existed in the West. And he was no insular ethnic Buddhist cut off from his surroundings: Tsuji rubbed shoulders with the likes of Alan Watts and attended major interfaith gatherings in the nation's capital, and he called for BCA to commit to "issues of world peace, hunger and poverty, and human dignity."[83]

Shin Buddhist modernism such as Tsuji embodied helps to nuance our understandings of modernist Buddhism as a phenomenon, because while it carries all the aspects identified as modern, it provides a particular inflection to them. Thus we see in Tsuji a modernist Buddhist who uses metaphorical interpretations but is comfortable with traditional language and motifs, who encourages meditation but decenters it in favor of chanting, who is thoroughly pluralist but committed to a single denomination, who seeks racial integration but spends most of his time among Asian Americans, who is interested in "original Buddhism" but mostly teaches and practices recent trends in Japanese and North American Pure Land Buddhism. Above all, we see that modernist Buddhism can exist in a passionately devotional form, which nonetheless affirms the value of science and reason and does not infringe on respect for the individual or insist on orthodoxy or hierarchical authority. And, what is essential, this modernist Buddhism has a spirit of engagement that can lead to missionary activity, which is what brought Tsuji to the South.

Distribution Effects on Buddhism in the South

I want to return now to the issue of regionalism specifically and examine the role it played in the founding of Ekoji Buddhist Sangha of Richmond, as well as in Buddhism more widely in the South. In chapter 1 I suggested five specific approaches to regionalism in American Buddhism: (1) distribution, (2) regional impact, (3) Buddhist impact, (4) intradenominational differences, and (5) built environment. The first of these, distribution patterns, is one of the most important aspects of regional influence on Buddhism in Richmond generally and on Ekoji specifically, especially in attempting to understand why Ekoji operates in the manner that it does.

Asian and Asian American ethnic groups with high percentages of Buddhists have historically been poorly represented in the South, and this is certainly true of eastern Virginia. Furthermore, Buddhism, whether practiced by ethnic groups with historic ties to the religion or by newer practitioners, has had a very limited role in this part of the country. Data on exact figures is hard to come by — one potential source is the American Religious Identification Survey (ARIS) carried out at the Graduate Center of the City University of New York in 2001, but it has specific drawbacks when examining Buddhists, as Andrew Walsh and Mark Silk observed in their discussion of the ARIS numbers for Buddhists in New England.

Those figures are almost certainly too low, for a variety of reasons. In the case of Buddhism, many practitioners do not believe Buddhism to be a religion. So when asked, as the ARIS protocol dictates, "What is your religion, if any?" many Buddhists no doubt answered, "None." Moreover, some Buddhists called by ARIS researchers never even got to that central question, since large numbers of Buddhist immigrants, particularly from Southeast Asia, do not speak English. In fact, in New England, the household language is something other than English in 19 percent of all homes. Because ARIS conducted its research in English only, its findings exclude nearly one in every five New England households, including many households of recent immigrants from Buddhist-dominated countries in Asia.[84] These same caveats apply to the ARIS figures on Buddhism in the South. Nonetheless, Walsh and Silk further state that "although there are reasons to mistrust the data on Hindus, Buddhists, and Muslims when it comes to nationwide percentages, they are useful for comparing the relative strengths of these religions in different states,"[85] I agree. While the survey surely fails to capture exact numbers, it can be tentatively applied when we are discussing relative strengths and proportions of Buddhists in different regions and the nation as a whole.

The ARIS report has been extensively analyzed by Mark Silk and his colleagues in the Religion by Region project. Unfortunately, they do not focus on Buddhism specifically, but instead use the far from exact designation "Eastern religions." This category includes Buddhists, but also Hindus, Daoists, and other religious practitioners. Nonetheless, it is relevant to our discussion, and it is significant to note that the South has the lowest percentage of self-identified practitioners of Eastern religions of any region in America: 0.5 percent. The national average is 1 percent, making the South's percentage of such persons a mere 50 percent of the national average.[86] The Religion by Region project authors also use the ARIS numbers to note that the South is significantly more Christian, and especially Baptist, compared to the rest of the country. As Mark Silk and Andrew Walsh note, "It is hard to overstate the extent to which evangelical Protestantism sets the South apart from all other regions of the country."[87]

Thomas Tweed notes that the foreign-born population of the South quadruped between 1960 and 2000.[88] In Virginia specifically, the Asian and Asian American population increased 195 percent between 1990 and 2000 alone.[89] Prior to the immigration reforms of the 1960s, Richmond's Asian American population was extremely small, with no public religious institutions of any type. Even after 1965 Asian American growth in this part of Virginia was slow, and Buddhist public growth was particularly slow. Today Richmond and the surrounding suburban counties of Henrico and Chesterfield have an estimated Asian American population of 26,857, about 3.4 percent of the total population.[90] This compares to 4.4 percent Asian American makeup of the total U.S. population; the percentages for whites are 74.3 percent and for African Americans 12.3 percent, nationally. If the number is restricted to those who, due to religious adherence patterns in their country of origin, may have arrived in the United States as Buddhists, the population drops to 16,968 in the greater Richmond area, and the percentage is a mere 2.2 percent of the local populace. Furthermore, it is hardly reasonable to assign a strong Buddhist commitment to all or even most of these persons, as the immigration of Koreans and other groups has often disproportionately favored Christians over Buddhists in comparison to their actual representation in their homelands — indeed, it is likely that the majority of these nearly 17,000 persons are non-Buddhist. Meanwhile, the total population of Richmond, Chesterfield, and Henrico is 787,857 people, of whom 488,705 are white (62 percent) and 244,291 are African American (31 percent).

This is not the entirety of the story, however. Southern demographics have been profoundly influenced by policies designed to manage and often separate specific racial populations, and the greater Richmond area shows the clear effects of such urban planning. The city of Richmond — especially its eastern and southern districts — has been largely ceded to the African American population, while the western end and much of the county suburbs have been maintained as white strongholds. Thus the city of Richmond, with a total population of 200,158 has 103,043 African Americans (51.5 percent) and 84,790 whites (42.4 percent). Beyond the city, however, the situation is very different: in Chesterfield there is a total population of 298,617, of whom 217,679 (72.9 percent) are white and 62,998 are African American (21.1 percent), and in Henrico the population is 289,082, with 186,236 whites (64.4 percent) and 78,250 African Americans (27.1 percent). Asian Americans are likewise unevenly distributed. The city of Richmond's Asian American populace is particularly low: 3,173, a mere 1.6 percent of the total, of whom 1.1 percent come from potentially Buddhist backgrounds. In fact, most of the area's Asian American population is located within the surrounding suburban counties of Chesterfield and Henrico, where they have clustered in the past three decades. Chesterfield has 8,939 Asian Americans (3 percent of the total county, of whom 2.1 percent are from possibly Buddhist origins), nearly three times the number in Richmond itself, though still in a lower ratio than the national average. Henrico has 14,520 Asian Americans, making it 5 percent Asian American, slightly higher than the national average; 3.1 percent are from Chinese, Japanese, Korean, Vietnamese, or other potentially Buddhist origins. Again, however, we have to realize that the actual number of Buddhists in this group is significantly smaller.

In summation, the number of Asian Americans, especially from countries with significant Buddhist populations, is not high, although these modest numbers are still far greater than the Asian American population of the area prior to the last quarter of the twentieth century.

Two of the largest groups are the Vietnamese Americans and Cambodian Americans, who have successfully started their own temples. As I will discuss below, Vietnamese migration to the area began in the 1980s, and for Vietnamese Buddhists their low numbers necessitated an extended stay at Ekoji before they were finally able to purchase their own temple. The next most significant group is Chinese Americans. As a specific ethnic group, they have not been able to rent or purchase their own space for the practice of Buddhism. Therefore those Chinese American Buddhists in Richmond who wish to practice within specific Chinese lineages (such as Tzu Chi or the Amitabha Buddhist Society) meet periodically in members' homes, especially when a traveling monk or nun is in town; occasionally they use the space at Ekoji if it is available. A modest number of Chinese Americans who enjoy meeting in a more mixed setting attend Ekoji regularly, where they make up the single largest contingent of the multiracial Pure Land group at the temple. As a result, both English and Chinese are commonly used during the group's services and discussions.

The low percentage of Asian Americans in the Richmond area makes them stick out on the street, a situation that makes some of them uncomfortable. As we sat at Ekoji one summer afternoon after services, a Chinese American member who moved to Richmond from San Jose discussed his feelings: "This is the South, so it's not like California. When I'm there in California, I don't feel like I'm a minority. When I go to a restaurant here I will be the only Asian there, and I can feel it. People are sensitive, and they will look at me longer than they should. When I come to this group [at the Buddhist temple], or I go to Ellwood Thompson, I don't feel that way. [laughs] Here and Ellwood Thompson are the only places where I feel at home [laughs]. When I come here I feel at home, that could be why unconsciously I keep coming here."[91] The low Asian American population density has led some families to cluster at ethnically based temples as much for ethnic solidarity and support as for any explicit religious motivation. I recall a late summer conversation that I had with a Vietnamese American youth as we stood outside the Chua Hue Quang temple in the Richmond suburbs. He had no clear idea of the meaning of the ritual we were watching — he came to the temple because he could eat good (Vietnamese) food, meet girls, and his family expected it of him, while he characterized his parents' interest in the temple as being a place where they could speak Vietnamese (a language he was less than proficient in) and be away from "non-Vietnamese."[92] In other cases, such as that of the Chinese American gentlemen quoted above, Buddhism provides a sufficient refuge: while many of his fellow temple members at Ekoji are not Asian American, he feels that "people who practice Buddhism seem to be pretty open-minded" and that he is racially accepted by other Buddhists.[93] Note, however, that he prefers to attend the Ekoji Pure Land group, which is racially mixed but has a particularly strong Chinese American component.

Besides ethnic distribution patterns, the occurrence or scarcity of particular types of Buddhism in different regions is important to pay attention to. English settlement began in the Richmond area in 1609 and was permanently established with the city's founding in 1737. Richmond's religion has been strongly dominated by Protestant denominations, although it has long had both a Catholic and a Jewish presence. The first recorded Buddhist in Richmond was Marie de Souza Canavarro, who in 1897 was the first American women to convert to Buddhism on U.S. soil. She lived on a farm outside Richmond from 1910 to 1913 before moving to California, and apparently she attracted a fair bit of attention from the locals due to her unusual ways.[94] In general, though, Buddhism was absent from Richmond until after World War II. Beginning in the 1960s a few Soka Gakkai Buddhists began to meet in Richmond, and in 1972 they formed the area's first Buddhist group, a small Soka Gakkai chapter that met in people's homes and had minimal public presence.[95] In 1981 a small Zen group was formed, called the Richmond Zen Group, which met in a local New Age store and eventually became part of Ekoji. When Ekoji opened its doors in 1986 it was the city's first Buddhist temple and one of the only representatives of Buddhism in the area.

Since then, a handful of other Buddhist groups and temples have been organized in Richmond and its suburbs. Theravada Buddhism is represented by a Cambodian temple, as well as by the Vipassana group at Ekoji. Vajrayana Buddhism has even fewer representatives: Ekoji's modest Kagyu group and a very small group of Dzogchen practitioners who meet in members' homes. Most Buddhism in Richmond, therefore, is Mahayana, but even that is not especially diverse. There are two Vietnamese temples (one a schism from the other), a semimoribund Korean Zen group (whose members are almost all white), a tiny Korean Won Buddhist temple south of Richmond in the town of Chester, the Soka Gakkai chapter, a Chinese Tzu Chi chapter that meets in members' homes, and the Zen and Pure Land groups at Ekoji. And perhaps we can recognize another category of nonsectarian Buddhists, into which we can place the Buddhist activities organized at the Unitarian Universalist church and the semi-Buddhist Meditative Inquiry group at Ekoji. Only the Vietnamese-, Korean-, and Cambodian-based temples have permanent local clergy—all the rest are lay-led. Thus in 2012 we can say that Richmond—from the Buddhist perspective—is more diverse than it has ever been, and that it is significantly less diverse than cities where other major American Buddhist ethnographic projects have been carried out, such as New York, Chicago, and Los Angeles.

The general paucity of Buddhists in the South, and the scant Buddhist diversity, is something many Richmond Buddhists feel acutely. As one Ekoji board member told me as we had dinner in a restaurant near the temple, "I know when I've spent time out in Marin County [California], where I lived for a couple of years, it's a whole other world. There's a Buddhist group or a self-help group or a rebirthing center or something on every street corner. Out there it's no big deal. Somebody told me there's a greater concentration of Buddhists in L.A. than anywhere else in the world. I don't know if that's fully true—but it sure ain't true here in Richmond! At all."[96]

The South remains a mission field for Buddhism, and not a particularly active one: there are few Buddhist teachers dedicated to advancing the religion in Richmond. In fact, this was the most-voiced complaint by my informants at Ekoji. When asked what challenges they thought they faced as Buddhists in the South, Ekoji members offered a range of answers. In nearly every case, however, the lack of Buddhist teachers was highlighted as the greatest challenge, or, occasionally, ranked as equal to the difficulty of being non-Christian, a position I explore further in chapter 5. Many combined the two challenges as a connected phenomenon, attributing the lack of teachers to fears of the South specifically. As one member of the Richmond Zen Group exclaimed: "I don't know why they don't have teachers around here! Is it this southern stigma? So they think we're all ignorant? Are they avoiding us? Half of the teachers don't even want to come past the Mason-Dixon line!" This leads to further problems, as she explained: "I think for all us in the South the biggest challenge is getting to a [Buddhist] center. You have to leave the South and when you get there you wonder if you belong there. Everyone else lives there and they talk about things that matter to them, and you don't fit in."[97]

Another member described the lack of teachers as "easily the biggest difficulty we have" and spoke about how it all feeds back on itself: teachers do not want to come to the South because it is perceived as anti-Buddhist, and there are not enough Buddhists to support a teacher; without Buddhist teachers new groups cannot be formed and Buddhism cannot establish a more public presence that would make it more respectable; those groups that do exist lack the leadership that would allow them to grow large enough to support a teacher by offering more attractive programs and trained spiritual guidance.[98] The Zen group at Ekoji courted many teachers from the San Francisco Bay Area, flying them to Richmond for teachings and meetings, but in the end none were willing to settle. The teachers typically wanted to move to a place where they would not have to work outside the temple for a living (i.e., they wanted to be supported by the temple membership from the very beginning), and many were wary of the generally conservative and Christian culture of Virginia. As one Zen practitioner told me, "When teachers or priests at [San Francisco] Zen Center decide they want to move out, they usually move out to Viejo or San Bernadino. They stay in California—they stay within the Pure Realm of the Bay Area! The Pure Land! And I don't blame them one bit."[99] This was a commonly voiced frustration. Another Zen group attendee aired his doubts as we sat in the temple after service one day: "It's really hard to convince someone to go from the beautiful San Francisco Bay area where you're completely accepted and you can do a peace walk and no one is going to say boo about it, to a place where they have a march with people in Confederate uniforms along Monument Avenue but they stop before they reach [African American tennis champion] Arthur Ashe's statue. It's a hard thing to convince someone to come out here and I don't know that we have the wherewithal to do it."[100] Burned by years of dialogue with nonsouthern teachers who inevitably refused to commit to moving to the Richmond area, the members at Ekoji have gradually reduced their expectations. Many have simply given up the idea of ever attracting someone to lead them permanently in Virginia.

Thus Richmond's Buddhist groups—whether at Ekoji or elsewhere—are often served sporadically by the Buddhist circuit riders I have described in this chapter: monks, nuns, and priests based in other parts of the country who itinerate through the Richmond area periodically to lead services for the local community. It is difficult or impossible in this situation to establish the strong master-disciple bonds expected by many types of Buddhism. Many Richmond Buddhists choose to leave Richmond (and often the South) periodically in order to train at centers in the North and West, where they can practice in a much larger sangha and work intensely for short periods with advanced meditation and ritual instructors. This puts a significant economic strain on these individuals, further reducing their ability to financially and otherwise support their modest sanghas in Richmond. For the itinerant teachers such as Tsuji too there is a considerable cost (including stress) in traveling to Richmond in order to minister to the flock there. And for the handful of Richmond-based teachers (who are often the only leader at their temple, or at best one of a handful of monastics) such as the monks at the Vietnamese and Cambodian temples, there is the responsibility of shouldering all of the duties of guiding a community, with less time and energy spent on specific disciples or training successors compared to larger and better-staffed temples.

The discussion of Ekoji's founding in this chapter sets the stage for an analysis of how the various groups at the temple interact with one another. As we will see in the next two chapters, specific strategies are employed to differentiate between the groups, yet there is nonetheless considerable overlap. Tsuji's modernist Buddhist pluralism is much on display among the current practitioners at the temple he founded, as they seek to carry forward in their own ways the Buddhist mission he put in motion.

Experiencing the physical dimension of religion helps *bring about* religious values, norms, behaviors, and attitudes. Practicing religion sets into play ways of thinking. It is the continual interaction with objects and images that makes one religious in a particular manner.

—Colleen McDannell, *Material Christianity: Religion and Popular Culture in America*, 1995

Chapter Three

THE BUDDHIST CONFEDERACY
Differentiation and Identity in Buddhist Spaces

Ekoji Buddhist Sangha of Richmond is the only temple in the country that shelters five distinct groups practicing in distinct lineages. These diverse groups have found that, in the decidedly non-Buddhist environment of Richmond, the shared label of "Buddhist" is fundamentally more important than their individual differences: that is, they share more in common as Buddhists than they share with the non-Buddhist religious world beyond the temple's walls.

However, while this shared Buddhist identity keeps the five groups together at the same temple, at the same time they are among the only local (or even regional) representatives of their specific lineages, and therefore each group must explore and create its own distinctive Buddhism. To this end, the members of each group work to maintain some degree of independent identity and character for themselves. One of my informants described Ekoji as "the Buddhist Confederacy of Richmond," a model that implies the voluntary association of five essentially sovereign groups, groups that guard their own rights even as they unite around common causes.[1] This book opened in the introduction with vignettes from two typical services at Ekoji, first the Pure Land and then the Zen group, the two oldest constituencies at the temple. As these descriptions suggested, the practices performed by the five separate groups of Ekoji differ from one another in significant ways. This chapter details some of the strategies for differentiation that are found between the five constituent groups of Ekoji. First, I describe the practice of each group, including some historical details about how and why their practices have evolved over the years. I then proceed to a general discussion of how the differing usages of material culture and spatial and bodily practices by Ekoji's members help them to imagine and enact the specific Buddhist lineages that they identify with.

The Pure Land Group

Pure Land is one of the main forms of Buddhism, with a long and complicated history. Although its origins lie in early Indian Mahayana Buddhism, its real flowering began in China, and it is only in Japan that specific, separate Pure Land denominations arose. Pure Land Buddhism focuses on the salvific powers of Amitabha Buddha, often accompanied by his assistant, Avalokiteshvara bodhisattva. Amitabha is believed to assist suffering beings through intervention during difficult circumstances and by providing teachings accommodated to that being's situation. According to Buddhist legend, Amitabha presides over a nirvanic realm (Pure Land) outside the ordinary mortal world. Devotional practices such as chanting the name of Amitabha Buddha can result in rebirth in this perfected land, where it is easy to become a buddha oneself. Pure Land belief is popular with both elites and common people in East Asia, and its motifs are interpreted in a wide range of literal and metaphoric manners.

One of the independent Japanese Pure Land lineages is Jodo Shinshu ("True Pure Land Buddhism," often called simply Shinshu or Shin Buddhism), founded in the thirteenth century by Shinran. Today Jodo Shinshu is the largest Buddhist denomination in Japan; the second largest, the similarly named Jodo Shu, is a Pure Land sect founded by Shinran's teacher Honen. Despite Pure Land Buddhism's major presence in Asian history and modern religion, and its presence in mainland America for well over a century, it is relatively unknown in American mainstream culture, where more recently established meditation-oriented forms of Zen overshadow Pure Land as the most recognizable representatives of East Asian Buddhism.

When Ekoji was founded by Reverend Takashi Kenryu Tsuji, it was envisioned as a Jodo Shinshu temple; today, the Ekoji Pure Land group combines elements of Shin and Chinese Pure Land, with a smaller percentage of material drawn from other traditions. There are currently no self-identified Shin Buddhists at the temple. While the temple has become multidenominational, for the entirety of its varied history there has been a stable — if often small — Pure Land presence. The present Pure Land group is the direct descendant of Tsuji's initial sangha. It continues to meet on the day and time he established, uses some liturgy and practice he introduced, and has members who began meeting with him at Ekoji in the late 1980s. Nonetheless, this should not obscure the significant changes that have taken place in the group's practice and membership.

When Ekoji officially opened in 1986, services were held on Saturdays at 2:00 P.M. This scheduling allowed Tsuji to drive down to Richmond from Northern Virginia. On the Saturdays that Tsuji did not attend, the temple remained closed. The services he conducted were only loosely structured, often changing to fit the circumstances, as Li Chen, a member of the group since 1989, explained one day after we had finished conducting the current, more ordered Pure Land services:

> Reverend Tsuji had a very loose style. . . . Sometimes you would do ten minutes' meditation, sometimes not. Sometimes he gave a little more elaborate dharma talk, sometimes not. So Reverend Tsuji is really, really flexible, depending on the attendance and what he wanted to talk about. He changed the service, he was not rigorous about it, not fixed. Three Refuges was always there. Juseige most times was there, sometimes chanting in Japanese, sometimes in English. He always used Pali for Three Refuges. . . . Sometimes [he would] have [the] Heart Sutra, sometimes [he would] have no Heart Sutra. . . . Sometimes I Gassho to Amida. . . . Of course you can find a common thread there. . . . He'd sometimes bring films or videotapes and he showed us Buddhist-related films.[2]

The service was a mixture of mainly English elements, sometimes with Japanese chanting; practically the only truly constant element was the opening chant, the Three Refuges, performed in Pali.[3]

During the earliest stages of the group, it was mainly composed of whites, with a handful of Japanese Americans and, eventually, the irregular attendance of a few of the Vietnamese Americans from the Richmond Buddhist Association.[4] In 1989, a significant new demographic began to visit the Shin services: Chinese Americans.[5] The Vietnamese services frequently included a significant minority of Chinese-speakers, but there is no evidence that they ever attended Tsuji's English-language services. But this new contingent, beginning in 1989, was to slowly increase until Chinese Americans became the backbone of the Pure Land group.

In the mid-1990s, the Jodo Shinshu group underwent a major modifica-

The Ekoji Pure Land Group chanting in the main room at Ekoji.

tion. Members decided to begin holding their own lay-led services when Tsuji was not in town.[6] So for the first time Ekoji was host to weekly Pure Land services. For these alternate services, a new script was composed, far more structured than Tsuji's typical service. The group began by chanting Buddha Vandana, more commonly known as Namo Tassa.[7] Next they recited the Three Refuges in Pali, followed by the Juseige and the Heart Sutra, both in English.[8] Then there was an extended silent meditation period of ten to fifteen minutes. The service ended with a homemade merit dedication chant and a gatha from the Diamond Sutra: "Thus shall you think of all this fleeting world: a star at dawn, a bubble on a stream, a flash of lighting in a summer cloud, a flickering lamp, a phantom, and a dream."[9] Participants then offered incense and chatted and drank tea before going home. More recently, the merit dedication chant has been replaced by verses from the *Way of a Bodhisattva* by Shantideva, commonly perceived as a text from the Tibetan tradition.[10]

Most of these elements are derived from things that Tsuji did at least occasionally: the Pali refuges, the English sutras, silent meditation, incense offering. Several others are entirely new: the Namo Tassa, merit dedication, and Diamond Sutra gatha, although these have equivalents in more mainstream BCA temples. Furthermore, by 1996, when the short-lived Chinese sutra study group melded with the Pure Land services, some even less familiar elements were added: fifteen minutes of chanting the Buddha's name in Chinese were inserted after the Heart Sutra, and the group began to stay and discuss important Buddhist texts in a bilingual session using both English and Chinese.[11] When Tsuji led services, they remained loosely structured, without the Chinese elements. But after his retirement in 1999 this hybrid Pali-English-Chinese service became the weekly standard and is still performed to this day. As the main person behind the creation of this hybrid service described to me, "I'm trying to construct — very very slowly — an eloquent Buddhist service. For me it's a matter of constructing a moving and affecting ritual. I've been trying to find Buddhist texts that are written in decent English, English that I consider to be eloquent or moving. I would like to have the dharma expressed in a plain way."[12]

One further alteration of the Pure Land group's practice must be noted. In 2002, following the request of a group member, a Chinese nun from the Foguangshan temple in Raleigh, North Carolina, began to visit every two or three months and lead the Saturday services at Ekoji; this continued until late 2004, when demands on the nun's time became too great for her to travel to Richmond. Foguangshan is a contemporary Chinese Buddhist form of Buddhism, based in Taiwan. It is heavily inflected by Pure Land but with many elements from other types of Buddhism, especially Chan, which I discuss below. The Venerable Jue Chuan's services were conducted entirely in Chinese and followed a completely different pattern, as Li Chen explained: "We chant the Small [Pure Land] Sutra, we do a lot of bowing. And we chant Buddha's name three times or six, then sometimes Guanyin's name, then the name of the one standing beside Guanyin.[13] And also other names. And also Amida's name. And then incense, there is [a] standard chant when you burn incense. So the chanting often goes about an hour.... She initiated that sutra study, so if when she come[s] we are doing that, she will pick out a section of that.... And then we eat, and that take[s] about another forty-five minutes, that's the highlight!"[14]

Visits in the late 2000s by a monk from the Amitabha Buddhist Society also brought modifications to the practice, especially the introduction of a hand-held bell used to keep time during chanting. As we see here, the Pure Land group has substantially changed its practice over the years and recently at times held two different types of services. Participation currently ranges from four to twelve people per Sunday, with an average of eight. Approximately 60 percent of the group is Chinese American, with the rest being whites.[15] One interesting aspect of the Chinese American contingent is that they are all foreign-born, in contrast to the overwhelmingly American-born non-Chinese temple members. According to my 2004 survey of the temple membership, 40.8 percent of Ekoji members have attended the Pure Land services at least once, and 22.5 percent report attending the Pure Land services regularly, while 20.4 percent identify themselves as Pure Land Buddhists.[16]

The Zen Group

Another type of Mahayana Buddhism is Chan, more familiar to Americans in its Japanese Zen form. Central to this tradition is emphasis on specific lineages of awakened patriarchs who embody a penetrating insight into reality allegedly passed down from the original Buddha. While frequently portrayed as a meditation-oriented tradition, actual Chan meditation in Asia has historically been rare, confined mainly to specialized monks or priests.

Chinese Chan, and its Korean (Son) and Vietnamese (Thien) versions, are primarily practiced by Asian Americans in the United States. However, Zen presents an interesting exception to this trend. Never enjoying particularly large representation within the immigrant Japanese population, Zen was spread instead by the missionary efforts of modernist Asian Zen teachers who portrayed Zen as a timeless, intuitive spiritual tradition focused on silent meditation and relatively unadorned with ritualistic trappings. This modern reformist Zen appealed to many whites beginning in the 1950s, resulting in the first significant groups of American Buddhist converts by the 1960s. Major centers include the San Francisco Zen Center, representing the Soto Zen sect, and Dai Bosatsu Zendo Kongo-ji in upstate New York, affiliated with the Rinzai Zen sect. A few convert-oriented versions of Son and Thien, often simply labeled "Zen," have also enjoyed considerable popularity since the 1970s. The most prominent ones are the Korean-derived Kwan Um School, represented by the Providence Zen Center, and the Community of Mindful Living, a remarkable network of small-scale meditation groups centered on the teachings of Vietnamese monk Thich Nhat Hanh. As with Zen in America, these convert-oriented Korean and Vietnamese lineages practice a form of Chan quite different from that typically followed in Asia.

Ekoji's Zen practitioners have one of the most interesting histories of all the temple's groups. Zen at Ekoji began in November 1990, when Tsuji allowed a small group to begin meditating at the temple on Sunday mornings. As an early document from the group states, they called themselves

Chimborazo Zen Group: "Zen groups often identify their groups with a nearby geographical point such as a mountain, river, or stream. The name Chimborazo was chosen as it is one of the (historical) seven hills of Richmond. It was also the site of a hospital during the Civil War and thus there is the identification with suffering and attempts to ease suffering."[17] Chimborazo Zen Group looked for guidance to Zen Mountain Monastery, a Zen temple in upstate New York that practices a combination of Soto and Rinzai Zen. As an older member who joined in 1991 noted one sunny afternoon while we sat in the temple's backyard:

> Based on his seminary training and based on the sutra book at Zen Mountain Monastery, he [Allen Galloway, the first leader of Chimborazo Zen Group] had put together what I thought was a very thoughtful liturgy. It was interesting though, in between sits we chanted a little bit, which I think is unusual. But there was a theme to what he was doing, and it was really nice. . . . It always started with the atonement gatha. . . . It was in English. The sits were thirty minutes. . . . And then we did the Tisarana [the Three Refuges], that was in the middle. And then we did the robe chant: "Vast is the robe of liberation." That was always in English. We did the Tisarana in Pali. We had more meditation, and then we'd do the Zen Mountain version of the Heart Sutra in English. . . . Before the first sit there was an offering of incense, by one person. The other person would be using the gong in a certain process and the person was bowing. . . . I remember for walking meditation we used wooden blocks, just to signal.[18]

Meanwhile, some members of a local Rinzai Zen organization, the Richmond Zen Group, began to attend the Zen services at Ekoji. Richmond Zen Group had been established in 1981 and met on Sunday nights at Aquarian Books, a New Age store located in the Carytown neighborhood close to Ekoji.[19] Whereas the Chimborazo Zen Group looked to Zen Mountain Monastery (led by John Daido Loori) for guidance, the Richmond Zen Group took its cues from Dai Bosatsu (led by Eido Shimano) in upstate New York.[20] Brian Ford, a long-time member who used to attend the sessions at Aquarian Books recalled their practice as we thumbed through a service book left over from that time:

> In terms of the form, it was similar to what we do here. It was sitting, walking, sitting, and then chanting. But they used a script that was more from Dai Bosatsu. . . . They did thirty-five minutes of sitting,

ten minutes of walking, thirty-five minutes of sitting, and then six or seven chants. We ended with floor bows. At the time that I was going there was no discussion period. From what I heard, originally they would serve tea and then they would have a discussion. . . . Once in a blue moon we would stay after and listen to a tape. But we didn't have that discussion. . . . We started off with Atta Dipa. We would chant it three times in Pali, and then we would recite it once in English. Then we would do Tisarana, which is the refuges, and we'd do it the same way. We'd do purification, in English. We would periodically do other ones, but I'm giving you the main ones. We'd do the Heart Sutra in English, then we'd do the Heart Sutra in Japanese. Sometimes we did the Sho Sai Shu. And sometimes we did the Dai Hi Shu. . . . We always ended with Shigu Seigan, the Great Vows. We'd do it three times in Japanese and once in English.[21]

Not long after Chimborazo Zen Group was founded, some members of the Richmond Zen Group, including Ford, began attending Ekoji Zen services. Soon merger discussions began, though it was not until 1993, when the two groups had significant overlapping membership, that they actually combined. The combined group was faced with the challenge of integrating two different practice styles of Zen. As Brian Ford explained, "The service we came up with was a hybrid between the two, to satisfy everybody."[22] This hybrid was named Ekoji Zen Group. The group sat facing each other, as Chimborazo had done (Richmond Zen Group had faced the wall during meditation).[23] All of the chanting was moved to the end of the service, following the established style of the Richmond Zen Group. Many different chants were used over the years, to the point that some members felt it was becoming chaotic; others appreciated the eclecticism. Those who felt unmoored by the looseness of the service began a steady push to affiliate with the Chapel Hill Zen Center (CHZC), located on the outskirts of Chapel Hill, North Carolina, about two and a half hours southwest of Richmond. CHZC is a Soto Zen temple in the lineage established in America by Shunryu Suzuki at the San Francisco Zen Center.[24] The abbess of CHZC, Josho Pat Phelan (also sometimes called Taitaku), had first visited Ekoji in 1993 and was coming up every few months to lead services and offer advice. As one of the group's current lay leaders and a major force behind the affiliation with CHZC explained to me at his home: "When it was just the blind leading the blind, it really didn't have any appeal for me at all. . . . We tried to shape the forms around what they do in Chapel Hill, when the bows come, when the bells come in, and how we begin, and doing floor bows in the beginning and the end [of the chanting section]. Those things came in at that time. It took a couple of years of discussion. A couple of people were really against it."[25] In 2003 the group officially affiliated with Chapel Hill Zen Center and its parent temple, the San Francisco Zen Center, the most prominent Zen lineage in America. Because groups in this lineage are usually named after the town in which they practice, this necessitated yet another name change, back to Richmond Zen Group.[26] The Sunday morning service of the Richmond Zen Group is now stable and consists of thirty minutes of silent sitting (known as "zazen"), ten minutes of walking meditation, thirty more minutes of seated meditation, three floor bows, the Heart Sutra chanted in English, the four bodhisattva vows (repeated three times, in English), a dedication of merit (also in English), and three concluding floor bows.[27] This more or less mirrors the typical service at Chapel Hill Zen Center, although the group in Richmond continues to tinker with the format. Afterward there is tea and discussion of Zen texts. Many Zen temples in America do not have such programmed postmeditation activities. Realizing that most visitors in Richmond would not have any sort of prior exposure to Zen and might be confused by the practices that seemed so different from the usual forms of religious activity in the South, the early leaders of the Zen group instituted a regular question and answer period following the meditation.[28] This eventually evolved into the present discussion period, which is today designed as a Zen study session rather than an informational session for newcomers.

A Wednesday evening service was also instituted early on by the Ekoji Zen Group. The meditation practice was the same, although the chanting style fluctuated somewhat.[29] With the Suzuki Roshi lineage affiliation this service has stabilized into the same format as the Sunday morning service, minus the book discussion. In 2009, a Thursday morning Zen session, identical to the Wednesday format, was also added.[30]

Chimborazo Zen Group had an attendance of roughly four to six people per week. Other than a couple of infrequent Vietnamese American participants from the Richmond Buddhist Association, all members were white.[31] The Ekoji Zen Group/Richmond Zen Group's membership has slowly but steadily grown over the years: services range from seven to seventeen participants, with an average of twelve. That the Zen group's membership has risen since the adoption of specific forms and greater discipline appears to confirm Henry Finney's assertion that imposition of moderate to strong discipline has been a successful strategy for American Zen groups.[32] This

argument is also supported by the findings of Finke and Stark in their research on American Protestant denominations, wherein they suggest that
making greater demands on members actually helps to retain membership
in American religious groups.[33] At the same time, the imposition of a more
formal Zen led some members to drop out and was a factor in the eventual production of a fifth group at Ekoji, one based on Meditative Inquiry.
The Zen group is overwhelmingly white, but some nonwhites occasionally
attend.[34] According to my 2004 survey, 83.7 percent of Ekoji members have
attended the Zen service at least once, and 46.9 percent of Ekoji members
report that they attend the Zen services regularly, while 40.8 percent pro-
fess to be Zen Buddhists.[35]

The Tibetan Group

Pure Land and Zen are both Mahayana forms of Buddhism, and share a
common history of interchange in East Asia. But in 1993 Himalayan Vajrayana Buddhism was added to the mix at Ekoji. Tibetan Buddhism is the
primary heir of the final stages of Indian Buddhism, and thus incorporates
significant levels of Buddhist tantricism. Many commentators classify this
tantric Buddhism, known as Vajrayana ("Diamond Vehicle"), as a separate form of Buddhism, while others include it as a special category within
Mahayana.

This outgrowth of the Mahayana tradition includes an even larger pantheon of deities and awakened beings, often manifesting both peaceful
and wrathful forms. Vajrayana Buddhism includes an additional cycle of
authoritative scriptures known as tantras, often couched in esoteric and
highly symbolic language requiring special initiations to understand. The
master-disciple relationship is particularly central to tantric Buddhism,
which claims to be able to help one become a buddha within a single lifetime. Vajrayana Buddhist immigrants come mainly from Tibet, Mongolia,
and Nepal, none of which have very large populations in America. Some
Japanese and Chinese Americans also practice in specifically tantric lineages, and tantric influences are common in many Mahayana Buddhist traditions. There are four main schools of Tibetan Buddhism — Gelug, Kagyu,
Nyingma, and Sakya — and two Japanese tantric sects, Shingon and Tendai,
as well as Tibetan (Bön) and Japanese (Shugendo) syncretic religions that
incorporate tantric elements and are considered by some scholars to be
Buddhist. Other than Shugendo, all of these groups have temples in the
United States.[36]

"Tibetan Buddhism" in America is in fact numerically dominated by non-Tibetans, most of them white.[37] Fueled in part by positive Hollywood portrayals and the international charisma of the Fourteenth Dalai Lama, but also by dynamic and highly trained teachers who have set up shop in the United States, Tibetan Buddhism has blossomed since the 1980s and has perhaps overtaken Zen as the most visible form practiced by newcomers to Buddhism. This type of Vajrayana includes a belief in tulkus, wise teachers who deliberately reincarnate life after life in order to continue teaching unawakened beings. The Dalai Lama, currently in his fourteenth incarnation, is the most famous example of this. He belongs to the Gelug school, represented in America by such centers as Namgyal Monastery in Ithaca, New York, and Jewel Heart in Ann Arbor, Michigan. Several members of the Ekoji Pure Land group had ties to a Kagyu lama in New York, who suggested that they start holding services at the temple.[38] Thus on a Tuesday night in January 1993, Kagyu Shenpen Tharchin (KST) was born.

KST traces its origins to several Kagyu lineages in Tibetan Buddhism, especially the Karma Kagyu branch.[39] The group met for the first several years in the hondo before moving upstairs to what is now known as the Tibetan room, which had recently been vacated by the Vietnamese group. The primary practice of the group has always been the Chenrezi (Avalokiteshvara) *sadhana*, a cycle of chants, mantras, and visualizations conducted entirely in Tibetan; this is followed by a series of long-life prayers for various lineage holders, also conducted in Tibetan.[40] All told this practice takes approximately forty-five minutes. The group would then read chapters from a book (usually by one of the lineage's gurus) and hold a discussion. After about four years, a second component was added—the Mahakala sadhana, a sonorous Tibetan chant accompanied by the beat of an enormous drum and the ringing of vajra bells; this practice takes about half as long as Chenrezi and came before the book discussion.[41] More recently, however, Mahakala has been moved to the end of the service, after the talk, allowing the group to end on a high note and not scare away newcomers with seventy-five uninterrupted minutes of Tibetan chanting.

KST has held a number of additional activities on other days of the week, such as Mondays, Wednesdays, and Saturdays. These have included Green Tara practice, ngondro, and Tibetan language lessons (often held at a member's home).[42] However, the Tuesday evening service, held at 7:30 P.M., is the only regularly scheduled practice at this time.

The membership of KST has changed quite a bit over the years, although the core founding group is still present. In the late 1990s KST was the largest group at Ekoji, with more than twenty regular attendees, but more recently the group has shrunk to become the smallest of the five groups.[43] Attendance ranges from four to seven participants, with an average of five. One reason for the small numbers is that several members have left for traditional three-year retreats, a fact the group points to proudly. A second reason was the establishment of another Tibetan Buddhist group in a nearby town, which drew away some members who had been attending Ekoji. And a third factor is that a scandal at a separate Tibetan center in Virginia seems to have disillusioned some former members about Buddhism.

Although they are known at Ekoji as "the Tibetan group," this refers to their practice style, not their ethnicity: the group is entirely white.[44] Among Ekoji members, 32.7 percent have attended the Tibetan services at least once, but only 8.2 percent of official Ekoji members report attending the KST services regularly. Those who identify as Tibetan Buddhists are 12.2 percent.[45]

The Vipassana Group

If KST's Vajrayana represented a new type of tradition for Ekoji, the Vipassana group was an even larger departure. Vajrayana is sometimes seen as a subtype of Mahayana Buddhism, but authorities agree that the Theravada tradition, from which the Vipassana group traces its lineage, is a separate tradition of Buddhism from Mahayana. Theravada ("Teaching of the Elders") Buddhism is primarily represented in America by Thai, Sri Lankan, Burmese, Cambodian, and Laotian immigrants and their descendants; there are also smaller numbers of Bangladeshi and Vietnamese American Theravadin Buddhists. This is the oldest surviving form of Buddhism, though like all religious traditions it has undergone significant changes over the centuries. Theravada is distinguished by its reliance on the Pali Canon, a collection of authoritative scriptures preserved in the Pali language. This relatively conservative form of Buddhism has a strong focus on the original Buddha Gautama and his immediate disciples, though various other saints, deities, and spirits also receive veneration in popular practice. Monks (the nuns' order officially died out in 456 CE, though there have been recent small-scale attempts to revive it) are held to a strict interpretation of the monastic rules, necessitating their reliance on the laity in most cases for food, clothing, transportation, and other needs. Donations to the sangha reap karmic rewards, such as birth in one of the heavenly realms or perhaps as a monk, offering the possibility of strenuous meditation and moral practice to achieve nirvana. Major Theravada temples in America include the New York Buddhist Vihara, Wat Thai in Los Angeles, and the Bhavana Society in West Virginia, which some Ekoji members attend for retreats.

Vipassana is a term with a number of usages. Classically, it is the Pali term for a certain type of insight meditation, distinguished from samatha meditation which is used for concentration purposes. In the last one hundred or so years, it has become associated with a range of modern reformist movements within Theravada Buddhism, mainly concerned with stressing the role of meditation practice and the quest for personal enlightenment. This often comes with a reduced emphasis on ceremonial ritual acts and a greater stress on the spiritual potential of the laity. Thus people sometimes speak of the Vipassana movement. As this movement has spread and developed its own unique institutions, some of which have even gone so far as to claim to be non-Buddhist, there has been talk about a developing Vipassana tradition, separate in some way from Theravada Buddhism. All three usages have been employed by various people at Ekoji at different times.[46]

Depending on how one frames the question, the Ekoji Vipassana group may be considered to have several different origins. In 1994 a Vipassana group was formed at the Richmond Friends Meetinghouse, gathering once, and eventually twice, a month. This could be one genesis of the group. On March 3, 1995, that group began to hold weekly meetings at Ekoji. This could be the second genesis. In December 1995, this group was officially disbanded. However, before the month was out Vipassana meetings were being held on Fridays at Ekoji once again. This is the third, and most plausible interpretation of the group's genesis, because the practice, meeting times, and membership of the current Ekoji Vipassana group derive directly from this end-of-1995 group. Darren Grant, the founder of this incarnation of the group, is clear: "It was a totally new group."[47]

Practice at the Quaker meetinghouse, as Grant describes it, had been "a real mixture of stuff." The group sat for forty-five minutes, listening to a guided meditation by one of the leaders. It included elements of mindful movement and took place in a space devoid of Buddhist imagery. When the group began to meet at Ekoji, this style was retained for alternate Fridays, while on other weeks the group simply sat silently for an entire hour. When the current Ekoji Vipassana group was formed, the sitting was still an hour of silent meditation. It also often began with ten minutes of walking meditation. Meeting times were sporadic from week to week until they finally

The Ekoji Vipassana Group meditating in the main room at Ekoji.

stabilized at 5:30 P.M. a few years ago. In the meantime, walking meditation had been eliminated. Several attempts have been made to add chanting
in Pali, particularly the Three Refuges and the five lay precepts, as well as
guided metta (lovingkindness) meditations. So far, none of these elements
has successfully been integrated into the group's regular practice, although
they have influenced individual members, who sometimes silently perform
the metta meditation while others are doing Vipassana meditation. In February 2004, Monday night sits at 7:30 P.M. were added.[48] Friday night meditation sessions are followed by a check-in period where participants describe their meditation experience and voice any thoughts or concerns that
have arisen in the past week. This is followed by a book discussion period
centered on a Theravada or specifically Vipassana text.

The first Vipassana incarnation at Ekoji typically drew about seven participants, all white.[49] When the second incarnation began at the end of 1995
it was extremely small, but has now grown to be one of the largest of the
five groups, with a range of eleven to seventeen attendees and an average
of fourteen. As before, all members of this group are white.[50] Among Ekoji
members, 55.1 percent have attended the Vipassana services at least once
and 36.7 percent report attending the Vipassana group regularly, while 30.6
percent identify as Vipassana Buddhists, Theravada Buddhists, or both.[51]

The Meditative Inquiry Group

The fifth group that meets regularly in the space at Ekoji is the Richmond Meditative Inquiry Group, which was started in November 2005. For years Brian Ford of the Zen group had been going to the Springwater Center for Meditative Inquiry in upstate New York. As I noted in chapter 2, this retreat center was founded by Toni Packer, a former disciple of Philip Kapleau of the Rochester Zen Center. Although recognized as his eventual heir, she found herself at odds with elements of the Zen tradition and decided to strike out on her own. The resulting center draws on her Zen experiences but has abandoned many of the Zen forms; Packer also has been influenced by non-Buddhist teachers.

Although Ford had been attending Springwater when his schedule allowed, he continued to meditate with the Richmond Zen Group. Then in 2005 Ben Harris, another person involved in Packer's form of meditation, moved to Richmond. He and Ford decided to start a Meditative Inquiry group in the style of Springwater at Ekoji. The group meets on Sunday evenings at 7:00 P.M. Their practice is quite simple in nature: at 7:00 P.M., whoever is facilitating rings a bell, and meditation begins. Participants sit in a circle for thirty minutes doing silent meditation. The default form is a type of simple awareness of whatever is occurring both internally and externally, although participants are free to utilize other meditation techniques if they wish. After thirty minutes, the group stands, puts the cushions and chairs away, and does ten minutes of silent walking meditation in a circle (the pace is faster than at the Zen group). When they are done, they sit in a circle again and bring out tea. In earlier years, the group used to listen to tapes of various teachers: Toni Packer was a frequent favorite, but the group has also listened to the New Age teacher Eckhart Tolle, who is often described as being somewhat Buddhist in approach but who is not formally affiliated with any Buddhist lineage or with the Springwater Center. More recently, Brian Ford has been giving talks after the meditation period. After listening for a while to either a tape or a speaker, attendees begin a discussion that uses the tapes or speaker as a launching point, but the discussion is allowed to meander into conversation about meditation, Buddhism, or any topic participants wish to raise. The Meditative Inquiry group has made an effort to cultivate a particular listening and speaking dynamic where people listen closely to what is being said and take their time in speaking.

Meditative Inquiry meetings at Ekoji draw between fifteen and twenty-five participants.[52] Most of the attendees are white, although a couple of African Americans attend as well. The group began meeting after I had already conducted my survey of Ekoji members, so I do not have the same sort of statistical figures for them as for the other groups. However, field observations show that many of the people at the Meditative Inquiry group also attend the other meetings at Ekoji. In particular, I have seen regular attendance by people who also are part of the Zen, Vipassana, and Pure Land groups. About a third of the Meditative Inquiry members are otherwise new to Ekoji and I have not observed them at gatherings of any of the other groups.

Thus in 2012 there are eight meetings held weekly at Ekoji (including three Zen and two Vipassana) with a total weekly attendance of about eighty participants on average. This includes a number of repeat visitors during the week (perhaps 20 percent overall) and works out to an average attendance of approximately ten participants per session at Ekoji.

Using Space, Objects, and Bodies to Negotiate Buddhist Identity

Ekoji's five groups strive to maintain harmony among themselves and to find commonalities among their various sects. Nevertheless, each group is officially aligned with a specific form of Buddhist practice and doctrine (or, in the case of Meditative Inquiry, looks to a quasi-Buddhist lineage), and each is constantly confronted by the reality of alternate models of Buddhism. Thus they must each find ways to understand and express their individual sectarian identities. Furthermore, this differentiation takes place within the same space, and budgetary constraints typically cause the groups to utilize the same materials. Therefore, I have found, the primary ways in which Ekoji's different groups construct their differences involve how they orient themselves within this shared space and how they use these common materials. Furthermore, their bodily practices — sitting, kneeling, and walking — are also sites of differentiation and identity-formation. They also differentiate themselves by selecting study materials from specific forms of Buddhism. While the close proximity of the other groups makes this an especially urgent concern, I have observed similar forms of Buddhist identity-making in other locations with only a single tradition. Thus Ekoji provides a highly useful arena in which to observe the sort of attitudes and approaches taken by other American Buddhists in these five traditions.[53]

To illustrate this identity-construction, consider again the various services held at Ekoji. To prepare for their weekly service, the Pure Land group arranges two rows of mats down the center of the hondo, oriented toward the altar. Thus the group faces the statue of Amitabha, the central icon of the Pure Land tradition. Three sections of the liturgy specifically draw on Pure Land imagery related to Amitabha: the Juseige, nianfo, and merit dedication. Furthermore, many participants continue to mentally (or, in some cases, inaudibly under the breath) chant the nianfo during the silent meditation period. When the final piece of liturgy has been recited, members individually go to the altar and make an incense offering. In most cases, this is accompanied by three full prostrations, going from a standing position to kneeling with one's head on the ground, palms open by the side of the head. In these individual acts the participant directly approaches Amitabha, embodied by the statue, and offers supplication and gratitude to the Buddha.[54]

Other elements of the service also point to sectarian influences. While Pali is the ancient language of the Theravada Buddhists, it is actually a common form for reciting the refuges in the Jodo Shinshu temples affiliated with the Buddhist Churches of America. This is how Tsuji, a Shin minister, performed the refuges.[55] So it is in fact a type of Jodo Shinshu chant, even if at first appearance it does not seem to be. Furthermore, the temple, the altar, the altar adornments, and many of the various bells and drums used to differentiate parts of the service and maintain rhythm during the chants were provided by Tsuji for use in Jodo Shinshu services.[56]

The occasional Chinese services by visiting monastics further underscore the way Pure Land Buddhists utilize space and ritual. When nuns or monks from separate Chinese Buddhist lineages visited and directed the group, they nonetheless faced the altar, spending virtually the entire service venerating figures of the Pure Land through chant. More specific sectarian association was temporarily enforced by the use of a different liturgy derived from the Foguangshan or the Amitabha Buddhist Society, but the fundamental structure and spatial orientation of the services were similar to the standard Ekoji format.

The real significance of the Pure Land arrangement as a sectarian expression only becomes apparent in comparison with the other groups that meet at Ekoji. The Zen group, for instance, lines the mats along the outside perimeter of the wall, and participants sit on their cushions facing the wall, in accordance with Soto Zen custom. They have consciously chosen not to face the altar but instead spend most of their time in an arrangement that cuts out distractions to meditation. The majority of the service is simply quiet sitting meditation, with a short walking meditation interlude wherein the mats are folded in half and the congregation proceeds in a slowly moving oval clockwise around the room. The sitting meditation is a constant source of discussion during the postservice conversations, and two main themes recur again and again: first, the proper form for sitting, and second, that seated meditation is itself in some sense a direct expression of enlightenment. This is a doctrinal point of the Soto school specifically, with which the group is currently aligned. The importance of this activity is further underscored by the attention paid to proper posture — ideally, legs crossed with feet on thighs in the full lotus position (a form only a minority of the participants are able to achieve), with the hands in the lap forming the symbol known as the cosmic mudra (performed by most members of the Zen group).[57] Effort is made to keep the back straight throughout the meditation period, and visiting teachers will periodically roam the room correcting people's posture. As Shunryu Suzuki, the founder of the Zen group's lineage, wrote, "These forms are not the means of obtaining the right state of mind. To take this posture is itself to have the right state of mind. There is no need to obtain some special state of mind." In a very real sense, at Ekoji to be Zen is to perform zazen.[58] Participants are expected not to move during seated meditation and may be politely chastised afterward if they prove to be too distracting.

Twice during the service — after each of the thirty-minute sitting periods — participants ritually fluff their cushions and wipe off their mats, expressing gratitude to the central objects that assist in their pursuit of enlightenment and ensuring that the meditation tools are kept in prime condition. This is a practice that none of the other groups engages in. Furthermore, at several points during the service participants actually bow to these cushions; they also bow to one another, acknowledging the assistance and buddha-nature of their companions. After meditation, there is a short chanting service. No benches are used; instead, the service books are simply pulled out from their hiding places under the mats and held, as the attendees chant the Heart Sutra, four bodhisattva vows, and a merit dedication celebrating the lineage of enlightened Zen teachers. The prostrations performed by this group are similar to those undertaken by the majority of the Pure Landers, but with two significant differences. First, they are done corporately, signifying a group enactment of humility, rather than an individual encounter with the figure of worship. Second, the hands are used slightly differently: after they are opened, they are raised to approximately

ear level. This is a specifically Zen form of prostration, moving one step beyond the Chinese Pure Land bows.

All of this contrasts with the Pure Land group, which prescribes no specific posture or hand gesture during meditation, and pays little attention to
the cushions while giving a place of honor to the service book that contains
the words of the Buddha. In fact, for years people at Ekoji simply sat on
homemade cushions with a floral design sewn by Tsuji's wife.[59] When the
Ekoji Zen Group began to grow, members purchased sturdy, neutral-toned,
specifically Zen zafus and zabutons from DharmaCrafts; the homey, floral
Pure Land cushions were put into storage.[60]

That sectarian ideals underpin the Zen service's forms can be further
demonstrated in the way they have evolved over the years. For instance,
while the Zen group currently faces the wall during meditation, this is a
relatively recent innovation. Until September 2003, the group had always
faced inward. This 180-degree reorientation of the central practice came
on the recommendation of a visiting teacher from the head temple in San
Francisco, reinforced by the leader of the primary regional temple in Chapel
Hill, North Carolina. The concern was that facing inward was a Rinzai style
left over from the days before the group was officially Soto.[61] Switching
the practice helped signify the sectarian affiliation of the group, and "wall-
gazing" is a specifically Soto Zen practice, derived from the meditation of
the legendary founder of Chinese Zen, Bodhidharma, who according to
Buddhist hagiography spent nine years facing the wall of a cave. Inciden-
tally, even the previous form was also a consciously Zen one, where one's
orientation was not toward the object of devotion on the altar, but toward
the community of fellow practitioners.

More than a decade prior to this innovation, the Chimborazo Zen Group
had already made a dramatic statement about its conceptualization of the
space by rearranging the temple adornments. Originally, the Pure Land
group had placed the altar on one of the long walls. People attending services at Ekoji thus sat in two wide rows that stretched to flank the Buddha.
This was a standard Japanese Pure Land hondo arrangement (although in
America such temples tend to adopt a Christian style, with the altar at the
short end of the room). Without consulting anyone, the Chimborazo Zen
Group one day picked the altar up and moved it to the far end of the room
where it is now, out of the way of the sitters who wished to meditate along
the long wall.[62] Between the Buddha and the cushion, it was the cushion
whose placement took priority.

The Zen group has also altered the altar by placing a small statue of Shakyamuni to the right of Amitabha. This figure is left over from the original Richmond Zen Group.[63] Additionally, the Zen group added the large Zen calligraphy and the Guanyin, a figure revered by both Zen and Pure Land.[64] An earlier study of seven American temples in the San Francisco Zen Center lineage buttresses my assertions about the important role of ritual objects: "Zen objects, both symbolic and utilitarian, play a crucial role in the daily life and practice of members of the Suzuki-roshi communities. They identify and categorize space, synchronize activity, facilitate ritual order, regulate and systematize time, aid meditation, enforce community identity, and reify tradition."[65] It is noteworthy that the figures added by the Zen group are all depicted seated in the full-lotus position associated with Zen meditation. This contrasts with the dynamic standing position of the Pure Land Amitabha statue, which leans forward slightly to show his intention to come and assist others. Even as they serve as objects of potential veneration, the Zen figures model self-sufficiency and proper behavior to onlookers. According to Jodo Shinshu understanding, by contrast, the Pure Land figure depicts a buddha prepared to come to the rescue of those who are unable to efficiently carry out strenuous meditative practices themselves.

The Vipassana group is also meditation-centered, but it arranges itself in the space in slightly different ways from the Zen group. Rows of mats and cushions line the walls of the hondo, but this group faces the altar. An additional row of mats is placed down the center if attendance is high at the Vipassana group, something the Zen group, which wishes to face the walls, cannot do. This means that the Zen group, due to its chosen sectarian usage of the space, frequently finds itself cramped at Ekoji. As we will see, space is one factor in the Zen group's possible migration to their own temple. That they might stave off overcrowding by switching to an altar-facing sitting position, thus allowing an additional row of cushions down the center of the room, is not a topic of in-group discussion, apparently because it would violate sectarian norms.[66]

Meditation in the Vipassana group begins and ends with three chimes from a special bell brought from Burma, a Theravada country.[67] Normally, the service consists entirely of silent meditation. The eyes are kept closed, following Theravada practice, and participants do not gaze at the statue. There is no liturgy, which is often devalued in the modern reformist Vipassana movement, only meditation, the key to liberation. Many participants perform prostrations before they sit. These prostrations contrast with those of both the Pure Land and Zen groups. They are individual, unlike the Zen prostrations, and unaccompanied by incense offering (in fact, this group does not burn incense at all), unlike the Pure Land. Incense is left out of Vipassana gatherings at Ekoji due to the allergies of some participants; this minor note illustrates the pragmatic nature of practice at Ekoji, where venerable Buddhist traditions are often easily modified or suspended to accommodate individual requests. At least some of the Vipassana participants understand the three prostrations to be a form of taking refuge in the Three Jewels, rather than an homage of the icon on the altar.[68] Perhaps even more significant, some of the members are unaware that the Buddha on the altar is Amitabha, believing instead that it is Gotama, the historical Buddha who is the primary one venerated in the Theravada tradition.[69] The form of the bows differs noticeably from that in the two Mahayana groups: Vipassana members bow from a kneeling position, with hands placed together in the anjali mudra, a form of prostration common in Theravada countries.[70] But the most significant fact is that these bows are not part of the group's practice — if participants want to do them before formal meditation practice starts, they are free to do so, but they technically are not part of the communal activities, and there is no expectation that anyone will necessarily bow (most do not).

The Meditative Inquiry group eschews formality in its approach to meditation practice but in fact manages to display clear group-specific approaches to bodily practice. The members arrange cushions and chairs in a circle, but they also do not exert pressure on attendees who prefer to meditate in some other fashion. For example, a regular attendee in 2006 typically laid on his back on top of two mats, due to an injury that made upright sitting uncomfortable for long periods. Sitters who are used to facing the wall during meditation are perfectly welcome to do so. Meditators are allowed to sit in whatever posture they choose, and no particular instruction is given as to what to do with their hands, so some sit with palms open, some with their fingers crossed, some with the cosmic mudra, some even with their arms by their sides. Likewise, during walking meditation participants may hold their arms at their sides, swing them, or hold them at their chest as the Zen group does — whatever they prefer. They perform no prostrations, have no liturgy, and include no devotional elements of any type. They do not face the Buddha image on the altar and do not interact with it in any manner: it is simply a physical obstacle to be avoided during walking meditation.

At first glance, it might appear that the Meditative Inquiry group does not use forms to enact its identity as the other groups do. But formlessness is itself a form in this situation, and the group has taken an extreme individualist approach as a way of expressing its ideals. Meditative Inquiry, as the name suggests, is about questions and process, not about answers and goals. Their basic orientation is toward openness to the present moment without any preconceived ideas or projections onto bare experience. They therefore sit in a circle—typically seen as an egalitarian form of seating arrangement in America—and encourage participants to sit and walk in whatever manner best meets their individual preferences and needs. Much of this openness is in fact a dialectic with the Zen tradition from which Toni Packer emerged. In her descriptions, she found Zen to be too rigid and authoritarian, and she sought a new approach faithful to what she considered the core of Zen without imposing any rules or expectations. In fact, people in all of the Ekoji groups regularly remark that the Zen group is the most formal of all of the traditions represented at the temple, both in terms of the strictness with which it expects members to embody the forms and gestures of the practice and the general atmosphere that the Zen group creates.[71] Meditative Inquiry is closest to Zen and draws some of its authority from the fact of Packer's Zen background, but it also must specifically differentiate itself as not just Zen (indeed, as implicitly at least equal to if not better than Zen), and this is expressed through forms that are very loosely Zen but consciously informal and without group consistency. The cofounder of the Richmond Meditative Inquiry Group was fully aware of this dynamic when we discussed the matter:

> Speaking for myself, and I think I'm also speaking for some people I know, we consider it a sort of very pure form of Zen, or at least a very austere or stripped down form of Zen. When I say pure I don't want to be making a value judgment, but you can understand what I mean. It's very pared down but still a very rigorous approach to meditation practice. My initial experience was like, "Wow, this is sort of like the core of Zen." And I remember thinking on my first visit, "This is what Zen might look like in this country twenty or thirty years from now." The Zen group is very formal, and it has become more formal over the years. Without a doubt. And that's probably a good thing, and the group supports that. But there were some people who wanted an alternative. This practice model works for me, it just does.[72]

Even subtle clues point to the varied ways the groups order the shared space of the hondo to produce their distinctive services. The Pure Land group places incense sticks horizontally in the burner (a style associated with Jodo Shinshu). The Zen group places a single stick of incense straight up in the burner. After complaints from people with allergies, the Vipassana group deemed incense unimportant and forsook it altogether. The Meditative Inquiry group sometimes burns incense or lights the candle on the altar to create a peaceful, introspective mood, but there is no particular consistency to this practice. The discussions which follow formal practice also reveal attitudes derived from doctrine and worldview: Pure Landers frequently read scriptures to learn more about Amitabha and other elements of Mahayana Buddhism, Zen folks read Zen texts, and the Vipassana practitioners give testimonials about how their meditation is proceeding and read from Theravadin books. The Meditative Inquiry participants listen to Toni Packer or to other teachers who provide the same sort of open, awareness-focused meditative approach without any formal tradition. Their discussions include substantial talk about Buddhism, especially Zen, but they always bring in non-Buddhist religions and thinkers as well, and even the discussion of Buddhism is often connected to Packer's experiences with it as a Zen student and how she talks about Buddhism now.

Thus each of the four groups that commonly occupy the hondo do so in intentionally different ways related to the practices that they most value and the lineages they identify with. And what of the Tibetan group? They too used to meet downstairs in the hondo. When they held services they placed on the wall above the radiator Tibetan thangkas depicting Chenrezi, the Kagyu lineage, and other figures important to their tradition.[73] These would be removed at the end of each session. Also during their services they would set up specifically Tibetan offering bowls on the altar, filled with things prescribed by the tradition. They sat facing one another, similar to the Zen group, but with an important difference. Though this meant that half of the group had their backs to the thangkas, in their practice the members of the Tibetan group unfold small covers for their scriptures that act as miniature altars. In addition to the pages of the sadhanas, these pechas[74] hold pictures of whatever deity is being honored (Chenrezi, Green Tara, etc.) and the gurus of the group, such as Lama Norlha, the Karmapa, and the late Kalu Rinpoche. Thus regardless of where they sit (and sitting in opposing rows is a tradition seen in Tibetan Buddhist monasteries), they face their honored figures of veneration and visualization. Also, the sutra benches used at Ekoji were constructed by the Tibetan group. Their lineage emphasizes reverence toward the sacred text, which should never be placed on the floor or stepped over.[75]

In addition to the thangkas, offering bowls, and pechas, there are other objects used only by this group — KST easily has the most unique and the most complex material culture of all the Ekoji groups. Much of what separates Vajrayana from Mahayana is the elaborate usage of specific symbolic gestures (mudras, formed by KST participants during the service), ritual objects (such as vajra-shaped bells, rung during the Mahakala practice), and phrases or syllables (mantras, such as "Om mani peme hung," invoked during the Chenrezi sadhana), as well as certain types of liturgy and meditation (including taking refuge in the guru and creating a mental picture of the deity, both performed during KST meetings).[76] Every aspect of the KST service is intricately coordinated to produce the bodily actions, speech, and mental habits of the revered bodhisattva.

The move to their own room allowed the full flowering of their impulses to enact their identity through spatial and material practices. Cloistered upstairs, they have painted the walls and altars in vibrant colors associated with Tibetan lineages, hung Tibetan images on all bare surfaces, and set up Tibetan-style stepped altars covered with Himalayan buddhas, bodhisattvas, and offerings, as well as photographs of their lineage's leaders. All of this contrasts in unmistakable ways with the room on the other side of the wall, which is primarily used by the Zen group. It has been decorated in clean, muted tones, with a minimum of adornment or objects (there is, however, a noticeable sectarian element: a poster tracing the Zen tradition's pedigree). The altars in the Tibetan room have been placed so that they are approached on entering the room. This is significant: the Chimborazo Zen placement of the altar in the hondo was a source of some discomfort for the KST members, as it meant that the altar was often approached from behind via the back door that leads to the parking lot — this is a taboo in the Kagyu tradition.[77] This contrasts with the Jodo Shinshu tradition that established the temple — in that school, it is proper for ministers to enter from behind the altar, something that Ekoji's special arrangements have never adequately facilitated even during Tsuji's time.

Though they have now left Ekoji, the members of the Vietnamese-based Richmond Buddhist Association, the previous occupants of the current Tibetan room, also used spatial and bodily practices to enact their identity. Their main altar sat where the large drum is now stored because that allowed the greatest number of people to crowd together along the longest wall, where they could then face the buddhas on the altar. That the Tibetan practitioners have used sect-specific ideas about space and proper relations to objects is underscored once again by their placement of the altar on the opposite wall from where the room's previous altar sat, so that one does not enter the room with one's back to the altar.

The colorful flourishes of Tibetan Buddhist culture are a significant part of what attracts converts to this form of Buddhism in the first place. Thomas Tweed describes a particular type of American convert to Buddhism, "the romantic or exotic-culture type, [for whom] the attraction to Buddhism was part of an immersion in, and attachment to, a Buddhist culture as a whole—its art, architecture, music, drama, customs, language, and literature as well as its religion."[78] Tweed was talking of nineteenth-century converts, who were most attracted by East Asian Buddhism, but the insight holds true today, when Tibetan religion and culture are seen as the most rich and interesting by many Americans, replete with fantasies of Shangri-La.[79] I heard echoes of these attitudes in many of my interactions with Ekoji members, both attendees of the Kagyu group and others.

By contrast, aesthetics play little apparent role in the attraction of Pure Land, Vipassana, or Meditative Inquiry, and Zen alternately repudiates aesthetics or champions an austere, minimalist aesthetic (seen in the former Zen room at Ekoji, a pure white space with a small, nondescript buddha, and the group's black zafus and zabutons) that allows it to function in the moderately adorned hondo. If the Tibetan group returned to meeting in the hondo, their ability to recreate the vibrant aesthetic that attracts many people to this form of Buddhism (and informs its practice, especially the core visualizations) would be severely diminished. This may indicate a potential hindrance to Tibetan Buddhism's spread in the United States— since a more permanent, religiously disciplined space is optimal for Tibetan rituals, they may be relatively restricted in the number and types of places that can be used for practice compared to the Pure Land, Zen, Vipassana, and Meditative Inquiry lineages, which can practice wherever a little time and space are available. This should be kept in mind during the next chapter's discussion of the effects of low membership and scarce resources in the South—these factors have different impacts on different Buddhist groups operating in America because their needs are not all the same.

A final note about bodily practices in the Tibetan space: KST members each perform three full prostrations when they enter the room. These are done in a specifically Tibetan style, with clasped hands touched to the head, throat, and heart before the practitioner stretches out flat on the floor, hands straight out before him- or herself. This activity is clearly different from the type of prostrations performed by the Pure Land or Zen groups.

Disputes over Boundaries in a Shared Temple

That the different groups at Ekoji use specific orientations in space, ma-
nipulation of objects, and bodily practices to differentiate themselves is
consciously recognized by many of their members. Consider anecdotes
that briefly demonstrate this awareness, such as this one told to me by long-
time attendee Sarah Strauss during a conversation in the Tibetan room: "I
remember there was a short period of time there where we had three different buddhas on the altar [in the hondo]. Because the Tibetans didn't want
to just have Amitabha, they wanted a Tibetan buddha. So then the Zen said,
'OK, if we're going to have a Tibetan and a Pure Land one, then we need
to have a Shakyamuni.' And then somebody put a Guanyin up there."[80] At
some point, the Pure Land object—Amitabha Buddha—failed to satisfy
at least some of the Tibetan practitioners. They felt a need to have their
own object on the altar, despite the fact that the Tibetan group had originally grown out of the Pure Land group. Thus they placed a Tibetan statue
next to Amitabha as a way of asserting their presence in the temple. But
this only managed to set off a kind of Buddhist "arms race" (icon race?),
as the Zen group responded to this development with feelings that they
too should be represented with an object from their own tradition. They
chose to put their own Shakyamuni Buddha, in the seated position, on the
altar, contesting the standing Amitabha Buddha of the Pure Land group
and the seated Himalayan-style Buddha of the Tibetan group. Eventually
the space was redisciplined: the Shakyamuni figure is now upstairs on one
of the Tibetan altars, the Zen Buddha was removed (though another Zen
statue subsequently appeared on the altar), and Guanyin ended up in the
kitchen.[81] Amitabha, who waited through the entire ordeal, remained where
he had always been.

It is worth noting that Amitabha is in fact a member of the Tibetan pantheon and that the KST group actually has images of Amitabha—depicted in
a Tibetan style—adorning their room. The conflict therefore seems to have
been that they wanted a Tibetan-*looking* buddha, rather than a Japanese-
looking one. Aesthetics also determined the removal of the Guanyin from
the altar to the kitchen—without consulting others, a member of the Zen
group who felt the cheap ceramic figure was "tacky" relocated the statue
from its prominent position on the altar to its current humble station in
the kitchen.

The Tibetan ambivalence about the Zen positioning of the downstairs
altar has already been noted. The Zen group also has occasionally had some

trouble swallowing the non-Zen elements of the space it uses, as Sarah Strauss noted:

> Before the Tibetan group moved upstairs (although everyone was always very nice) I think the downstairs room was just getting a little too Tibetan for some of the other groups. Just having the thangkas on the wall and the offering bowls on the altar, things like that. We kept them on the mantle during the week and just set them on the altar during the service, and then put them back. But sometimes somebody would forget to set them back. It was never a problem, but I had the sense that, "Oh no, the Tibetans are taking over!" . . . I remember some comments being made in the Zen group. . . . There was just a sense that, "Eek, every week we come in here and there's more Tibetan stuff in this room. This is turning into a Tibetan zendo! We like it plain!"[82]

At this time, the Zen group was facing inward, with eyes downcast and half-closed during meditation. This means that the presence of Tibetan objects would not have posed a significant distraction to the Zen practice. Nonetheless, the increasing encroachment of objects from outside their tradition began to unsettle some people. In fact, for years there has been talk within the Zen group about possibly leaving Ekoji to establish an independent Zen center. One primary motivation that frequently comes up is the desire to practice in a solely Zen space. As one regular Zen group attendee, Henry Kelvin, noted: "In two or three years the Zen group might pull out so that it can be 'pure' Soto Zen with a resident priest. And we can have the altar the way we like it, we can have the kitchen the way we like it. Don't have to fuss with other groups about 'Why don't you sift the incense?' and all the little particulars."[83]

In another example of the sort of contrasts that appear between groups based on their differing preferences around material culture and bodily practices, Fred Brown, a lay leader of the Tibetan group, nearly bounced with eagerness to relate an anecdote as I sat with him and his wife at a café in Richmond's upscale Carytown neighborhood: "I have this great story about that. I was talking to a Zen person at Ekoji, and I said, 'You know, we have different traditions. Like for example, in the Tibetan group we have to put the texts up on a table, we never think of stepping over the text. But I just take the cushions and I *toss* them over to where I want them to be. You all in the Zen group *sit* on the texts but would never even *think* of tossing a zafu!'"[84] This anecdote produced a huge burst of laughter from the listeners. Brown had put his finger on an important difference between the way Zen and Tibetan groups in America understand the sacredness of material objects, which allows them to draw boundaries around themselves. For Tibetan practitioners, cushions are just tools for sitting on, while liturgical texts are holy scriptures composed by enlightened teachers. For Zen practitioners, cushions are bodhimandas—seats/places of awakening to true reality—while liturgical texts are just paper and ink, mere auxiliaries to the true practice of zazen. At the root of these attitudes are differing conceptions of where liberation comes from in the Buddhist tradition. Zen practitioners conceptualize enlightenment as the result of silent seated meditation—in some cases they call silent seated meditation itself enlightenment. Tibetan practitioners of visualization techniques, meanwhile, look to the deities generated in meditation (as described in the texts) and to the gurus who write and transmit the texts as the forces that bring about buddhahood. Thus the texts are in some sense an extension of the holy teachers themselves and are looked on as sacred.

With five different groups meeting in the same space, it is natural that issues of what it means to be Buddhist are regularly provoked. Perhaps the clearest example in the recent history of Ekoji emerged from the formation of the Meditative Inquiry group. Compared to the other groups that have met at Ekoji, the Meditative Inquiry group's connection to Buddhism is the most ambiguous, since the teacher it looks to, Toni Packer, underwent full Zen Buddhist training but later renounced her position as a Zen teacher and stopped considering herself Buddhist. Since she also draws frequently on Buddhism (especially Zen) in her teachings, and since her style of meditation, experiences, and basic orientation to religious practice have been indelibly stamped by her Zen training, she inhabits what her admirers at Ekoji freely admit is a "gray zone."[85] Many of them appreciate that Meditative Inquiry seems to have one foot in Buddhism and the other foot outside, so to speak. As Ben Miller, a cofounder of the group at Ekoji, told me:

It's different from Zen, but also I've heard some people say that under the surface maybe Toni is offering a very pure form of Zen. Zen is the absence of everything but the pure work of awareness. There's not a sense of striving for attainment in Toni's work. But Zen is about sitting yourself down and seeking attainment. . . . I [am] attracted to Zen for its simplicity, its stripped down efficiency. Toni is interested in the whole person. In traditional Japanese Zen there can be a denial of some emotional sides of one's nature. Toni is more sympathetic to these sides of our nature than traditional Asian Zen. I think Toni's style appeals to people for whom self-reliance is a virtue. She draws people who don't like gurus, or authority, or organized religion.[86]

Packer and her students are thus able to draw on the mystique and authority of the Zen tradition, while holding themselves at arm's length and being able to disclaim responsibility for what they see as problems in strict or formalistic organized religion.

The ambiguous position of Meditative Inquiry promotes reflection on its relationship to Buddhism by other people at Ekoji; if the group were clearly non-Buddhist, it would not raise the same sort of questions. When Ben Miller and Brian Ford approached the board about starting the Meditative Inquiry group, it set off a fairly intense discussion. One board member wondered aloud (and somewhat skeptically) about the issue in an e-mail: "Ekoji is a Dharma Center—is the Richmond Meditative Inquiry Group a Buddhist group?" This prompted the board to closely question the co-founders at a meeting where they discussed the issue, seeking to know specifics about what texts Meditative Inquiry venerates, what its lineage is, and what its practices are. There was clear concern that the group might be non-Buddhist and about what this might mean for the temple.[87] In the end, however, Ekoji is characterized by a very liberal religious style that does not seek to impose standards or rules on others, and no one felt enthusiastic about preventing the group from meeting.

More than anything, the respect for Brian Ford—a member of the temple since 1991 and a well-regarded meditator and lay leader—enabled the board to swallow any misgivings and grant the group permission to become part of Ekoji. Board members and other Ekoji attendees almost always mentioned Ford as a factor in how they reconciled themselves to the presence of an at best quasi-Buddhist member of the Ekoji family of groups: "I think that the Sunday night group is in there because we know Brian Ford so well. He's an old-timer and his Buddhist bona fides are well-established. I don't see him turning Ekoji into a New Age place: unicorns and crystals and stuff like that."[88] That Ford has a strong Buddhist connection was at least as important as the fact that Toni Packer comes from a Buddhist background. Thus even without an overtly Buddhist lineage the temple members could recognize that there was an organic connection with Buddhism within the group. This contrasted with other possible groups, such as yoga meetings. A board member flatly rejected the latter possibility: "I know if a yoga group came I wouldn't have any problem saying, 'I don't think it's a good fit, no thank you, you should go to the Yoga Source in Carytown and have your class there.' I'm very clear that I think that would be going too far. Because there's no Buddhist connection there whatsoever. Except in the sense that the Buddha used to be a Hindu, and yoga comes out of the Hindu tradition. So I would sort of see that as moving beyond the acceptable range for Ekoji."[89]

Ekoji's Buddhists frequently looked to practice to discern whether Meditative Inquiry was Buddhist or not. As one of the oldest members of Ekoji put it matter-of-factly as we discussed the issue in her home: "I assume it is a Buddhist group. We meditate and we walk, that's what Buddhists do. Christians pray, Buddhists meditate."[90] A former president of the temple agreed: "Personally, I would think that anyone who studies meditation from a nontheistic point of view could be considered Buddhist."[91] This was not enough for some, however. The sort of formless meditation advocated by Meditative Inquiry struck one member of the Pure Land group not only as non-Buddhist but also as actually dangerous. He claimed that "it [could] become a poison" and, frowning, said that it was "no good."[92] What seemed to be lacking for many was a formal commitment to Buddhism, especially as embodied in taking refuge in the tradition's "Three Jewels": the Buddha, the dharma, and the sangha.[93]

Many Ekoji members also indicated that a group would be considered Buddhist if it consented to or taught some core doctrines. Typically, the essential doctrine was that of the Four Noble Truths: (1) that life involves suffering; (2) that suffering is caused by attachment; (3) that suffering can be overcome by achieving nirvana; and (4) that the path to nirvana is found through Buddhist training in such areas as correct meditation, correct livelihood, correct action (morality), and so on.[94] Sometimes other concepts were added to the list, such as "emptiness," but it was striking how minimalistic this list of required Buddhist doctrines really was for Ekoji's Buddhists. It did not, for example, include belief in reincarnation, other realms of existence (such as heavens or hells), or transcendent buddhas or bodhisattvas. Some felt that the Meditative Inquiry group taught these implicitly even if it did not overtly affirm them, and that this was enough to classify them as Buddhist; but others said that this implicit approach was not enough. People who attended Meditative Inquiry regularly equated this with a liberating sense of freedom, while those who preferred other groups at Ekoji often puzzled at what the group's approach meant, as one Zen practitioner expressed: "I wonder if that connects up with the people who say they've learned Buddhist meditation or Buddhist spiritual practice, and then they want to get rid of all the icons, get rid of any association with the Buddha and the Buddhist teaching and everything and sort of wash that away. I think anything like that is going to eventually peter out, when you try to deny and expunge any connection to the lineage and the teaching and the tradition and all of that."[95]

All religious groups must establish boundaries that differentiate them from other groups, defining in some manner who is inside the group and who is not. The strategies that Buddhists take in America are especially easy to observe in a place like Ekoji, where the limited opportunities of Richmond have forced several groups into close proximity to one another. Attempts at identity production and maintenance are especially clear in the spatial and bodily practices of these Buddhists, as well as in their use of material culture; these differences, in turn, are often rooted in some basic philosophical or "theological" understanding particular to each specific Buddhist tradition. However, despite these many attempts to demarcate boundaries and distinguish the groups from each other, the various boundaries at Ekoji are easily crossed by people and practices, resulting in hybrid combinations of Buddhist practice that draw on multiple traditions. These crossings and mixtures are the subject of the following chapter.

A task that confronts those who do fieldwork with local religion is to discover routes from the particular gestures enacted by members of a religious group to the worlds of meaning manifested by such actions.
—Ruel Tyson, James Peacock, and Daniel Patterson, *Diversities of Gifts: Field Studies in Southern Religion*, 1988

Chapter Four

THERE'S NO SUCH THING AS "NOT *MY* BUDDHISM"

Hybridity, Boundary-Crossing, and the Practice of Pluralistic Buddhism

It is a bright, chilly January afternoon outside, but it is warm inside at Ekoji as I sit on the floor enjoying a casual after-service discussion with the Pure Land group. Their plan was to study a booklet about bodhisattvas, but as we have spent the time sipping tea and passing a plastic baggie full of pistachios, the subject has drifted to the unusual nature of Ekoji. "Is this really one temple?" I wonder aloud. "Or is it more of a bunch of different groups that happen to share a space out of convenience?"

Li Chen, a member of the temple since before the Zen, Tibetan, Vipassana, and Meditative Inquiry groups arrived, shakes his head. "We don't differentiate between groups so much." Martin Boyd, who first arrived at the temple on the same day as Li, pushes the point further. For instance, even though the gathering this afternoon is a Pure Land group, they do not just stick to Pure Land texts. "We spent a year discussing the Vimalakirti Sutra, and then we did two Zen works. We only recently began the Smaller Pure Land Sutra."

George Zheng, a thin, elderly Chinese American man who has been attending Ekoji for many years, agrees. Maybe there might be Buddhists who think that you should only stick with one tradition, but that seems strange to him. "Chinese Buddhism is more liberal, there is more freedom than in Japanese," he asserts. He tells us about his grandmother and his great-grandmother, both of whom were Buddhists in China. People from other Ekoji groups visit this one all the time, he claims. "Fred often joins us, even though he's deeply committed to the Tibetan sangha." Li says that he some-times attends guest lectures put on by the Tibetan group. George says he does, too. "I visited the Vipassana group in October," Martin adds. "And I've been to the Zen services." He has also driven to upstate New York with the Tibetan group in order to visit the monastery of their guiding lama.

"In that case, why do you think people choose one group over another?" I ask.

George thinks for a minute, absently plucking at his white hair. "Time of services is important—this group's timing is more convenient," he finally replies. Li is even more adamant. "I think most people choose the time and style, not so much the content of the service. Especially this group. If I go to the Zen or Tibetan group, so what? They still have Amida [Amitabha], Guanyin too. It isn't important."

George nods. "Buddhism is Buddhism. There's no such thing as 'not *my* Buddhism.'"[1]

This universalistic approach to Buddhism is shared to some degree by nearly all the participants at Ekoji, regardless of which groups they prefer to primarily attend. Not all are so expansive—for some, there are types of Bud-dhism that do indeed seem strange, though they commonly assert that such traditions are perfectly legitimate, just not appealing to them as individual practitioners. And George's ecumenical comment has to be juxtaposed with his implication moments earlier that Chinese Buddhism is superior to Japa-nese Buddhism, precisely because it is more open to multiplicity. While tim-ing and convenience, as my informants speculated, were indeed often rea-sons that people attended one group or another at Ekoji, many of the people I talked with also cited other reasons—often they had read a book from one tradition (such as Zen) and decided to try that type of Buddhism specifi-cally. In chapter 3, we saw how the various Buddhists at Ekoji make efforts to distinguish their groups from each other. So there are significant sec-tarian undercurrents at this multidenominational temple. But at the same time, the conversation that opens this chapter demonstrates that there is another important, opposing dimension to the life of Ekoji. As much as members tend to align themselves with particular forms of Buddhism, they have nonetheless chosen to practice in a shared space where they can inter-act with forms beyond their own — and indeed they often do so.

This chapter considers the meaning of Ekoji's diversity and how it aligns with a pluralistic attitude often encountered in American Buddhism. I sug-gest that the temple's diversity is a compelling reason for many people to attend, and that despite attempts to inscribe sectarian identity, many of the participants at Ekoji are drawn into new, hybrid manifestations of Bud-dhism that escape easy categorization as simply "Zen" or "Pure Land" or some other tradition. This hybridity — which is manifested in both con-scious and unconscious ways at Ekoji — is one of the most noteworthy as-pects of the temple, and once again use of space, objects, and practices re-veals information about the influences active in these Buddhists' religious lives. In analyzing the pluralistic Buddhism that is operating at Ekoji, I de-scribe some of the factors that tend to create hybridity in American Bud-dhism, whether at single-tradition or multigroup temples. Many of these factors are especially prevalent at temples in smaller cities, and Buddhism in the South may be more likely to display such characteristics than Bud-dhism in the North or West.

Before I go further, I need to further unpack my use of the term *hybridity*. For some readers, this may be a less than ideal term, as they associate it with racial ideas of original purity that is then diluted when two stocks are intermingled. I intend it in no such facile sense. *Hybridity* in fact is the term many of my informants used to describe their own situation at Ekoji. They saw themselves as consciously hybrid practitioners who celebrated their ability to draw on two or more Buddhist traditions, such as Zen and Tibetan, or Zen and Vipassana. But at the same time, they did not consider these two or more traditions to be truly, "genetically" distinct. Rather, they viewed these multiplicities as the conjoining of streams with a common source — the teachings of the Buddha — that over time had developed into different cultural forms in different parts of the world. For my informants, therefore, bringing them together was not the creation of a mongrel Bud-dhism but the utilization of multiple forms or techniques that naturally complemented each other and in some sense belonged with each other. Hybridization thus had an affirmative value for most of my informants. This was true even when they described themselves as being hybrid Buddhist-Christians or some other combination with non-Buddhist religions. For these informants, both religions originated in the awakened mind (of the Buddha or Jesus) and therefore ultimately traced back to the same source, though they had diverged widely in their manifestations.

I do not argue that all Buddhisms really do trace directly back to the Buddha, or that all religions spring from a common, same experience. But I do use the term *hybrid* in a manner that does not expect or require the two streams being brought into a mixed practice to be themselves fully distinct, pure sources. All religions are in fact historically conditioned and constantly evolving, composed of elements derived from many sources (acknowledged or otherwise). But at the same time, there are degrees of hybridity, and there are religious practitioners who are unaware of or seek to minimize hybridity, as well as others who are conscious of and revel in diversity. The Buddhists at Ekoji fall into the latter category, and they proudly wear the label *hybrid*. Because I consider this an interesting phenomenon that reveals important aspects of American Buddhism more generally, I believe it is worthwhile to consider exactly what it means to be a hybrid Buddhist in America.

Benefits of a Shared Sangha

Over the years that I have researched Ekoji, I have asked many practitioners about the advantages and disadvantages of having different traditions housed in a single place. Some complained that it can be hard to schedule activities because other groups use the space, too. But no one found fault directly with the temple's housing multiple forms of Buddhism.[2] Rather, it was striking how frequently Ekoji members sang the praises of the multidenominational temple. I encountered this attitude in the Pure Land group:

> *Reggie Han*: I really appreciate the persons who made the house into a place to practice or a place to get together, and we are very thankful. I think this is a really nice place, especially when you have four different groups. And we can have more groups to share the space, and it will be nice to have in-between communication and interaction between the groups. . . . We are actually pretty harmonious between the groups, there are no conflicts at all.[3]
>
> *Li Chen*: The reality is we are helping each other to maintain this sangha. Personally I think it helps. I am reading the Flower Adornment Sutra, and more and more I feel that all different flowers should decorate the garden, and the more variety the prettier the garden will be. I would say they add something.[4]

And I found it in the Zen group:

> *Christina Baine*: There is a kind of a nice sharing synergy that we have. It's nice to see the Pure Land people from time to time, and the Tibetans. They just give a grace to our communal life.[5]
>
> *David Simpson*: I think it's been really advantageous. Just because all these Buddhists in Richmond of different traditions have a common place to meet and know each other and exchange information and ideas and that kind of thing. . . . We have the chance to experience each others' practice if we want to. So I think that's worked out really well.[6]

The Tibetan practitioners also expressed this view:

> *Frances Brown*: I think it's very advantageous in just about every way. It's advantageous because we're sharing resources. . . . I think it's good to be exposed to other traditions. . . . We have the Greensville [prison] sangha and I don't think any one group could support that. Because we're all together we can do something like that.[7]
>
> *Sarah Strauss*: I don't know how many hybrid people you've talked to — I know there are some around. To me, one of the great benefits of having a place like Ekoji where everyone is practicing together is just that: that you have that opportunity and that you also know that they're all here. Because if they were all sprinkled all around town you might not even know that the other groups existed. And I've noticed that a lot of new people come to Ekoji and they will visit the different groups to find the one that fits them. I think that's a really wonderful opportunity for people to have. They have one place that they can come [to].[8]

And the Vipassana group also:

> *Darren Grant*: I like it. I think it's really good. The Pure Land group actually opened it up to all the other groups. The fact that we have a multigroup, I think it's really nice. It's really making good use of the facilities.[9]
>
> *Harry Nugent*: It's sort of like having one church and having the Catholics and the Lutherans and the Methodists and the Episcopalians and Baptists. . . . I think that's a wonderful thing. One of the great experiments or blessings is that all these places that are ethnically identified — Laotian Buddhism, or Tibetan Buddhism, or whatever — there's something that is going to come out of the whole thing, they're going to be, or they already are, informing powers to

one another. What Tsuji predicted, I think is entirely true: if you're only going to cater to your Laotian group, or your Japanese Pure Land people, it's going to die out or be very, very small; very, very insular; very, very exclusive. And Buddhism, there's just one thing you can say about it: it's not exclusive.[10]

Members of the Meditative Inquiry group agreed:

> *Trevor McNeill*: I think having multiple groups here is the best. It takes the dogma out of religious aspiration. At the temple you see that there's five approaches, so right away you're made to start thinking, "I have to do some thinking of my own."[11]
>
> *Garth Huntson*: I love that there are five groups here. There's cross-fertilization, to some extent the Meditative Inquiry group came out of that cross-fertilization. One of the strengths of Ekoji is a new group like Meditative Inquiry can get started. It's a wonderful incubator. I think it should be a model. I'd love to see it spread. If I won the lottery and had $100 million to spend, I'd buy little places all over and say anyone could come there to start Buddhist groups.[12]

Another indication of the value placed on attending a multidenominational temple is the strong feelings that were provoked by the Zen group's possible departure a few years ago. Most people I talked to conceded that if the Zen group thought they needed to leave, they should go, and my informants understood why it might be beneficial to have a space of one's own. However, this did not stop many people from hoping the group would find a way to stay. One middle-aged informant from the Vipassana group, who also meditates with the Zen group, expressed this firmly as we talked at the temple one afternoon: "I would be upset if they broke up Ekoji and the Zen group left. I want to express that very clearly. There are a number of people that come to both groups, because they like to sit and they like the community. . . . I think it's good that there's the ability to learn from the other groups, see these other teachers. I've been here when Lama Norlha was here. . . . For me I feel like this is sort of a home, because this is where I started. So that's my feeling. I would hate to see it broken up."[13] In a conversation the following week, another Ekoji member agreed that the Zen group should not leave: "I think it's a mistake. I think it's a mistake. It's pretty simplistic where I'm coming from. My whole thing is inclusion. When you withdraw into yourself and become exclusive, I don't think it's a good thing."[14] Some people put it in even stronger terms, such as this lay leader of the Pure Land group, who has attended nearly all the various groups that have met at Ekoji over the years:

> *Jeff Wilson*: What do you think about the fact that the Zen group might leave?
> *Martin Boyd*: I don't like it. I wish they wouldn't do it. One of the unforgivable sins is to destroy the sangha. One of the five biggies. This is really a bad thing to do, to fragment the sangha. And I see this as a little bit like that.... I would probably express deep regret that that was going to happen. . . . I think it's the wrong thing to do. I think we've got a good operation working here, and it's been working for years. I just believe what I've said. I *mean* what I say.[15]

Ekoji members saw several specific benefits in their temple's diversity. First, it allowed newcomers to Buddhism to try out several different types of Buddhism and discover for themselves which one they found most appealing. Second, it provided an opportunity for Ekoji members to learn from other forms of Buddhism and apply various techniques in their spiritual pursuits. Third, it reduced sectarianism and exclusivity, forces that they opposed and believed to be both antithetical to Buddhism and dangerous in general. Often they pointed to the example of conservative Christianity and the conflicts it has caused. Fourth, it allowed the various groups — each of which was too small to sustain itself alone — to pool their resources in order to accomplish goals that would have otherwise been impossible, such as owning a temple or supporting the Greensville Buddhist prison ministry. Each of these speaks to a value system that not only seeks to support a range of different types of Buddhism but also often actively supports intra-denominational Buddhist contact and mixing.

Buddhist Hybridity and Boundary-Crossing

Ekoji's shared space is constructed and reconstructed along particular sectarian lines throughout the week, as five different groups use the temple to hold services according to their own traditions. However, while the groups do make an effort to differentiate themselves, their interactions, whether directly or through the shared space and material culture of Ekoji, inevitably lead to a certain level of amalgamation.

The Pure Land group, established by Tsuji as a Jodo Shinshu gathering, has been at the temple the longest, and in some ways it has picked up the most outside influences along the way. At first glance, the group appears to be following a fairly standard Pure Land format (of course, the BCA is itself a rather hybrid organism at this point—besides the introduction of Pali chants and other non-Shin elements of Buddhism, BCA temples have been highly impacted by American religious forms, particularly those derived from Anglo-American Protestantism).[16] However, evidence of other influences is everywhere, once one begins to look for it. During the Saturday afternoon meetings, the group sits on zafus and zabutons brought in by the Zen group. They use sutra benches created by the Tibetan group, a practice they picked up after encountering the use of the benches at one of the temple-wide events. The wooden fish drum which is used to keep time during recitation of the Buddha's name was bought by the original Richmond Zen Group, while the hand-bell they use was introduced by a monk from the Taiwanese-based Amitabha Buddhist Society. The Zen group buys most of the incense that the Pure Land group burns, and it is often the source of the flowers the Pure Landers face on the altar. The altar itself has been moved to one end of the hondo by the Zen group, whose members have placed a second buddha on the altar. The Pure Land participants chant under the watchful eyes of the Guanyin statue that the Zen people purchased, and they sit in the shadow of a large calligraphy inked by a Rinzai priest. They include chants in Pali, the liturgical language of Theravada Buddhism, as well as the Heart Sutra, which is identified by members as being a Zen influence, and use a verse taken from Shantideva, a figure in the Tibetan Buddhist tradition.[17] No BCA temple performs extended silent meditation in the middle of its services.

In the Zen group, traces of outside sources are also clearly evident. The large and small bells that the Zen practitioners ring come from Tsuji's original Jodo Shinshu group. The altar they bow before was built by Tsuji, and the main icon is Amitabha Buddha, the central figure of the Pure Land group, who is almost never the main object of devotion in American zendos. Of course, the building itself and most of the other adornments, such as the pictures of scenes from the Buddha's life, also originate with the Pure Landers. Their primary meditation space has been modified by the Tibetan group, which removed a curtain that used to cover the window.[18]

The Vipassana and Meditative Inquiry groups also meet in this space so deeply influenced by both the Pure Land and Zen groups. They use Zen-derived cushions and, if they look up at the mantle, see pictures of teachers from the Karma Kagyu, Soto Zen, and Jodo Shinshu lineages. Members sometimes put cards with the names of sick or deceased loved ones on the altar, a practice that began with the Pure Land group.[19]

The Tibetan group is relatively more isolated due to having its own room, but hints of influences from the other groups can still be found. For instance, one of the Tibetan thangkas—of Amitabha—was given to the group by Tsuji.[20] They have used cushions taken from both the Pure Land and Zen groups. The Vipassana, Meditative Inquiry, and Tibetan groups participate in the annual Buddha's Enlightenment Day and Buddha's Birthday celebrations, which come from outside their tradition. For the Tibetan practitioners, the December and April dates of the holidays differ from those ascribed by their own customs. For the Vipassana group, the difference is even greater: Theravadin Buddhists normally observe Wesak, the simultaneous celebration of the Buddha's birth, enlightenment, and death. By participating in two separate events based on a Mahayana calendar, they are operating in an arena outside their own tradition. Meditative Inquiry groups do not typically celebrate Buddhist holidays at all.

Beyond direct exchange of materials or practices between the groups, evidence of hybridity is especially apparent at the individual level. Many people at Ekoji have been influenced by the alternative traditions at the temple, whether through participation in their services or exposure to their material culture. For example, Denise Fielding, one of the Vipassana group members, who has never been to another group's service, nonetheless learned about Pure Land Buddhism through her experiences at Ekoji, as she explained to me one evening at the temple:

> I read a book that was in the box there. You know these Buddhist books don't come with labels. It just said something about the Buddha, and I borrowed it from the free box, and it was actually a history and description of Pure Land. So I went ahead and read it, because Pure Land is here and I had no idea about Pure Land. So that gave me some background in Pure Land. . . . I learned about the chanting of the name, and to reach the Pure Land, and from there you go to enlightenment. A lot of it seems much more faith-based. I also read that it doesn't even matter whether you believe that or not. If you chant that name it will still help you even if you don't believe that. Which was an interesting thought.[21]

For another member of the Vipassana group, the opportunity to sit with a Zen group in a familiar space gradually caused her to rethink her ideas about this different tradition:

Gail Leonard: I tried the Zen group, and it was so foreign to me. They were doing a lot of chanting in Japanese. I stayed for the whole service. It was too . . . there's too much I don't understand about Buddhism, and then on top of it you've got the whole Japanese overlay. It just felt like too much and I never went back.

Jeff Wilson: But you have been back since then?

Gail Leonard: Oh yes, I have, since then, yes. . . . The summer before last, I had a fair amount of free time, and I started going on a semi-regular basis on Wednesday nights. And I really liked that, that was fun. . . . I've gotten over my chanting-in-Japanese phobia at this point, so that's not a problem.

Jeff Wilson: What was it that drew you to go back there?

Gail Leonard: Well, I guess I just became more comfortable, I began spending a little bit of time and getting to know some of the people in the Zen group. . . . I've read a lot more about Mahayana now and I have a better understanding of it now, so I don't have that knee-jerk, "Err, I don't know," kind of thing. . . . I do still identify, if I had to choose, as Theravadin. But I feel like I'm moving, and it feels like a process. I feel like as I get to know more teachers, and not just sitting with the Zen group—because sitting with the Zen group and talking with the people doesn't feel very different to me than sitting with the Theravada group. It really doesn't. Except they sit a little bit less, and walk a little but more. It doesn't feel really very different. Which kind of is nice.[22]

I heard similar stories from many others at Ekoji. The longer they practiced at Ekoji, the more likely they were to attend a service of another group, either because of an invitation or out of curiosity. For some, this led to a greater understanding of other Buddhist traditions, even if they did not go back. Others found a commonality that they appreciated, as expressed in a telephone conversation with a member who mainly attends the Vipassana group: "I've really learned more about Zen, and about the differences. Zen is really external. And Vipassana is really internal. Everybody does the precepts, there's definitely some commonalties. And the silent sitting meditation."[23] In some cases, uncovering this commonality leads to regular attendance at multiple groups—this trend was especially strong between the Zen and Vipassana groups. As Richard Kraft, one such practitioner, said, "I lived in a Theravadin monastery for a while, so I got indoctrinated into that tradition. But I've also been studying Zen. I come to the sits, it helps my practice. It's like going to the gym — once you're there you have to exercise."[24] Another Vipassana member explained his motives in greater detail as we ate at a Thai restaurant in Carytown:

> *Harry Nugent*: Specifically in reference to Zen . . . It seems to me that even though the one is Mahayana and the other is Theravada, there are tremendous similarities, comparisons, and parallels, more than contrasts, between Theravada and Zen. There's just so much there, that even though they're from two divergent schools, there's something about Zen that wants to go back to the Theravada. That's one of the things that I've found most helpful. Theravada is the only one that's survived from the most ancient of times, so it's connected most directly to ancient Buddhism. I think that that directness and that simplicity, Zen emphasizes. . . . That specifically is one reason why I come pretty regularly to Wednesday and Sunday Zen things.[25]

These boundary-crossers act as cross-pollinators, seeding the various groups with ideas from the other traditions. During the discussion periods they sometimes bring up viewpoints, practices, or concepts they learned elsewhere; sometimes members of one group will notice the presence of someone from another group at their service, often resulting in a conversation about the different practices of each group.

And finally there are the people who join two or more groups and begin to incorporate the views and practices of multiple lineages into their own religious lives. Sarah Strauss, who has been attending Ekoji for many years, explained how diverse her Buddhist practice has become over time:

> *Sarah Strauss*: In 1994 I started practicing Tibetan Buddhism. . . . But my original interest had been in Zen, and I couldn't seem to forget about that. So I finally decided, I have the perfect opportunity here at Ekoji, we have all these different groups. So I'm going to go visit the different groups; I'm going to go sit with the Zen group and get it out of my system. And I've been sitting with the Zen group for five years now, and I haven't gotten it out of my system! So I've kind of gone along practicing both for about five years. . . .
>
> *Jeff Wilson*: Could you describe your practice now?
>
> *Sarah Strauss*: Well, it's rather hybrid. I get up about six in the morning, and I sit zazen for about half an hour, and then I chant the Zen morning service. . . . And every evening I sit zazen for a half hour

and I do the evening service. I chant the Enmei Jukku Kannon Gyo.[26] And the refuges . . . Then every evening I do the Tibetan chod practice.[27] And I do [a practice] that Lama Norlha gave me.[28] So I do those two every evening. If I'm home all day—I usually try to have two days a week when I'm home all day, those are kind of my retreat days. And if I'm home all morning, I often chant the Tibetan morning practice, which is Green Tara and Medicine Buddha.[29] And I do what they call the tsang practice, which is like a little fire puja offering. Then I do the Zen noon service. And then sometimes—now that I'm taking care of my mother I rarely have this much time anymore—sometimes if I have two or three days straight where I don't have to go anywhere, I just do my own little sesshin.[30]

Jeff Wilson: This Zen stuff has been added in over the last five years, bit by bit.

Sarah Strauss: Right.

Jeff Wilson: Mainly by your exposure to the Zen group here?

Sarah Strauss: Right . . . I was doing ngodro, I do that.[31] I don't do it daily, I do it those two or three days when I'm home. . . . Right now I'm doing both every day, but I don't mix them. I do this, and then I do that—I don't do them at the same time. I'll do the Tibetan practice usually about eight o'clock or nine o'clock, because that takes about an hour and a half. And then I'll usually go and get ready for bed, turn out all the lights, and then I sit with just my candle. I start with the Zen in the morning and then I go have breakfast. I do floor bows. Zen does nine in the morning service, and then three at other times, at the beginning and end of service. Tibetan prostrations I do when I'm doing ngodro. . . . I guess one thing with my personal situation, because I have this depression thing, and it's particularly bad in January and February, I find it difficult to sit sometimes. So I find it helpful to do Tibetan practice, because I'm doing something—I'm either physically doing something, or I'm chanting, so I can't think. It's more engaging. So there are times when I find that very helpful to focus my mind. And then there are other times when I just feel like I just want to sit. And all of that kind of gets in the way of being with my mind.

Jeff Wilson: Do you see any conflict between these different types of Buddhism?

Sarah Strauss: No, I don't see any conflict. . . . A lot of the teachings that I got in Tibetan were very . . . not straightforward, or maybe "metaphoric" is the right word. I find Zen teaching much more straightforward. And then when I ponder the Zen teaching, the next time I do the Tibetan practice I think, "Ah! I get that now!" And I'm not sure I would get it totally. (I'm not sure I get it totally, anyway.) I really think my Zen practice has helped me understand my Tibetan practice more than if I had not had the Zen practice.[32]

This is only one of many such stories I heard at Ekoji. Consider, for instance, the Vipassana practitioner who found that "while I walk down the street and out and about elsewhere, repetition of the nembutsu has been keeping me more present and less mindless";[33] the Pure Land member who took the refuges with Lama Norlha;[34] the Theravadin who chants "Om mani padme hum" in his car;[35] and the long-time Zen attendee who switched her home practice to meditation on the Pure Land within herself.[36]

All told, according to the questionnaire that I distributed in 2004, 55.1 percent of Ekoji members had visited the services of at least two groups; 26.5 percent had visited all four groups that were present in 2004. Those who regularly attended more than one group made up 20.4 percent of Ekoji members, while those who had attended a temple-wide event, such as the Buddha's Enlightenment Day celebration, Dharma Movie Night, or the Buddha's Birthday, were 77.6 percent. Every group had at least four members who had visited all of the other groups, as well as at least one member who attended the services of another group regularly, and the de facto lay leaders of each group were especially likely to have attended multiple groups. Finally, 18.4 percent reported multiple sectarian affiliations.[37] Thus we can discern significant amounts of intergroup contact.

All religious groups use a variety of practices to display their particular affiliations. While the shared nature of Ekoji increases the need for such displays, it also leads to the crossing of boundaries as soon as they are drawn. The borders between the five groups at Ekoji are not only fluid but also highly permeable. Whether passively through environmental influences or actively through participation in the services of several lineages, Ekoji's groups and individual members have constant contact with other forms of Buddhism, and they seem to value this juxtaposition of differing Buddhist traditions. As might be expected, hybrid practices result from this contact across sectarian lines. For groups, hybridity appears when they incorporate the established practices or ritual objects of other groups. For individuals, hybridity occurs when they draw on the ideas or practices of multiple tradi-

At a temple-wide celebration of the Buddha's enlightenment, members of Ekoji's Zen, Tibetan, and Vipassana groups listen with interest to a presentation about Pure Land Buddhism.

tions. People, objects, ideas, practices, and texts constantly circulate among the various traditions represented at Ekoji. Often efforts to exert sectarian identity result in increased hybridity: several groups have placed pictures of their teacher on the mantle in the hondo, but this attempt to mark a place for themselves has only resulted in the further display of Ekoji's multiplicity. Sometimes this increased multiplicity is not even noticed by the actors involved. For instance, when the Zen group placed a Japanese Buddha on the altar in response to a Tibetan Buddha recently placed there, it was a reproduction of the famous Kamakura Daibutsu. This seems to have been done without the awareness that this gigantic monument is in fact Amitabha Buddha, not Shakyamuni, the intended figure. Furthermore, the Zen group also does not seem to have been aware that the Tibetan Buddha already on the altar was in fact Shakyamuni, depicted according to Tibetan motifs.

Factors That Create Hybridity

How is it that this multiplicity is generated and sustained at a single temple? I propose seven factors that tend to increase the level of hybridity in American Buddhist communities: (1) the lack of resident leaders, (2) the presence of pluralistic attitudes, (3) limited resources, (4) low membership, (5) sustained contact with other Buddhist lineages, (6) the new Buddhists' need to familiarize themselves with an unfamiliar religious practice, and (7) the devaluation of creedal formulas for religious identity.[38] Any or all of these may be operative anywhere in America, though as we have already seen a number of these factors are particularly likely to appear in the South. I will now explore each of these seven factors in turn.

Resident Teachers

Unlike many Buddhist temples in the United States (to say nothing of Asia), Ekoji has never had a resident monk, nun, or priest or even a designated lay leader. Even Tsuji only came to town for a few hours once every other week. This has led to considerable fluidity in Ekoji's practices over the years and is a major source of intra-Buddhist contact. First, the lack of a local teacher means that there is no one to closely monitor Ekoji's activities. Anyone with enough initiative can usually get a group to shift its practices, whether this means adding, subtracting, or revising ritual elements. Each change tends to lead the group further into hybridity as lineages mix. The Zen group has arguably been the strongest example of this phenomenon, so much so that they affiliated with a specific lineage to counteract this trend.

Second, the lack of a single leader means that each group is obliged to invite teachers from outside. Thus, Ekoji has been visited by various Zen priests, Tibetan nuns, Shin ministers, Vipassana teachers, and others. Each visitor impresses portions of his or her own tradition and personal perspective on the practices of Ekoji. Furthermore, the novelty of these teachers tends to draw people from outside of the teacher's specific tradition. For instance, when Teah Strozer from the San Francisco Zen Center visited in early 2004, there were people from all the Ekoji groups in the audience; the Vipassana contingent was particularly conspicuous.[39] Likewise, a Vipassana teacher who visited in 2010 gained attention from the Zen group and others at the temple. Attending these talks by various teachers, people learn about many approaches to Buddhism, some of which they incorporate into their own. Thus the yearly parade of various guest teachers at Ekoji actually increases the temple's hybridity: each speaker stays long enough to pass along new practices and ideas but not long enough to root out undesired concepts and behaviors or to impose any sort of lasting discipline.

Third, when someone does step up to act as an unofficial leader or facilitator, that person has a surprising amount of power. I experienced this first-hand during my time at Ekoji. Because their meetings are not large and many people are uncomfortable acting as leaders, I was occasionally asked to serve as the ritual facilitator for specific Saturday sessions of the Pure Land group when members who often facilitated could not be there. Usually I managed to beg out of the job, concerned about my insider-outsider status at the temple. But finally in January 2004 I received an e-mail from Pure Land group member Martin Boyd. He was going out of town, and Li Chen had to be somewhere else on Saturday afternoon. Would I please facili-tate the Pure Land rituals? With much trepidation, I agreed to do so out of a feeling of indebtedness to my informants. On Saturday I found myself seated in Martin's usual place, the large bowl-shaped bell beside me. As I lifted the striker to start the service, I was struck by the power that I held at that moment. I could lead the service however I wished. If I wanted to leave out elements I found distasteful, they would be gone. If I felt like im-posing my particular opinions or sectarian practices on the others, I could do so with ease. Given the chance to lead for several weeks in a row, I might well succeed in completely transforming the group, perhaps causing it to realign with a lineage of my choosing or completely overhaul its activities to suit my whims. It was a moment of revelation, even temptation. I brought the striker down on the bell firmly and proceeded to do my very best im-pression of Martin Boyd for the next forty-five minutes, imitating even his speech intonations during the chants and his way of sitting. Through this experience I discovered firsthand the potential of teacherless sangha to be molded and remolded continuously.[40]

Existence of Pluralistic Attitudes

Of course, teachers themselves can create hybridity, especially if they are of the type that I designate below as "pluralistic Buddhists." Tsuji was argu-ably an exemplar of this type of hybridizing teacher: even though he was committed to the Jodo Shinshu tradition, his services included elements of several types of Buddhism, he frequently showed videos about sects other than Jodo Shinshu, and he invited other Buddhist denominations to share his temple. While teachers may rein in influences from beyond their sectar-ian affiliations, those who are themselves hybrid or who have a strong ori-entation toward drawing from multiple traditions will naturally cause their groups to develop an eclectic form of practice.

Even when pluralistic teachers are absent, if the lay members of a Buddhist group have the sort of positive attitudes toward multiplicity demon-strated by Ekoji members then they will be likely to result in hybridity. For example, a given Buddhist group might be Zen in basic orientation but lack any specific guiding teacher and have a significant number of members with pluralistic attitudes. Such groups will naturally accumulate perspectives and perhaps practices from across the Zen spectrum and beyond Zen as well, as participants bring in preferred elements gleaned from their reading or encounters with other Buddhist groups. Many of the other factors pre-sented in this chapter are more or less passive in nature: lacking a teacher or having few resources can allow outside influences to "seep in," as it were. A pluralistic Buddhist attitude, however, is an active agent for change, as it en-courages American Buddhists to seek out new forms of Buddhist practice and philosophy in order to enrich their spirituality. When they share their discoveries with their fellow practitioners, the groups they attend become more hybrid in nature.

Limited Resources

Many Buddhist groups in America start from scratch. As minorities in a pre-dominately Christian country, Buddhists have less access to local religious institutions, teachers, and materials. Furthermore, many groups begin with a limited financial base. They cannot build new temples, and they may be unable to purchase facilities to convert into temples—they may not even be able to afford to rent space for their meetings. Some Buddhist tradi-tions require specific artifacts—sacred images, special meditation cush-ions, ritual implements, musical instruments, and so on—and their prac-tices are impaired or even impossible without the presence of these items, which can be expensive and hard to come by in the United States. Lacking the ability to rent or purchase their own space, groups or individuals from different backgrounds that lack significant funds or access to Buddhist ma-terials may find it advantageous to band together, pooling their resources. In such situations the sharing of materials—texts, ritual objects, worship spaces—results in a mingling of sectarian influences. This is often linked to the next factor, low membership, but not necessarily: the Vietnamese group at Ekoji served several hundred people, more than many churches start with, but it took time for the refugee members to accumulate suffi-cient resources to move to their own temple. In the meantime, they used the facilities at Ekoji and came into regular contact with the other Buddhist traditions represented there.[41]

Even when groups do not decide to join with other local Buddhists in order to buy or rent spaces, limited resources can contribute to increased hybridity. Without the ability to acquire the perfect practice tools and study materials, groups can be forced to settle for whatever they are able to come by. This can mean borrowing practice tools from other local groups, purchasing cheaper implements from lineages outside one's own tradition, or other strategies that raise the likelihood of hybridity.

Low Membership

The small number of participants at a temple affects the level of hybridity. This may seem counterintuitive, since one would think that the larger the number of participants in the group, the more likely the group is to have diverse views and people with exposure to other forms of Buddhism. My fieldwork at Ekoji, however, suggests that this may not be the case. First, if a group has a low membership, it is likely to be unable to afford its own separate space and materials, possibly leading it into partnership with other groups, as I have just discussed. Second, when the pond is small, everyone is a big fish. The individual opinions and influences of each participant loom large, allowing a single person or a few people to change how a group operates. Again and again I heard stories about how one or two people had joined a group at Ekoji and then caused its practice to be changed to fit their personal preferences. Larger groups are more stable and a critical mass of participants can exert a form of passive pressure that keeps things operating in the way that the majority is used to and comfortable with. Also, I once again found that my own presence altered things. For instance, before I ever came to Ekoji, I had been taught at other Buddhist sites that it is appropriate to raise the service book to my forehead in a sign of reverence and gratitude. Operating on such assumptions about proper behavior, I repeated this practice when I began attending Ekoji as a participant-observer, and when I did so, my actions were clearly visible to the dozen or so other participants. On more than one occasion I saw that others observing me mimicked my actions, raising the service book just as I did. As I became more familiar with the practices at Ekoji, however, I realized that no one ever did so independently, but only if I had done so automatically while sitting next to them. Thus I was myself inadvertently introducing a practice from other Buddhist traditions into the space at Ekoji, something that the low membership numbers—which made my actions more visible and increased the impact of every participant on the others—clearly affected.

Membership is low in many southern Buddhist groups, and often there is little attempt to change this fact. Some Richmond Buddhists actually take pride in their small numbers and unwillingness to bring others into Buddhism, contrasting this approach with what they depict as an evangelical Christian obsession with membership numbers that measures success in terms of head counts and spirituality in terms of notches on one's belt (conversions). Tired of being proselytized, these Buddhists explicitly avoid attempts at outreach and try to argue down any movement toward temple marketing. These are phenomena they associate with southern Christianity, and they want to participate in a religion that definitively does not approve of such activities — indeed, they feel that the nonproselytizing nature of Buddhism is one of its superior features. Buddhism in fact has been an active missionary tradition, but for these southerners it is practiced as quiet and inward-oriented, with, at best, an attitude of welcome toward those lucky enough to seek it out on their own initiative. Low membership is thus an acceptable norm for these Buddhists, which can open them to greater degrees of hybridization as a result.

Sustained Contact

Hybridity necessarily assumes the presence of two or more different sources of tradition that can meet and possibly influence each other. When one Buddhist group comes into contact with another group from a different tradition, there is always the potential that it may absorb something of the practice or ideology of that second group, especially if other factors that promote hybridity are present as well. This is obviously most likely to occur in situations where multiple groups or various lineages are in frequent contact with one another. Contact may occur because of immediate proximity, as at Ekoji, where five groups are housed together and can easily influence one another. Proximity need not be so dramatic, of course — having more than one Buddhist group in an area can provide sufficient occasional contact to increase hybridity. Or the contact may be through other sorts of channels, such as electronic or print networks that bring new information about the range of Buddhist phenomena to groups that have no other Buddhist neighbors.

Contact with forms of Buddhism beyond a group's own lineage may also occur through participation in outside events or organizations with other groups, whether these are explicitly Buddhist or not. One particularly likely location for such contact and exchange is inter-Buddhist organizations, a growing phenomenon in America that Paul Numrich has studied.[42] These organizations bring many Buddhist groups together for mutual support. Cross-sectarian dialogue is guaranteed in such situations and often actively encouraged by the leaders of these organizations. Contact may be sought out by certain groups, may arise from contingent circumstances that bring multiple lineages into contact, or may even be forced on groups. Regardless of the reason for the contact, interaction with other Buddhists naturally increases the level of hybridity displayed by a group compared to those that never interact with any tradition outside their own.

Convert Needs

Whether one is raised in a Buddhist household or comes to the religion as an adult, every Buddhist has to go through a learning process to discover what exactly it means to practice Buddhism. Most members of Ekoji came to Buddhist practice as adults, which means that they are not operating on Buddhist principles passed on to them by their families and communities from an early age, and their learning process takes place in a regional location where Buddhism is very poorly represented. Nearly all have gone through a process of looking at various Buddhist lineages, often through reading texts from a number of different traditions. I heard this story many times in my conversations with Ekoji members, which appears to substantiate James Coleman's claim that books are the major way in which newcomers are introduced to Buddhism.[43] However, when I asked them where they found out about Ekoji, the largest number of respondents indicated that they first heard of the temple through a friend who knew they were sympathetic to alternative approaches to religion. Thus personal networks perhaps play a larger role in American Buddhism than suggested by Coleman, whose arguments continually focus on the individual as an isolated entity.

In order to create themselves anew as Buddhists, converts in America must develop practices through which to define themselves. Often, the initial openness and searching causes newer Buddhists to mingle aspects of different traditions, in many cases without any awareness of the distinct origins of the practices they are exploring and appropriating. The result is a hybrid Buddhist practice, even if the practitioner may believe that what they are doing is "fully Zen" or "entirely Tibetan." Because most Americans undertake their quest in an area without strong Buddhist numbers, new Buddhists usually cannot rely on the larger community to point out to them which practices or ideas are specific to this or that sect. If the group that they are participating with is itself relatively new or composed mostly of other converts who do not have a strong lifetime background in a particular tradition, hybridity is that much more likely to occur. Such amalgamations are naturally increased when other factors I have listed are present, such as sustained contact with multiple groups or a lack of authoritative teachers.

Lack of Creeds

Groups or individuals that do not put a strong stress on creedal tests of membership are more likely to demonstrate hybridity. Many (but certainly not all) forms of Buddhism do not require professions of faith from their adherents. None of Ekoji's groups subscribes to a formal creed, nor does membership at the temple require any statement of allegiance. In fact, there are no requirements at all for people who come to Ekoji, other than that they not disrupt other people's practice (by making noise during silent meditation, for example). Furthermore, Buddhism in the United States is in many cases heavily influenced by liberal religious sentiments. Religious liberals, such as Unitarian Universalists, Quakers, and Reform Jews, are disproportionately represented in American Buddhist circles, and they bring with them a tolerance and acceptance, even an encouragement, of exploring multiple paths. Many practitioners of Buddhism come to the religion specifically because there is a perception in some quarters, particularly within the so-called New Age community, that Buddhism is open, free, nondogmatic, and nonjudgmental. To what extent this is naturally true, and to what extent it becomes a self-fulfilling prophesy as people with a preference for creedless religion become Buddhists, is difficult to determine. Buddhist history exhibits fewer "holy wars" than such religions as Christianity or Islam, though it is hardly free of sectarian disputes, including even clashes between rival monastic armies.[44] But either way, the result is that Buddhism is shaped in ways that promote openness to other traditions and flexibility, increasing the hybrid nature of many groups.

This openness may take both weak and strong forms. In the weak form, Buddhism is felt to be a relatively noncreedal religion, and outside influences are not resisted with particular vigor. In its strong form, people may seek out different traditions to augment their practices, or join groups perceived to be pluralistic. In these cases, the ability to learn from more than one tradition is valorized and hybridity is embraced as a beneficial state. This type of pluralism conforms with William Hutchinson's definition of pluralism, as opposed to mere diversity. Both attitudes are displayed by various members of Ekoji.

Regionalism and Hybridity

In my opinion, the presence of these seven factors will always tend to increase the level of hybridity in a group, wherever they may be. At the same time, that Ekoji has *all* of these aspects is related in part to its being a Buddhist temple in the South, as well as to the size of Richmond. As I will argue more explicitly in chapter 5, Buddhists (and other religious minorities as well) face different challenges in different places. Here I want to focus on the interaction between Ekoji's location in the South, its small-city environment, and the seven phenomena discussed above, including attention to how these shape differences among groups in the same Buddhist lineage that exist in separate regions of the United States.

It is important to consider what sort of environment a temple is located in: urban, suburban, or rural. If the location is urban, the city's size is crucial. Ekoji is located in a residential area of Richmond, a medium-small city. With just over two hundred thousand residents in the city itself (there are more in the county suburbs, which are larger than Richmond's own population), Richmond is not among the one hundred largest cities in America, although it is the fourth-largest city in Virginia.[45] Ekoji is the only permanent Buddhist temple within the Richmond city limits that owns its space outright. Property values were low enough in 1985 to allow for a well-financed outside Buddhist organization to purchase a house for renovation as a temple (something that might have proved prohibitive in a larger, more expensive city), but are high enough now to prevent the midsized current membership from moving on to a new building with much-needed space. All other local Buddhist groups either remain small and meet in homes or rented spaces—such as the Richmond Vipassana Group—or purchase or build their temples in the suburbs outside of Richmond proper: the area's other large, permanent temples, which draw overwhelmingly from Asian American population bases that began settling in the suburbs in 1975, are all located in the counties surrounding Richmond. The size of Richmond means that Ekoji is able to enjoy a certain level of automatic anonymity that a smaller city or town could not afford; but Richmond is not so large and cosmopolitan that many of its members feel comfortable announcing the temple's presence. On an individual level, reactions to Richmond's size vary: some Ekoji members are frustrated by the lack of opportunities that a larger city might afford, while some others who have lived in large cities actually find the somewhat less hectic pace of life in Richmond to be a boon to Buddhist practice.

Many of the factors I have discussed in this chapter are mutually reinforcing. A temple that lacks a teacher is likely to attract and retain fewer members, which limits the financial resources and manpower of the organization, which in turn may necessitate greater contact with other Buddhists for support, which can provoke pluralistic attitudes.[46] Having a pluralistic attitude can lower interest in maintaining creeds and is often associated with newcomers who are exploring and imagining what Buddhism is in the first place, often through encounters with a wide range of Buddhist and non-Buddhist traditions; because they are eclectic they are hesitant to commit to supporting any single teacher, and because they are seekers more than joiners, such new Buddhists are often unwilling to commit significant amounts of money and time to specific sectarian groups. Newcomers to noncreedal traditions are rarely interested in the hard work of proselytizing their neighbors, which prevents groups from rapidly expanding their membership rolls and bank accounts, which makes them unattractive to teachers seeking a community to lead.

In the South, these trends can be especially exaggerated. As I discussed in chapter 2, the South has few trained Buddhist teachers given its geographical and population size, and teachers who are Buddhist circuit riders are rarely available to the satellite groups they manage. The same is true for smaller cities such as Richmond, which cannot boast a large number of Buddhist teachers. If interest in Asian religions such as Buddhism is inherently limited to a certain percentage of the population, then Richmond's size does not afford a particularly large pool of potential converts for Ekoji and the other Buddhist groups in the area. Social pressures in the South further decrease the number of people interested in exploring Buddhism — as I show in chapter 5, families, churches, and others with a connection to evangelical Protestant Christianity disapprove of the exploration of non-Christian religions and attempt to bring Buddhists back into the Christian fold or cut off relations with ex-Christians. Many who decide to leave Christianity are disenchanted with religion in general and therefore unlikely to explore Buddhism. For those who do decide to become Buddhists, the low number of Buddhists and lack of teachers in the South and in smaller cities makes reimagining themselves as Buddhist and developing a sense of what Buddhism is that much more challenging, which contributes to the need to draw on whatever resources are available, such as books and the Internet.

Without a guiding teacher or a large Buddhist peer group, newer Buddhists naturally cast a wider net in their explorations and come into contact with more types of Buddhism, even if only through reading.

So the feedback properties of these factors are especially heightened in the South and smaller cities. Low numbers and resources in the South have many subtle impacts. One is the tremendous challenge of mounting effective Buddhist programs for children. In California the many temples in the Buddhist Churches of America, as well as a large number of other institutions, provide degrees of religious instruction for children, which helps to bring them into the fold. These institutions also assist young parents who seek some sort of moral instruction for their children and may go elsewhere if the Buddhists cannot provide it (in Richmond, such alternative sources include the Unitarian Universalists). In addition, the programs such institutions offer provide young parents with regular relief from their childcare responsibilities, allowing them to meditate, chant, or otherwise focus on their own religious practice and social interactions. Child-based social networks at churches and temples are a strong engine for growth, as they knit parents and children into religious community and increase the likelihood that families will support religious activities through pledges and volunteer work. But without sufficient resources, Ekoji has made almost no attempt to include children or young parents. The situation is exacerbated because nearly everyone is a convert to Buddhism (or, at least, began active Buddhist practice as an adult). A typical Ekoji member, like many involved with Buddhism in the South, is an adult who has rejected a more creedal and restrictive form of Christianity that he or she was raised with, either turning to liberal forms of Christianity mixed with Buddhist practice or, especially, leaving Christianity for Buddhism. These newer Buddhists are poor candidates for Buddhist Sunday School teachers and supporters. They have relatively less knowledge about Buddhism, as they are only learning about Buddhism themselves. They have no experience of Buddhist childhood and therefore little understanding of how to make Buddhism (especially extended silent meditation sessions and complex philosophical ideas such as no-self) accessible to children. And they have—to greater or lesser degrees—turned away from their own religious upbringing, often rejecting the very concept of "indoctrinating" children in a specific religious tradition.

As a result, even within the same school or lineage of Buddhism, American Buddhist practice may differ from one part of the country to the next. For example, the prevalence or absence of clergy or teachers has a clear impact on Buddhist groups: most forms of Buddhism assume that the proper functioning of a Buddhist community requires a trained leader to provide expert meditation guidance, advanced spiritual insight, doctrinal instruction, ritual mastery, or the ability to generate and distribute karmic merit. And the teachers in a lineage are often concentrated in one region.

The Ekoji Zen group has fluctuated in practice style and lineage orientation throughout its existence. With no Zen masters resident in Richmond, the group has done its best to establish ties with teachers beyond Richmond. For years many Ekoji Zen practitioners sought guidance from Dai Bosatsu Monastery in upstate New York, while others looked to the Springwater Center, also in upstate New York. These distant networks ultimately did not prove satisfying, and the group was reorganized to follow the guidelines of the Shunryu Suzuki lineage of Soto Zen as exemplified by the San Francisco Zen Center. This came about because of the presence of the San Francisco–affiliated Chapel Hill Zen Center two and a half hours away in North Carolina. Although this distance still poses difficulties, the connection to the Chapel Hill center has at least afforded the opportunity to work with a teacher who could come to town on a regular schedule and whose own center could be visited occasionally for retreats. Many members are satisfied with this connection to the San Francisco lineage and are pleased with Josho Phelan as the Richmond group's guiding teacher.

There are, however, voices of dissent. Some people were so upset at the reorientation toward Soto Zen and the Suzuki lineage that they quit the group. Among those who stayed, some do not like Phelan and wish for a different teacher. Others do not like having a teacher at all—used to the basically teacherless approach to Zen established over the years at Ekoji, they chafe at even this level of long-distance authority and resist by criticizing Phelan or not attending Ekoji when she is visiting. Thus the Zen group at Ekoji is indeed a part of the Suzuki lineage in America, and yet it differs from what can be found in other regions. In the San Francisco Bay area, for instance, one can choose from a wide range of Buddhist traditions, including numerous types of Zen, and even different teachers in the Suzuki lineage. Thus any given Suzuki-based Zen group in the San Francisco area is likely to be composed of members who have chosen it out of all the other options and are relatively content with their teacher and fellow practitioners. Not so at Ekoji: in a region with no local Suzuki teachers and only one teacher two and a half hours away, the Richmond Zen Group is attended by people who both like and dislike the Suzuki lineage, people who approve of and disapprove of the group's guiding teacher, and people who accept and oppose the notion of Zen religious authority in the first place. For the discontented members, there are no other good options, so they attend a less than perfect group; those happy with the Suzuki connection are unable or unwilling to eject their disgruntled peers and thus must practice in a group that is much less united than might be expected elsewhere in their own lineage.[47] Of course these issues affect the ability of the group to grow and attract both new members and permanent teachers.

A further regional difference that can be seen at the Zen group is a sort of lag in practice style. When changes are made to the practice styles in a lineage, they take time to filter out to associated groups that are further from the centers of concentration, and groups at the very end of continent-wide networks (such as Ekoji) may be quite late in adjusting their practice. For example, the rise of female teachers and feminist concerns in general at the San Francisco Zen Center led to the addition of female names to the roster of venerated ancestors whose names are chanted at every service. Yet well after such changes had been made on the West Coast, members of the Richmond Zen Group were still venerating an all-male lineage—not out of actual resistance to the idea of incorporating female ancestors, but simply because no one had told them to change. Resistance does occur sometimes though, as a member told me over lunch one day: "I've been practicing these forms, and somewhere inside I feel like eventually I'm going to get them right, I'm going to perfect them. But they keep changing it on us! Every time the teacher visits from Chapel Hill, she seems to change a little something. And when Chapel Hill is visited by people from San Francisco, they say, 'Oh, we don't do it that way anymore.'"[48] Thus at least in some cases, Buddhist groups farthest afield preserve old, now outdated forms, while more central groups change more often.

The dynamic in the Vipassana group is also noteworthy. Because there is no local teacher, those members who have been meditating with the group for many years get thrust into positions of de facto leadership and guidance for newer members. Yet this is a situation that they resist and resent: they see themselves as average lay practitioners and have neither pursued nor desired leadership responsibility. Indeed, they often ache to *receive* guidance and support from truly advanced, trained teachers, perceiving that their own practice has been retarded over the years by their inability to get regular help with their meditation practice. Thus older and more experienced members of the Vipassana community in a teacherless region such as the South come to be pressured into roles they find frustrating for their own spiritual advancement.[49] And unable to actually provide expert guidance, they watch as their groups go through cycles where newer, younger people join, fail to find proper guidance, and leave, to be replaced by another round of newer, younger people, and so on and on. This contrasts with Vipassana groups in other places where teachers are more readily available: such groups may in fact be chronologically much newer than groups established for years or decades in places like central Virginia or smaller cities like Richmond, yet their practice may be perceived by members as much more disciplined and "deep," and their group dynamics may be significantly different even if the number of members is approximately equal. There is also a difference in the type of people who come to Ekoji — they tend to have less experience to draw on than some Buddhists in other parts of the country, as one perceptive temple member noted:

> I have experience in Rochester at the Zen center, at San Francisco Zen Center, and Spirit Rock [in California]. In terms of sheer numbers, there's a difference in the South. We don't draw the crowds, not by a long shot. Buddhism seems to be younger in the South, it's still a growing thing. My friend in Kentucky confirmed this: they just don't get so many visitors. One thing I would say is different is that we don't tend to get many people with a practice history. Often people who show up in New York or California have done a lot already. They've tried all sorts of other kinds of Buddhism, have done Hinduism, you name it. My sense is that the people here in Richmond are really new, this is their first brush with trying something different.[50]

The Buddhist Churches of America afford another example of interdenominational differences between regions. The BCA is strongest on the West Coast and much weaker on the East Coast, most especially in the South. Ekoji began as a BCA effort to plant a new temple in the South. In terms of bringing Buddhism to Richmond, it has succeeded: after more than twenty-five years the temple is still self-sufficient and has a stable core of members. But in terms of bringing Jodo Shinshu to Richmond, Ekoji is a failure. The temple is still nominally associated with the BCA, to which it sends a token $100 donation each year, and there are weekly Pure Land services held every Saturday afternoon. But there are no Jodo Shinshu Buddhists at Ekoji, even among the Pure Land members.[51] The Pure Land services have shifted away from most of the specifically Shin elements introduced by Tsuji. At the very edge of the American Jodo Shinshu frontier, Ekoji has become a casualty of regional realties: Richmond has never had a large Japanese American community (the primary supporters of American Shin temples), and efforts to draw Shin converts from the larger community have been both minimal and ineffectual. Without a settled resident minister, such efforts are most likely doomed. The general prospects for Jodo Shinshu are not strong: when told about it, most people in Richmond relate Pure Land Buddhism to Christianity, and they are either satisfied with Christianity and thus see no need to pursue a seemingly Christian Buddhism, or they are turned off by Christianity and want something completely different, such as Zen or Vipassana.[52] Thus if the practice of Zen in Richmond is difficult, the Pure Land experience is even more fraught. It is noteworthy that Tsuji's successful Shin temple, the Ekoji temple located in Fairfax Station, is at the very northern tip of the South, in the Washington, DC, suburbs, and while its membership is ethnically mixed, there was a core group of Japanese Americans from the start. It was from this base in a relatively friendly location that Tsuji launched his missionary efforts southward, and the further he traveled from Northern Virginia, the less successful his southern groups have been over time. The northernmost Ekoji remains Jodo Shinshu, while the eastern Virginia Ekoji in Richmond has a Pure Land presence but is no longer Shin; the group in central North Carolina is now completely nonsectarian and lacks any Pure Land focus, and the groups in Georgia and Texas have completely disintegrated.

One further way that regionalism interacts with the seven factors listed above is in the types of Buddhism that local Buddhists have contact with. Buddhist traditions are not at all evenly spread in the United States, and if contact with other Buddhist groups is likely to increase hybridity, it is worth noting that outside influence is not automatic. Some Buddhist traditions must lend themselves more readily to influence by other forms of Buddhism, and there must be a range of degrees to which specific traditions are permeable to practices and ideas beyond their own lineage. In the South there are fewer other Buddhist groups to interact with, and the mix of traditions is regionally specific. With few Suzuki Zen teachers, Buddhists are more likely to encounter Zen practitioners from other lineages; with one of the country's only concentrations of Bön practitioners, central Virginia Buddhists have the opportunity to be influenced by a quasi-Buddhist tradition unavailable to most Americans in even the most heavily Buddhist areas of the country. These intradenominational interactions may be unprecedented in Buddhist history: Tibetan-derived Bön has rarely found itself in close proximity to Burmese-style Vipassana or Japan-based Soto Zen, and the hybrids that can result from these encounters may be rare or even basically unimaginable in Asia.

Practicing Pluralism

While the pluralism of American Buddhism in general has been often remarked on, pluralism within American Buddhist temples is a largely un-
studied phenomenon. The only sustained investigation of Buddhist multiplicity at specific sites is Paul Numrich's work on parallel congregations.[53]
While Numrich's work has added important insights to the field of American Buddhist studies, his model cannot be applied to a temple such as
Ekoji. Parallel congregations are typically divisions within the framework
of a single tradition—they point out diversity, and often a certain level of
conflict, within individual temples as different clienteles move in opposite
directions despite allegiance to a shared school of Buddhism. Ekoji, by contrast, is a situation of multiple congregations from separate traditions that
tend to move closer to one another over time.[54] Furthermore, Numrich's
work emphasizes the disjunctions between the parallel congregations. What
he discusses is a situation of multiplicity, but not pluralism per se. Diversity
or multiplicity is a phenomenon; pluralism is an attitude toward diversity.
Coleman has also noted that his subjects freely borrow from across multiple Buddhist traditions. But he makes the mistake of attributing this to
an emergent form he calls Western Buddhism. This analysis, unfortunately,
is much too sweeping. It is not at all true that all Western Buddhists are
pluralists in their orientation, nor are all Buddhist converts (the particular
Western demographic he is interested in). Rather, we need to analyze the
various different orientations and approaches swirling in American Buddhism, of which pluralism is only one. I hope here to provide a corrective
that builds on Coleman's pioneering work but restricts eclectic attitudes
and approaches to their appropriate places.

To account for the sort of phenomena we see at Ekoji, I suggest adding
another category to the burgeoning typology of American buddha-dharma
practitioners: *pluralistic Buddhists*. Simply put, pluralistic Buddhists are
those who (at least part of the time) practice or attend the activities of
more than one type of Buddhism. They may strongly identify with a particular lineage but have one or two practices picked up from other sources,
or they may actively seek to incorporate multiple forms of Buddhism into
their religious life. Perhaps a further term, *pluralistic Buddhism*, would be
warranted to describe the form of hybrid tradition that informs or results
from this approach.

In this study I have considered how different Buddhist groups interact
with and influence one another. However, there is yet another level of hy-

bridity that has been left out: influences from non-Buddhist religions. The factors I delineate above also apply to this case. For instance, limited resources cause Ekoji to use space at other religious institutions when a larger meeting place is needed. In a case of temporary hybridity, the Ekoji Vipassana group kept strict kosher when it held a workshop at Temple Beth-el.[55] Obviously, the presence of members with childhood connections to non-Buddhist religions also increases the likelihood of hybridity, since practices and material culture from prior religious affiliations often persist after the beginning of Buddhist practice. A large number of Ekoji members go to church or synagogue at least occasionally. I found the number of crucifixes, mezuzahs, Native American objects, and other non-Buddhist elements on the home altars of Ekoji members to be surprisingly high—the large majority of Ekoji members I spoke to kept non-Buddhist religious objects on their personal Buddhist altars. One informant told me that he uses the Jesus Prayer ("Lord Jesus Christ, have mercy on me") as a mantra, while yet another does a tantric visualization of Christ. The opportunities for contact with non-Buddhist religions are abundant in the United States—not only is America a largely Christian nation, but also the urban environments where Buddhism usually appears are typically hotbeds of religious diversity. The pluralistic impulses of some Ekoji members sometimes find quite vivid expressions, as in this response I received to my questionnaire:

> I honor, respect, and celebrate all religious traditions throughout the world which I have experienced and come to know, except for the intolerant and fundamentalist forms in any of them. I feel equally at home in a Christian church, a Jewish synagogue, an Islamic mosque, a Hindu mandir, a Buddhist temple, and a Sikh gurdvara, and try to relate, know, and participate as an insider, not as someone looking in, observing, or a tourist. All aim for an apprehension, realization, and manifestation of the divine presence in each person's life and in the external world as well. For there is no distinction, division, or duality. The first line of the Islamic Shahada, or creed, comes to mind: "La ilaha il Allah / There is nothing that is real which is not G-d." The names of this reality, or divine presence vary, whether personal as in most theocentric religions or spiritualities, or impersonally/non-personally, as is in the Buddha dharma.[56]

This Ekoji member does indeed interact with a wide range of religious communities in Richmond, although he is a committed Buddhist practitioner who puts more time and energy into Buddhism than into non-Buddhist activities. So another type of pluralistic Buddhist, or a subtype, might be one who combines Buddhism with one or more non-Buddhist religions. Such practitioners might be termed *Buddhist pluralists* — they are pluralists at heart, who happen to practice most frequently with Buddhist congregations.

In employing this new term, I acknowledge that religious boundary-crossing has been a frequent theme in Buddhist history — Buddhism has been variously amalgamated with Daoism, Confucianism, Shinto, Bön, and other religions in Asia.[57] I am not arguing that hybridity or multiplicity as such are new phenomena for Buddhism. But in the American Buddhist situation I do perceive what may be a difference in scale, as well as in motivation. Many of the American Buddhist pluralists self-consciously affirm the value of diversity for its own sake, actively seeking to add other Buddhist or even non-Buddhist strains to their individual Buddhist practice. In fact, for many of my consultants the perception that Buddhism is particularly supportive of pluralistic attitudes was an important factor in choosing to practice it. Of the questionnaire respondents at Ekoji in 2004, 28.3 percent singled out attitudes supportive of pluralism — "inclusivity," "tolerance," "open-mindedness," "compassion for others" — when asked what they liked *best* about Buddhism. This contrasts with 11.7 percent who said their favorite aspect was meditation. And whereas blended traditions in Asia have grown from centuries of slow on-the-ground contact and mingling over many generations, pluralistic American Buddhism is developing from some of the first generations to pursue Buddhism in the West and arises in part from pragmatic considerations as a survival tactic.

The pluralist approach to Buddhism highlights one of the ways that Buddhism often functions as a liberal form of religion in America, especially in the conservative South. Scholars of American religious history are quite familiar with the differences between liberal and conservative forms of religion, especially as embodied in the battles over modernism, evolution, and Biblical authority in the Protestant churches, the struggles over kashrut, gender, and other issues in Judaism, and the splits between liberal and conservative Catholics over issues such as abortion, female ordination, and lay authority. Buddhism has historically supported a wide range of approaches and in Asia continues to undergo modification and evolution. What is striking in America, however, is the extent to which Buddhism is conceived of and practiced as a liberal religion that supposedly affirms individual conscience, reinterpretation or abandonment of traditional doctrines in light of modern science, and progressive political agendas.

This trend is especially pronounced among converts in the South. Whether they are rejecting a conservative upbringing they have found too restrictive or simply reacting against a conservative surrounding environment they disagree with, southern Buddhist converts are prone to imagining Buddhism as representing the "holy grail" of an ancient religion that is nondogmatic, individually affirming, and naturally aligned with liberal politics and social mores. Whether or not Buddhism actually is or has been these things is beside the point—in the South, many Buddhists pursue Buddhism in ways that cause it to take on these aspects. Thus the Buddhism found at places such as Ekoji is explicitly welcoming to homosexual members of the community, invites full participation and leadership by both men and women, and encourages nonliteral interpretations of traditional texts. Ekoji members overwhelmingly support liberal political causes (health care reform, nuclear nonproliferation, affirmative action, abortion rights, environmentalism, etc.), and discussions at the temple often highlight ways Buddhist principles can be applied to strengthen these political agendas. The Mahayana concept of universal buddha-nature, for example, is cited as proof that everyone has worth and discrimination is wrong, while the notion of interdependent coorigination is interpreted to mean that an ecological consciousness is natural to Buddhism and should lead to activism to save the Earth (or, at least, to recycling). Members of Ekoji organized a local chapter of the Buddhist Peace Fellowship and held monthly meditation vigils in Richmond's Monroe Park to oppose the U.S. invasion of Iraq, an action interpreted as American imperialistic warmongering by a misguided conservative president. This attitude of Buddhism as the "better," more liberal religious alternative in Richmond will be explored further in the next chapter.

Conclusion

Hybridity and pluralism have their limits. We should not lose sight of the way that boundaries clearly continue to operate within Buddhist communities such as Ekoji. Chapter 3 details the many efforts at identity separation, and indeed most Buddhists at Ekoji, no matter how much they may dabble in various traditions, nonetheless fundamentally stick to a single Buddhist lineage as their primary orientation. We can also note that for all their affirmation of boundary-crossing and multiplicity, Ekoji's Buddhists reproduce (or, at least fail to dismantle) many boundaries that can be seen in American Buddhism and religion more generally. Ekoji is good at attracting people who are relatively new to Buddhism, but other than the long-departed Vietnamese group, it has mostly failed to serve as a refuge for Buddhists born into the religion.[58] Like nearly every religious institution in Richmond—liberal or conservative, pluralistic or exclusive, Buddhist or Christian—Ekoji is strongly dominated by a single racial demographic, in this case whites. Beliefs that race is a mere social construction and that all people are equal members of the human race are not in themselves sufficient to develop multiracial congregations, it seems.

Pluralism also provokes its opposite. When Ekoji's groups have become too amorphous, there have been efforts to align them with specific lineages in order to instill discipline and ensure that a coherent practice is maintained. Nor is hybridity a constant phenomenon. It can appear and disappear, and it changes over time as individual practitioners and groups absorb new influences and cull their practices. For my informants, Buddhism is a moving target, a source of identity and form of practice that is frequently revised and adjusted.

But despite these observations and caveats, it is clear that Ekoji is a place of considerable mixing and that this exploration is affirmed by most of its members. Particular factors especially prominent outside the large cities and in regions of relatively little Buddhist penetration help to strengthen a sort of natural pluralistic orientation often found in American Buddhism. These factors illustrate the need to always pay attention to the regional influences on American Buddhist groups when conducting our research. In the following chapters I thus analyze the role of southern religion and culture in shaping Buddhist experience in Richmond.

Such an intricate world allows us neither to reduce Richmond to a part of a monolithic South nor to easily assume the attitudes of its people.
— Gregg D. Kimball, *American City, Southern Place*, 2000

Chapter Five

BUDDHISM WITH A SOUTHERN ACCENT
American Buddhists in a Southern Culture

In chapter 1, I laid out a basic approach to studying regionalism in American Buddhism. Throughout this book, I have referred to the fact that Ekoji Buddhist Sangha of Richmond is located in the South, and that this has an effect on the temple. Now in this chapter I turn to the question of regional Buddhism directly and use Ekoji as a case study for American Buddhist regionalism. Specifically, in this chapter I am concerned to investigate how and why particular elements of Ekoji's southern location might shed light on the various phenomena one finds at the temple and among its membership more generally, as well as what effects Ekoji may have on Richmond as a southern locale.

Historian Gregg Kimball characterized antebellum Richmond as an "American city" and a "southern place." It is this continuing dual character that concerns us as we study Richmond in a very different era. On the one hand, Richmond is an American city, the capital of the state of Virginia. Richmonders have many of the same social concerns (crime, education, jobs, racial issues, etc.) as their peers elsewhere in the country. They tend to belong to one of the two major national political parties. Like other Americans, they watch baseball, basketball, and football; they go to movies and dine out at restaurants; they are mostly Christian and many attend church regularly. Richmond is a city where most consumer goods available in other parts of America can be found, and it is tied into the same interstate highway system and national communication networks (cable television, the Internet, and so on). On the other hand, Richmond is not a generic space—it is a specific place. And that place is in the region of the country known as the South. Thus Richmond is a city with a long history of slavery, legal segregation, struggles for civil rights, and ongoing tensions between blacks and whites. In terms of sports, it is Redskins territory. Diners can enjoy pad thai and sushi here, but it is easier to find collard greens. For both blacks and whites, the average religious institution is evangelical. And Richmond is not just any state capital in the South: it was the capital of the Confederacy until the waning hours of that failed nation's existence, a fact marked on the landscape and local consciousness by museums, monuments, cemeteries, voluntary societies, and battle-flag-waving marches and rallies. It is also a place with a legitimate claim as the birthplace of religious freedom, where Thomas Jefferson penned the Virginia Statute for Religious Freedom that became the model for the First Amendment to the U.S. Constitution. Richmond is not American *or* southern—it is both. Likewise, the Buddhism that exists here operates on both levels.

Buddhism with an accent: that is what southern Buddhism is. The southern drawl is not a different language from English, and saying "y'all" does not make you non-American. In the same way, Buddhism in the South is not a different religion from other American Buddhisms, it is just a local version of a national phenomenon that has its own particularities tied to a certain place and a certain history. Those who speak with a southern accent are understood throughout the country, though they sometimes stick out, and they understand what others are saying, though they are occasionally confounded or amused by it. Like southerners in general, the Buddhists of the South are fully American and well integrated into national culture, and many can travel about the country and overseas. They are increasingly knit into national and international webs of communication, business, and culture, yet they are still marked out in ways by their local experiences and circumstances. Far from arguing that southern Buddhism is not American, I say it is 100 percent American, just as West Coast Buddhism is. But to be American is not 100 percent the same in either of these places, and to be Buddhist is not 100 percent the same in these places either, and the distinctions—I believe—are worthy of our attention.

In chapter 1, I suggested that we divide the country into eight different regions as one possible approach to regional interpretation. Ekoji falls into the subregion that I termed the Coastal South, and that is worth bearing in mind. However, because I did not conduct comparable long-term fieldwork at another site in what I term the Inner South, here I will not stress the "coastal" part of that area, but the "South" aspect. Many, but not all, of the topics I discuss will be relevant to Buddhists in both the Coastal and Inner Souths, so rather than draw too artificial a line between them, I will instead mainly only bring up their differences when directly relevant to Richmond as a specific southern site. Buddhism anywhere in the South has been neglected by researchers. Let this be a first direct attempt at such work, and let us hope that future work will further break the South—a place of great intraregional diversity—into more useful subunits for our analysis.

Regional Impact on Buddhism

One of the most important forms of regional analysis that I laid out in chapter 1 is the examination of how the local environment is impacting Buddhist development and practice. This can be approached in several ways, such as through attention to climate and topography, to forces such as economics, and to the general cultural and religious milieu of a region. Climate and topography have minimal effect on Buddhism in Richmond. Like most parts of the South, Richmond has hot summers and relatively mild winters, but since it is in the upper South it is not as warm as many other southern locales. Being on the East Coast the city experiences four distinct seasons and significant precipitation. Spring thunderstorms, summer heat, and winter snow necessitate some planning for events, and occasionally cause cancellations, and activities that occur outdoors (such as meditation vigils) are most likely to be affected; there is some effort to schedule outside activities for milder parts of the calendar, such as spring and fall. But overall the weather does not significantly affect the Buddhists at Ekoji. Buddhists at the Cambodian and Vietnamese temples in Richmond have a greater chance of being negatively impacted, since they hold periodic large gatherings that draw Cambodian Americans or Vietnamese Americans from throughout the Southeast and necessitate the attendance of additional monks from other parts of the country: if the weather is particularly uncooperative on the day of a special event, it can spoil months of planning and preparations. But while weather is not a significant variable for most of the year in some places, such as Southern California, on the whole it does not inhibit or drastically alter Buddhist practice in Richmond. Nor is topography especially important to Buddhists in this area. Richmond is a city of hills and valleys, with the James River a prominent feature. The Atlantic Ocean is less than ninety minutes to the east, while the Blue Ridge Mountains are less than two hours to the west. But none of these features factor into the practice of Richmond Buddhists in any noteworthy way.[1] Thus it is possible to say that climate and topography do not have a great impact on Buddhism in Richmond, although they may play a greater role for Buddhists elsewhere in the South.[2]

Economic forces are a more clearly important set of factors to contemplate. Richmond's economy is fairly diverse, with some of the most outstanding features being the large number of universities; the tobacco industry; the seat of Virginia government; the financial, energy, and advertising industries; and Civil War–oriented tourism. The universities, financial sector, tobacco industry, and utilities account for a majority of the employers of Ekoji members, mostly in white collar positions. The rest of Ekoji's membership tends to fall into the helping professions (nurses, therapists, social workers, etc.), small business, and the arts. Blue-collar jobs are uncommon at Ekoji.

Among these various sectors the universities must be singled out for special attention. Virginia Commonwealth University (VCU) and the University of Richmond, as well as some of the smaller colleges and seminaries, are clear engines for the growth of Buddhism in Richmond. The universities are highly overrepresented at Ekoji compared to the overall population, with a very significant number of professors and students present at Ekoji, as well as some university staff. Many of the core members who have provided long-term lay leadership to the various groups that meet at Ekoji are university professors, and students are a significant portion of participants. Ekoji has little in the way of a formal liturgical calendar, but the groups' practice schedules do show patterns of fluctuation that correspond to the academic school year. When the universities are in session, there are generally more attendees at every group, especially the Zen group, which meets in the relatively student-friendly Sunday-morning timeslot. During the summer when students leave town and professors often go on vacation, there is less attendance at Ekoji meetings, and combined with the summer heat and humidity, Ekoji takes on a sort of sleepy feeling that persists until the increased school activity and crisper temperatures reinvigorate things in the fall. Late December is also a time of relative inactivity—groups still hold their regular meetings, but attendance is noticeably lower—as students go home after the fall semester and Ekoji members in general are distracted with holiday family gatherings, whether traveling out of Richmond or hosting out-of-town relatives.

With so many professors and students, there is a tendency toward intellectualism in the practice and discussions at Ekoji. This is supported by the high rate of education among the total membership — the large majority of Ekoji members have a college degree or are pursuing it, and graduate degrees are also very well represented at the temple. This intellectualism can be hard to quantify but is clearly recognized by many sangha members themselves, manifesting in such ways as the preference for postmeditation book discussions; the high regard for science in the membership; the attention given to the role of the mind in Buddhism and mental faculties as somehow possessing the key to spiritual development; preference for quietistic personal meditation over devotional practices by the majority of participants; and skepticism toward many core Buddhist concepts and practices (such as prayer and more literal interpretations of karma, gods and spirits, heavenly and hellish realms, etc.).[3] Many of my informants at Ekoji characterized Buddhism as a relatively rational religion that fit better with their individualistic and intellectual orientations than their native traditions or those generally available to the Richmond populace did; some frankly characterized it as atheistic and totally scientific, with no faith element or dogma, calling Buddhism a "way of life," "practice," or "philosophy" rather than a "religion." When responding to a question about what he liked best about Buddhism, one Ekoji member gave a fairly typical reply that seems to sum up this common attitude well, pointing to Buddhism's "experiential emphasis and cogent philosophical interpretations."[4]

As magnets for intellectuals from other parts of the country, the universities bring outsiders to Richmond, a certain percentage of whom are Buddhist and thus cause the religious diversity of Richmond to rise.[5] The universities are also places where ideas from around the world are explored and exchanged, exposing not only students but also professors and staff to concepts and religions not otherwise well represented in Richmond. Nearly all the practitioners at Ekoji began their exploration of Buddhism as adults, and in narrating their spiritual journeys many said their initial exposure came in classes at VCU or the University of Richmond, or in some cases at universities elsewhere in America. Students regularly visit Ekoji to fulfill class assignments, and even those Ekoji members not affiliated in some way with the universities frequently venture onto their campuses for cultural and artistic events, especially if one of the schools is hosting a program related to Asian culture or Buddhism, such as an art exhibit or calligraphy demonstration. For those who did not encounter Buddhism in college, another major source of initial exposure was through books, underlining the fundamentally intellectual nature of much of Ekoji's Buddhism.

I have observed similar correlations between the presence of universities and the degree of local Buddhist activities in other southern locations, such as Charlottesville, Virginia; and Chapel Hill, Asheville, and Boone, North Carolina. I suspect, therefore, that this is a general phenomenon that applies well beyond Richmond. For regions with historically little Buddhist practice, such as the South, universities provide an important entry point for Buddhism and contribute to a generally "university-type culture" that develops at some nearby Buddhist institutions.

Being a Buddhist in the South

A further regional influence on Buddhism is the local culture and religion. This is significant enough in the South that I have given it its own separate discussion here, although technically I consider this just one further aspect of the sort of overall regional influences that also include climate, economics, and other forces. It manifests in many ways, but above all it is especially defined by Buddhism's relationship with Christianity.

Perhaps a good entrance into this discussion could be provided by a quick look at how older minorities have dealt with life in the South. David Goldfield is one of the most perceptive southern historians, and his comments on southern Jews are relevant to the Buddhist situation as well:

> Jews, as quintessential outsiders, have developed a sixth sense to take cues on public behavior from the host society. Survival has often depended on their relative invisibility to the Gentile population. They have had to balance the pursuit of their culture and religion with the necessity of maintaining a low profile. This tension between preservation and invisibility has lessened in recent decades in the United States, but it still forms a theme of Jewish life in the South. For the South remains the most evangelical Protestant region of the country, the most conservative part of the United States, and the place most imbued with rural culture.[6]

For Buddhists in Richmond, there is often a reflexive tendency to minimize their public presence and avoid any possible conflict with non-Buddhists. Most of the attendees at Ekoji feel that they are a small religious minority in a sea of conservative, potentially hostile evangelical Christianity. Many avoid drawing attention to themselves both at the temple and elsewhere. One result is that Ekoji looks like any other house in the neighborhood and only very modest efforts have been made to display its religious identity to the outside public. A former president of the temple was very matter of fact about the situation when I asked him whether there would be an effect if Ekoji became better known in Richmond: "We would get people denouncing us. Every so often you get paranoid feelings. Christians come through and put flyers on the buildings. That's happened. Martin got a really strange invitation to the Baptist Mission Board to come and speak with them. They wanted to know what the weaknesses of our path were so that they could train missionaries and convert Buddhists to Christianity. I was like, 'Why are you asking? If I thought it was weak, why would I be a Buddhist?' . . . One person who visited the temple asked, 'How can you follow those terrorists?'"[7]

The attempts to keep a low profile have generally been successful—in fact, there are neighbors who have lived on the same block as Ekoji without ever knowing there was a Buddhist temple nearby. This contrasts with the prominent public face of the city's many churches, including churches near Ekoji on the same street. Naturally, this felt need to "fly under the radar," as one informant put it, makes it more difficult for the temple to attract members, since most people in Richmond are unaware that Ekoji even exists as a potential spiritual resource. "The South is a strongly religious place, and it's assumed you're Christian," explained a woman who was born and raised in Richmond: "In other places it's probably more recognized as a normal thing to be Buddhist. I follow the advice that I got from a friend at Ekoji, who said that what we do doesn't have to be called anything. We don't need to wear T-shirts that say 'Buddhism!' We can just do it quietly and not cause problems. I work with seniors; they're very strongly Christian. There's no way I could mention Buddhism at work. It would cause unnecessary problems. . . . I'm not comfortable with saying I go to Ekoji. People always ask me where I go to church. I wish I could say I go to the Buddhist temple. But I don't talk about it with my family."[8] Most of Ekoji's attendees have been invited to church by neighbors or coworkers at some point in their lives, but the Buddhists very rarely extend such offers to visit the temple unless they know that an acquaintance has an active interest in non-Christian religions. As one put it, "I've never brought anyone to the temple. I live in a very redneck, Christian area."[9] Efforts to fundraise for the temple are suppressed as well. A member active in the Zen group just shook his head at the idea of letting outsiders know about their temple and asking for help: "You can't go door-to-door to raise funds when the temple wants to expand. I think you could if you're a Christian group. But we can't go into the wider community and make our needs known."[10]

In their personal and work lives, most Ekoji participants weigh seriously how open they wish to be about their commitment to Buddhist practice. For many, the answer is to simply deflect questions about religion and to hide the fact that they are Buddhist.[11] This strategy can sometimes manifest in dramatic ways. A long-time Ekoji member and local business owner contrasted his approaches to revealing his sexuality and his religion:

As far as being a Buddhist in the South goes and dealing with my relatives, it's sort of funny: I'm out of the closet to my immediate family and some of my extended family as a gay person, but not as a Buddhist person. I think that actually would be even more difficult for them to understand than the gay part. I talked to a person in the Chapel Hill Buddhist community and she agreed. She said she told her family she was a Buddhist and that was really hard for them to deal with. When you come from a fundamentalist Christian background, they interpret it as your decision to turn away from God, which would mean you're going to Hell. So it's very negative. And I think that in the fundamentalist mind there's a religious continuum where fundamentalist Christianity would be on one end and Buddhism would be all the way at the other end, maybe just one step up from atheism.[12]

Many other Ekoji members have likewise decided to keep their Buddhism "in the closet" in order to avoid friction with their Christian relatives. Indeed, whether they kept their Buddhism secret or told others about it, people frequently drew parallels between the Buddhist and gay experiences. "I recently 'came out' to my mom as a Buddhist," explained a relatively recent Ekoji member from elsewhere in Virginia. His experience was not too harsh, since the family reacted with ignorance and concern but not anger: "She said, 'Is that related to Hinduism? Or Islam?' So she was confused, but didn't freak out. I told my grandma about a world religion course I took and mentioned how the Dalai Lama is chosen while still a boy. She said, 'So they brainwash a little kid?'"[13] Others face more serious penalties for publicizing their commitments, as a gay teenager in Kentucky described in the book *Queer Dharma*:

I came out as a Buddhist before I came out as gay. . . . I was constantly criticized for being Buddhist. I was often attacked verbally and once physically. On one occasion, as I sat in class, someone asked who I prayed to; but before I could respond the teacher jumped in and said, "Those Buddhists worship wooden statues! We Americans should go overseas where they come from and teach them who the real GOD is!!!" Suddenly the whole class burst out laughing and were yelling, "You're going to Hell, stupid! If you don't believe in God you're crazy! You had better never come around me, or I'll knock your teeth down your neck! You Buddha boy!!!" . . . I decided to come out to the small group of friends that I had gained in hope that if one of them were gay knowing that they were not alone would comfort them. . . . [My mother] tells me she knew she should have stopped me from being Buddhist and "this wouldn't have happened." Similarly at school the rumor spread that all Buddhists were gay.[14]

The necessity to hide their religious practice sometimes leads Ekoji members to elaborate smokescreens and deceptions that violate Buddhist precepts against falsehood, a factor which bothers some informants who feel trapped between the positive things they feel their Buddhist practice brings them and the lies necessary to maintain it; but being open about their Buddhism would lead to anger and hurt, including causing pain for others, which Buddhism strongly seeks to avoid. There are simply no good solutions for southern Buddhists who feel caught in this way.

The story of Oliver, a practitioner from the Tibetan group at Ekoji, illustrates the problems that develop as one's Buddhist spirituality deepens. Increasingly committed to the Buddhist path and recognizing that he could not get the training and support he wanted in Richmond, Oliver made plans to seclude himself for a traditional three-year-long Tibetan retreat at a monastery in New York. But he knew that his Christian parents from rural Virginia would believe he was damned to Hell if he discussed it with them. Therefore, he told his family that he was going abroad with a church group to work with poor children in Africa. During his three years of absence from the South, he wrote letters to his family about his alleged adventures in Africa—but rather than mailing them directly, Oliver sent them to a friend who really was living and working in Africa, who then mailed them back to the United States so they would arrive with an African postmark. By the end of his time in New York he had become a monk, and he returned to the South to work and offer Tibetan teachings, using his Tibetan ordination name which would not be recognizable to his family. When he returns home for gatherings, no one there has any idea of what he went through: on the first visit some church ladies invited Oliver over and told him they were sure that "the children must be missing you already." The comment confused him and he stammered in bewilderment momentarily, before realizing what they were talking about and trying to recover by agreeing that the children in Africa whom he had been teaching for the past three years must indeed be missing him now.[15]

Evasions were also sometimes necessary at work for my informants. A young man who works for a financial corporation in Richmond offered his experiences:

> It's kind of a pain in the ass to practice Buddhism in the South. I'm not in the Deep South, but I'm in a really conservative state. This is as red of a state as you can get in many ways. It's hard. You don't tell people you're a Buddhist right up front. Some of them will stop talking to you. Some of them will start preaching to you. And actually Jerry from the Tibetan group, he was on a job site — he works in construction — and he mentioned that he was Buddhist and he thought that he was going to get lynched. Just mauled by these people who were so adverse to it and honestly and truly believed that it was devil worship. This is a very Christian community. They believe that God is as they are told it is, and that nothing else is right. God bless America — and nobody else. It's not very accepting of that. It's places like this where notions that Barack Obama is a Muslim carry water. So I don't tell people that I'm Buddhist. And I had to change my schedule at work so that I could start coming on Wednesdays, since they needed a facilitator for the Wednesday night Zen meetings, and my boss was a very openly conservative Christian, a fervently Christian woman, and I knew that if I told her what religion I was, it was going to create a problem with her. So I told her I had to help lead a service, it's religious reasons and I don't really want to explain it. And she asked what church I went to, and I said I'd rather not share that. She was OK with that because she assumed it was a church that she knew downtown, and she never went downtown. She actually thought that there was a connection between her and I because she thought we were both strong, active members of a Christian church. And I know that if she had found out otherwise, that would've created conflict.

This was not the only person with whom this Buddhist had run into trouble at work. Another coworker had recently decided to become an evangelical Christian and spent a year and a half trying to convert him. "He would ask me questions about Buddhism, and at first I didn't pick up on it — maybe I'm not that bright — and I thought it was genuine intellectual curiosity, but he was just trying to find ways to convert me, basically. Which was comical in some ways, since he has the theological sophistication of an eight-year-old in a Sunday school. I just had to tell him, 'If you're going to always be trying to have a religious discussion with me, we're not going to be able to be friends,' because he's coming at it from the view that what I'm doing is wrong. I've had issues with him since."[16]

This last informant is also an example of the negative experiences that may occur when Ekoji members do decide to reveal their Buddhist interests to family, friends, and coworkers. In the most extreme cases, southern family members shunned them completely. Other Buddhists who had not told their families also said they felt they would be "ostracized" if they did so. Still others' experiences were also serious but not necessarily as shattering. The most common experience that people related was being told that they were going to Hell because of their Buddhist beliefs, a reaction many had received from family members, old friends, coworkers, and even strangers on the street who happened to learn about their Buddhism. These encounters did not necessarily result in a severing of relationship, but they strained the ties and afterward the Buddhist would typically be the target of pressure to stop practicing Buddhism, to go to church more often, or to convert to Christianity. One older lady who has lived in both Richmond and California described an encounter with her brother, a devout Baptist. She was performing a type of Buddhist-derived healing touch on her sister-in-law, and her brother pulled her aside and asked, "What do you think will happen when you die?," a frequent opening salvo for evangelical Christians looking to scare others about Hell and bring them into Christianity. She was "pissed" by his attitude but also touched by his concern.[17] Another woman related being ambushed by her father's religious community. Word had gotten around that she was involved with Buddhism, and she was invited to a gathering after she attended a memorial service for her father. At the gathering, she was put through an "inquisition" that lasted over an hour about the fact that she was Buddhist.[18] Even those Ekoji attendees who felt that they had not experienced any significant problems with non-Buddhists nonetheless almost all had ready stories about times when they were baited or poked fun at by Christians for being Buddhist. Often these anecdotes took place at public functions, such as a group of Baptist ministers who made dismissive remarks about a professor's interest in Buddhism at a wedding, and a doctor who equated Buddhism with exploitation and scandal when another professor came to comfort a hospitalized Buddhist.[19]

Even those who are not carefully hiding their Buddhism are automatically affected by being non-Christian in the South. As David Goldfield has pointed out: "Church and urban society remain closely connected. Religious affiliation is as important as lineage in describing a person today. The southern urban church is the best place in the city to attain and maintain social and business contacts."[20] This is an advantage that Buddhists are unable to enjoy. And southern temples — typically smaller than their denominational counterparts in other areas of the country — can be meager sites for social and business networking. As one Ekoji member who grew up in Richmond put it, "I'm a single guy, I'm looking for a lady, and I'd love to find someone who's into Buddhism. But there's just a small sprinkling of people in the South. It's a small pool. I'm less able to have a network of Buddhist friends. There's a lack of variety and social connection."[21] Not only are most Buddhist groups small, but the emphasis many put on silent meditation and individualism also makes them inherently poor locations for socializing and community building.

Same South, Different Experiences

Whatever else it may be, the South is multiple-choice. . . . There are numerous
Dixies from which to choose, and the real one is the one *you* perceive.
— Sharon McKern, *Redneck Mothers, Good Ol' Girls and Other Southern Belles*, 1997

Despite my observations in the preceding section, it is important not to depict the situation of Buddhism in the South as monolithic. While a clear majority of my informants indicated that they hid or downplayed their Buddhist practice in some way when interacting with non-Buddhists, others did not feel they experienced any significant conflict over Buddhism and did not find the South — or, at least, Richmond — to be hostile to Buddhism. Most people did not want to do anything that would draw attention to the temple, but a smaller number wanted to erect a more prominent sign and do more to advertise the Buddhist presence in Richmond.[22] There were temple members who related very positive experiences with Christians, and we should not forget that some Ekoji attendees choose to affiliate with Christianity or other non-Buddhist religions to greater or lesser degrees. As I spoke with more people about Buddhism and the South specifically, gradually a pattern began to emerge in the type of person who felt there was a serious disadvantage to being Buddhist in Richmond and the type of person who did not. The key to understanding most people's experiences turned out to be geography and proximity: specifically, whether my informants came from the South and how close by their relatives were.

Most of the people who felt that there was not a significant hardship to practicing Buddhism in the South due to the surrounding cultural and religious environment were not themselves natives of the South. They had migrated to Richmond from other parts of the country, including the Northeast, the Midwest, the West Coast, and Hawaii. They were far away from their families and childhood networks, beyond the surveillance of people who knew them from their pre-Buddhist days (all of them were adult converts). Many did not come from deeply conservative religious backgrounds to begin with, or at least they came from areas where their Christian family members were used to having contact with non-Christians in their neighborhoods and workplaces. Furthermore, when they moved to Richmond they created new local networks and communities chosen in ways to insulate themselves from the more conservative elements of central Virginia. Such newer Richmonders often shopped at grocery stores, bookstores, and other businesses patronized by a progressive-leaning clientele, joined yoga studios, met friends through Ekoji or other liberal religious sites (many have spent at least some time attending the Unitarian Universalist or Quaker churches in Richmond), went to peace rallies and vegetarian festivals, joined the local Democratic or Green Party, and tended to be active in the arts scene. The largest percentage of them worked at the universities, where they were enveloped in a relatively academic and liberal atmosphere and could expect that their coworkers would not make an issue of their religious beliefs. Having successfully ensconced themselves in the liberal subculture of Richmond, they had few or no direct ties to evangelical Christianity or political conservatives, such as local relatives, friends, or colleagues. For these Buddhists, Richmond was a city much like any other early twenty-first-century city, not a distinct part of America. Their feelings about the South tended be abstract, and if they had complaints about practicing Buddhism in the South, it was often just that there were so few Buddhist teachers and practitioners, making it hard to develop an advanced personal practice.

Buddhists with families from the South tended to paint the situation in quite different terms. The level of stress caused by being Buddhist often increased the nearer one's family was to Richmond: Buddhists with families elsewhere in the South were cautious but did not have as many "horror stories," Buddhists with families in other parts of Virginia were often reticent about speaking to their families about Buddhism, and Buddhists who were actually from the Richmond area were the most likely to be actively hiding their practice from their families, avoiding any mention of

Buddhism at work or in public, and to depict Richmond and the South as having a religious culture that considered Buddhism to be alien and unwanted. Some worried that they would be exposed as Buddhists and suffer social sanctions. For these Buddhists, Richmond was not just another American city, and the South was not just a generic part of the United States — it was a place with a serious and problematic history, both public and personal. Their personal narratives were full of anecdotes about attending local schools and (most often conservative) churches, and they lived within social webs that brought them into regular, often daily contact with fundamentalist Christians who were relatives, childhood friends, neighbors, and coworkers. These local Buddhists also attempted to create buffers by shopping at stores preferred by liberals, supporting progressive political causes, and cultivating friendships with people they knew would not be upset by Buddhism, but these Buddhist-friendly networks were usually more partial and compromised than those of more recent arrivals to Richmond.

In other words, being a Buddhist in the South exacts a higher social toll on people who are themselves from the South, while newer residents of the South (especially in urban areas) who lack local roots can often find ways to thrive in alternative subcultures. This is not an unbroken pattern — I had informants who were from the North and were bitter about the religious and political conservatism of Richmond, as well as Richmonders who traced their local roots to the American Revolution and felt no particular social pressure — but it was a quite common trend, one that my informants at Ekoji readily recognized and agreed was substantially correct when I raised the matter with them. Therefore we cannot talk simplistically about "*the* southern experience of Buddhism." We need instead to be aware that there are *multiple* experiences of Buddhism in the South, and that the regional Buddhist experiences of two friends who meditate together at the same temple may in fact be highly disparate. One person may find the South to be an ideal place to practice Buddhism and feel that there are no social or cultural difficulties involved, while the other may fear that if his or her Buddhist practice became public knowledge it could threaten his or her job, social support system, family ties, and even housing. *Both* are southern experiences that we should acknowledge.

Buddhism as Positive Alternative

Beyond attempting to hide their Buddhism or minimize conflicts with non-Buddhists, Richmond Buddhists find their practice influenced in other significant ways by the dominant conservative Christian environment of central Virginia. The most noteworthy of these is the way Buddhism comes to be conceptualized by its practitioners as a positive, liberal alternative to the common religion and culture of the area, and to some extent as resistance to mainstream America in general. At a conference held at Ekoji in April 1990 the temple president proclaimed: "The U.S. needs the Dharma; there is a great future for Buddhism in the South." One of the other participants agreed: "This society needs Buddhism as an alternative." An Ekoji Pure Land group member was even more emphatic: "We're in the burning house; it's on fire; we need Buddhism!"[23]

I encountered these ideas frequently during group discussions at Ekoji and when talking privately with Richmond Buddhists. A typical vignette from a meeting of the Vipassana group illustrates some of these themes. After an hour of silent meditation on a weekday night in late May 2008, the group began its usual discussion period. This started with basic check-in about people's meditation experiences, and proceeded to a reading from a book by Bhante Henepola Gunaratana. Before long, the conversation began to veer pretty far from the book. A frequent attendee at this and several other Ekoji groups remarked, "Henry and I were talking. And we decided that to be a good Buddhist is to be a bad American. Because to be a good American is to be a consumer, while to be a good Buddhist is to see through that consumeristic mindset."

Laura, a middle-aged woman in a white shirt, spoke up: "That depends on how you define American. It sounds more political."

Walt, one of the group leaders, who was still wearing his uniform from work, offered another perspective: "I was listening to this country song about this guy's identity as a southerner. 'I'm a hard-drinking, truck-driving, macho man.' And I was so struck by that and how it was all about this guy's identity as a man born in the South. And how it seemed to me that, on the contrary, we are really a constant flow of different changing parts."

Laura agreed: "There is no self. People get attached to an identity that isn't their true identity."

Walt took a sip of chamomile tea and continued: "Most of us attach an identity to our life and that identity becomes self. But it's not really that way. You see that it's really constant change."

The conversation turned back to the book momentarily, as the participants tried to analyze the author's use of the term *mindfulness*. But it soon returned to non-Buddhist topics. The subject of Christianity was raised. Several people commented that Christians are too close-minded and act in hateful ways. Ron, a brown-haired man in his early thirties, said, "It amazes me how archaic people's ideas are." Robert, a middle-aged man in a shapeless gray sweatshirt, said, "I was baptized Presbyterian. Forced to go to Sunday school. But I was totally disinterested. When I came here [to the temple] I felt like I'd finally found what I was looking for. I felt like, 'Gosh, I wish I'd found this when I was fifteen years old.'"

Another participant, Chris, chimed in: "I was talking to a Baptist preacher, and he said that I chose Buddha over Jesus. He asked me what my problem was with Jesus. I said I didn't have a problem with Jesus, but with the Church."[24]

Conversations such as these are common at Ekoji. We can see an interweaving of several different significant themes. First, there is question as to whether Buddhism fits in America or is in fact anti-American or countercultural in some way. Some Buddhists feel that Buddhism is in opposition to mainstream American culture, and that this is a positive thing. Such Buddhists characterize American culture (in general, not just in the South) as materialistic and consumption-oriented. A member of the Pure Land group echoed such sentiments in a conversation in his living room later that same week: "Buddhism doesn't fit in with people who buy houses as investments and people who drive SUVs. It doesn't really fit with the most materialistic side of America. It fits in with people who are concerned with environmental issues and people who are really concerned with sharing the wealth. It goes back almost forty years to 'hippie America.'"[25] These sentiments intentionally place Buddhists in Richmond outside of a mainstream that they view as decadent, wrong-headed, selfish, and destructive, allowing the Buddhists to position themselves as a vanguard of affirmative, forward-thinking values living in resistance to the failures of non-Buddhist culture. Most informants believed that America would be better off if there were more Buddhists in the country, because this would create a more conscious society that was less materialistic, militaristic, stressed, and self-aggrandizing.

A second theme is the creation of a stereotypical southerner and subsequent criticism of such a person. In the current example, the southerner in the country-and-western song is described in terms that carry significant class and regional associations in the South: hard-drinking, truck-driving machismo puffed up with southern pride. The Buddhists then disassociate themselves from such a person, indicating that their Buddhist practice has allowed them to rise above such immature projections and self-attachments. They thus project an alternate image of themselves as superior to a sort of common cultural figure assumed to be representative of basic life in the South. A similar encounter was described by the man who connected Buddhism to "hippie America." He recounted an incident that took place a few blocks from the temple, at the Arthur Ashe memorial statue on Monument Avenue. When the statue was put up in 1996 there were protests and marches against including a black figure along with the southern war heroes of the avenue. Ashe was involved in Zen practice as well as Christianity, and his widow is Buddhist, although their religious practices do not seem to have been the target of protest.[26] My informant characterized the protestors as "Confederate jerks. They said that putting that statue up was 'cultural genocide.' Oh boy, I tell you, someone got their thesaurus working when they came up with that one." He and his son, who does not attend Ekoji regularly but does do Buddhist practice, counterprotested with a sign celebrating the spirit of Arthur Ashe.[27] His description of the event paints the anti-Ashe protestors with the negative stereotype of the southerner clinging to a backward view of culture and having to use a thesaurus to come up with big words. By counterprotesting, he publicly repudiates a racist, essentialist vision of the South.

A third theme seen in this vignette is rejection of Christianity. With very little provocation, discussion participants volunteered negative past experiences with Christianity. One person described a process whereby he left his conservative Christian upbringing in Richmond and found instead Buddhism, rejecting his background for something implicitly better. Another Buddhist positioned himself as superior to a Baptist minister — the Baptist could not understand Buddhism or anyone's interest in it, whereas the Buddhist not only understood Christianity but also actually had a better grasp of Jesus' teachings than people who remained stuck in institutional Christianity, implied to be corrupt or barren. In these conversations, Richmond Buddhists are clearly highly aware of Christianity (one hardly imagines that Buddhism comes up as often at local Christian meetings). And not just of any Christianity but a conservative evangelical Christianity that is used to represent the religion as a whole. This conservative Christianity is raised in part because it is one of the anxieties of southern Buddhists, and the discussion allows them to gain some control over it by deprecating it: my field notes from 2002–8 visits to all five groups at Ekoji are littered with terms like "ignorant," "fundamentalist," "rigid," and "judgmental" on the many occasions Christianity came up as a topic, and they record a great many stories of people exiting their childhood Christianity for Buddhism or arguing over religion with evangelical Christians.

A conversation at the Richmond Zen Group in December 2003 further illuminates some of these trends. During the postmeditation discussion period, one of the readings happened to use the word *faith*. Brian, a frequent attendee, immediately remarked that he had been a Southern Baptist and so has trouble accepting the idea of faith. "I think of it as blind belief. But I do accept ideas of trust and confidence. I stumble when I encounter demands for faith like in that passage you just read."

A young man replied, "I understand this idea of faith. I mean, it takes a certain amount of faith to just sit here. Sometimes you're sitting and all you're doing is thinking about *Magnum P.I.*[28] And you're wondering how thinking about *Magnum P.I.* is possibly going to help you. So you just have to have faith. Not faith in *Magnum P.I.*! I mean, faith in the sitting."

With the issue of Christianity raised, many people began to speak up. Doug, who later moved away from Richmond, said, "I dislike the 'my way or the highway, my God is bigger than your God' approach to religion I often see. I prefer the Buddhist approach of just being aware, focusing on waking up yourself and being conscious of our surroundings and other people."

Another issue that some people had was with thinking that strongly categorizes things as right or wrong. Jason, a tall silver-haired man, was adamant. "I hate this way of thinking, it drives me nuts. I don't think you tell people this is good and that is bad. I don't think it works. I think it's emptiness. You see emptiness and it is from that that good arises. I hate holiness, I can't stand it. [sarcastic voice:] 'America is a holy place.' It hits a bell for me. When I smell holiness I go off."

Bob, an often quiet man with a serene air, asked, "Do you mean self-righteous holiness?" Jason nodded.

Mike, one of the Zen group lay leaders, was struck by the reading, too. He said it sounded like something from the Gospels. Bob added that the reading also talked about "being saved." Mike said, "Yes. I grew up hearing that being saved meant avoiding Hell."

Brian: "And in my religious upbringing Hell was a real place you went to."

Henry, another Zen group leader, contributed his opinion: "In Buddhism it's that we're saved from suffering. And being saved means awakening and being freed from delusions."

Bob said, "My guess is that much hinges on the word 'saved' here. A Buddhist teacher doesn't save people, he teaches them the way to be saved and shows kindness."

Brian replied, "By residing in that place of peace and awareness, when I'm in relationship with someone, I can't save them. I can't reach into them and change them, but my energy can affect them. And trying to break down that separation is part of it."

Jason nodded. "That is absolutely on the mark. I can't save you."

Henry brought the discussion to a close by quoting the Zen master Dogen, founder of the lineage the Zen group practices in. "'To study the Buddha way is to study the self. To study the self is to forget the self. Forgetting the self we realize how all things are connected' . . . except George Bush." Everyone laughed, and any tension from the discussion of salvation and Hell was dissipated.[29]

Here we again see the tension that Richmond Buddhists feel with Christianity, a force many of them wish to explicitly reject. Even use of terminology that has both Buddhist and Christian meanings—such as *faith* or *salvation*—is fraught, since the fundamental associations with these terms are conservative Christian ones for this group. Thus they seek to avoid elements of Buddhism that overlap with Christianity (such as faith—or Hell, for that matter, which was part of Buddhism long before Christianity was created). They steer instead toward Buddhist features that contradict the forms of Christianity that they disavow, in the process reshaping Buddhism to be more congenial to their search for a radical alternative way of being religious in Christian-dominated Richmond. They assert that their practice of Buddhism—unlike Christianity as they understand it—is self-reliant, rational, allegedly not self-righteous, based on personal awareness, with an insight into the emptiness and interconnectedness of all things. It does not prefer simple dichotomous characterizations of right or wrong, us or them, saved or damned, such as are important to the surrounding evangelical religious culture.

The joking insult toward George Bush, president of the United States at the time, is also important. The greater Richmond area is predominately Republican, like most of central and southern Virginia. Ekoji's Buddhist members, by contrast, are virtually all liberals; some are Democrats, while many feel they are too liberal for the Democratic Party and prefer the Green Party or political independence. I never heard conservative political opinions voiced at Ekoji. Indeed, it is taken for granted by most Ekoji members that Buddhism is an inherently politically liberal religion that supports progressive social programs, feminism, racial equality, environmentalism, separation of church and state, and pacifism. That this agenda does not necessarily match the actual manifestations of political Buddhism in Asian history is a dramatic understatement. But at Ekoji resistance to conservative politics, fundamentalist Christianity, conceptualizations of southern identity that value a racist past, and "mindless" mainstream American culture all converge to form a practically seamless whole that creates Buddhism as the antithesis of these forces. The Buddhism practiced at Ekoji is in many ways as much about *not* being something (Republican, Christian, stereotypically southern, narcissistically American) as it is about believing or doing something (accepting the Four Noble Truths, meditating, seeking enlightenment).

Countless further examples could be offered in a similar vein. We can see, therefore, that the impact of local culture and religion on Buddhism in some southern locations is significant.[30] While this is not true for all of them, Richmond Buddhists often modify their Buddhist practice so that it is less visible to the outside, diminish their contacts with non-Buddhists or seek to mask their Buddhist practice from many non-Buddhists whom they cannot avoid, harbor resentments toward evangelical Christians whom they have encountered, and pursue Buddhism in part because they believe it to be and adapt it so that it becomes highly differentiated from a sort of political conservatism, fundamentalist religion, consumeristic Americanism, and quasi-Confederate identity that they believe surrounds them. There is no need to accept such depictions of the South as accurate (and let us remember, those who have been most dramatically burned by the mainstream are the ones who are most likely to seek out radically different alternatives — such as Buddhism) to observe that such a widespread understanding of southern culture affects how Buddhism is pursued in parts of the South.

One further theme is worth noting here. Instead of Buddhism as a better alternative, I sometimes encountered the claim that Ekoji and Buddhism are actually *more* faithful to the *true* spirit of America, the South, Virginia, or Richmond than their conservative Christian competitors: that is, that Buddhists are the *real* Americans, and so on. In Richmond this was almost always made in reference to the Virginia Statute for Religious Freedom, written in Richmond by Jefferson. Thus when discussing how Ekoji came to be pluralistic, for example, the president of the temple gestured not only to Tsuji and the temple founders but also to Jefferson and the establishment of Virginia as a place of religious tolerance.[31] Likewise, in promoting the slave trade meditation vigil I discuss in the next chapter, the organizers specifically referenced the Virginia Statue for Religious Freedom, legitimating their event as somehow connected to the early history of the South prior to the rise of the Confederacy.[32] In gesturing to the role Jefferson played in setting in motion the events that — far later — would help make it possible to practice Buddhism in Virginia, Richmond Buddhists not only staked a claim to the legitimacy of their religion in the region but also appropriated Jefferson and the idealized early republican period in ways that suggested that the Buddhists were the rightful heirs of the best aspects of the country's foundation. In this sense, they were not positing an alternative America but suggesting that they were somehow the mainstream, while less tolerant forms of religion and society were illegitimate divergences from the founding ideals.

Buddhist Impact on the South

Beyond distribution and regional impacts on Buddhism, the third form of regional analysis that I recommended in chapter 1 is examination of Buddhists' impact on the regions in which they practice. For most of its history, the South has been empty of Buddhists, and Richmond as a specific southern place only began to develop permanent, public Buddhist communities in the last few decades. Although the South certainly has not become "Buddhacized" in any substantial fashion, can we nonetheless detect the smaller-scale effects of the growth of Buddhism? If so, where might we look? I suggest that interactions between religion and government, educational efforts, and relations between Buddhists and non-Buddhists are three useful areas to examine.

Ekoji came into direct contact and conflict with the city of Richmond after it incorporated as a temple in the mid-1980s. Religious organizations in Richmond, as in the United States generally, are exempt from taxation on properties used for religious purposes. Such exemption is particularly important for new, small, minority groups like Ekoji, which do not have a large pool of members to draw on for financial support and whose growth potential may be limited compared to mainstream Christian congregations. Ekoji was the first Buddhist group in the Richmond area to organize as a tax-exempt property-holding religious organization.[33] Richmond authorities had no precedent for dealing with Buddhism, a nontheistic Asian tradition without a sabbath or congregational model, and which in the case of Ekoji at least had no formal minister or specific creed.[34] The multidenominational nature of the temple that evolved after the first few years was particularly perplexing to them. In early 1989, an assistant city assessor visited the temple several times, mainly when the Vietnamese group was holding services. He found strange religious events he could not understand, conducted by a group that did not seem to be the same as the titleholders, and he was not able to locate someone who could speak adequate English. When told on a subsequent visit by one of the white temple trustees that the Vietnamese gatherings were the largest events at the temple, he ceased further investigation.[35]

The city assessors were naturally disinclined to overlook opportunities to collect funds. The city faced a possible crisis due to a shrinking tax base as the population of the city declined. One of the primary ways that many southern cities had dealt with finances and other urban problems in the past — outward expansion — was unavailable to Richmond. The city of Richmond had expanded via annexation of land in the surrounding counties many times before, but it began to run into difficulties in the 1960s. By then the nearby counties had become somewhat urbanized and no longer lacked the services provided within the city, and they had become overwhelmingly white (due to white flight), while Richmond was on the fast track to African American numerical dominance. An attempt at annexation or merger in Henrico Country failed in 1961; Richmond successfully annexed part of Chesterfield County in 1969 — in a blatant attempt to acquire white residents and thus dilute the black vote — but thereafter Chesterfield also resisted annexation attempts. Thus the city of Richmond's borders became set, seemingly permanently, as it became clear that after the 1960s both the white counties and the now majority-black city would never allow the power of their respective racial constituencies in their separate spheres to be diluted by future annexations. Meanwhile, the numerical dominance of Richmond proper by African Americans added urgency to the continuing migration by whites to the counties, and some middle-class blacks also moved away from the perceived urban problems of Richmond, all of which continually eroded the city's tax base. Richmond thus has to diligently exploit every opportunity for tax collection within its set boundaries. This created the situation that now confronted Ekoji. Rather than recognizing that a Buddhist temple might be legitimately used by multiple constituencies or making efforts to discuss the matter further with temple leaders who might better explain the situation, the city decided to pursue aggressive property tax claims against Ekoji, in violation of the temple's tax-exempt status, asserting that it was taxable because it allowed the Vietnamese group to meet in the building.[36]

Tsuji and several members of Ekoji felt that this was a clear case of "unjust and illegal discrimination that would not be attempted against a Christian church."[37] Temple members furthermore felt that the investigation had been prompted in the first place by prejudiced neighbors, and that the assessor was "looking for a reason to deny the exemption application."[38] The case dragged on for several years, until in 1993 Ekoji contacted a lawyer with the American Civil Liberties Union (ACLU) asking for help. The ACLU sent a warning letter to the city, and in a matter of days the city moved to dismiss the ongoing claims against the temple.[39] With the help of a community tax law group, Ekoji drew up further documentation to underline its status as a tax-exempt religious corporation and received notification from the city assessor's office the following year that its status had been officially changed from "taxable" to "exempt" in the city's records as of January 1, 1994.[40]

The story does not end there, however. Despite personal assurances to the temple leadership from city employees that the matter was resolved and to ignore any future bills, the city in fact moved again to collect money from Ekoji. Bills for back taxes continued to arrive, and in 1995 the city tax collection and enforcement department began proceedings to put the temple building up for auction as a way of collecting more than $16,000 in back property taxes that they had levied against Ekoji.[41] The temple leadership was not informed about this imminent seizure and sale of its building—the leaders only learned of it after bids were already underway, when a prospective buyer who had seen the property listed for sale for tax delinquency happened to contact the temple president seeking to learn more about the property.[42] Naturally enough, this development seriously alarmed the Ekoji membership, and they sought assistance from the community tax law project again. Several stern messages were sent to the city alleging religious prejudice, explaining in detail how Buddhist temples function and why their situation met the Virginia Constitution's code for tax-exempt circumstances, and requesting a cancellation of the sale process. The issue was finally resolved in November 1996, when the city attorney acknowledged that Ekoji had always qualified as tax exempt, had submitted the proper paperwork at the appropriate dates, and was not taxable in the future.[43] Since then, the temple has mostly been left alone by the city, but the process provoked a deep-seated anxiety that has yet to fully dissipate. In 2012 the temple leaders feel fairly confident that their property will not be seized but they nonetheless worry about it from time to time, and the clash with the city seems to have induced a low but permanent level of fear surrounding the issue.

Not only did the temple feel the impact of this series of events, but also, over the course of several years, the city of Richmond learned quite a bit about Buddhism. First, the municipal bureaucrats learned that at least some Buddhists in their city were well connected enough to call on the ACLU and community activist organizations, and that they would fight for their religious rights just as other groups would. Second, they learned that Buddhist temples were indeed religious organizations even if they did not conform to the congregational Christian model implicit in the state's constitution. Third, they were exposed to a significant amount of information about Buddhism as a religion. Here, for example, is one paragraph from the documentation presented by the temple to the city:

> In Buddhism, a sangha is a community. One does not "belong" to a denomination; rather, one shares denominations. Despite the name of the individual's main area of practice, his or her standing in the Sangha would be [the] same; only the methodology (or practice) would be different. The Buddhist denominations are not as stringent in the membership requirements of its congregation as the Christian denominations. The Christian denominations reflect the different divisions of thought in the Christian faith. Because the methods in Western religions are theologically and organizationally significant, one must undergo a ceremonial ritual in order to change from one denomination to another. The Buddhist denominations, on the other hand, reflect different paths leading towards the same goal. There is more fluidity between the denominations.[44]

There are many similar examples of Buddhist doctrine, practice, and organizational principles in the correspondence. The temple took the position of educating the city about Buddhism, arguing from a Christian model that the city took for granted to display how other models might exist and be equally legitimate in their own context. Thus city officials in the tax and attorney offices learned about Buddhism and became aware of the need to be more flexible in their approach to the non-Christian religions that began to appear in their midst at a greater rate in the 1980s and 1990s.[45] Through its attorney at the Community Tax Law Project, the temple argued that it was "time for the City to recognize the legitimacy of diverse religious faiths and practices,"[46] and the end result of the process seems to have indeed been such recognition.

Another type of government institution that was impacted by the arrival of Buddhists in Richmond is the prison system. Ekoji runs a satellite meditation group at a prison in Greensville, Virginia, and members sometimes visit inmates at other institutions, as well as supporting inmates throughout the state by sending them materials on request and educating prison chaplains about the needs of Buddhist inmates. Nearly all of Virginia's prison chaplains are Christian, many of them Southern Baptist or another form of evangelical Protestantism. Some are openly hostile to the introduction of Buddhism into the prisons; even those with a more open mind typically approach the situation with Christian assumptions, such as the idea that someone needs to formally belong to and identify with a specific denomination of a religion rather than being able to simply engage in religious practices (such as silent meditation) as a sufficient form of religious activity. Ekoji has attempted to provide a Buddhist perspective to the chaplains at prisons where there are Buddhist inmates, such as in the following example taken from a letter to a chaplain at the James River Correctional Center:

> I'm sorry you could not help the inmate in question, assuming that he really feels himself to be a Buddhist. I hope he is not in the Catch-22 position of only having access to Baptist preachers in his attempt to prove that he is a Buddhist. What if someone wanted to convert from Baptist to Catholic while incarcerated? Would he be permitted to see the priest, or would the Baptist preacher have veto power over the inmate's desire to leave the Baptist fold? I would also like to comment that one does not have to renounce one's membership in another religion to become a Buddhist. Buddhism is based upon faith that human beings can become enlightened by working with their own understanding and life situation, albeit with help from outside, e.g. from Buddha and other holy persons. If the deity of another religion is able to help someone in this task, then Buddhism would consider this a benefit, not a problem.[47]

The actual Buddhist activities carried out in Greensville include regular group meditation sessions led by visitors from Ekoji, as well as discussions of Buddhist principles.

The sort of educational outreach efforts directed at prison chaplains occur in other relationships beyond the temple's walls as well. For example, the temple sent invitations to its tenth anniversary gathering (along with some information about the temple and Buddhism) to the ministers of local Methodist, Presbyterian, and Catholic churches and to the rabbi of a nearby synagogue, as well as inviting Richmond's mayor and the district councilman. Members have spoken when invited at a range of local congregations, including Episcopalian, Methodist, Disciples of Christ, and Baptist churches. In June 1999 members of Ekoji held a ceremony in the chapel at the Richmond International Airport, attended by the airport chaplain, the airport executive director, and various other airport employees. At this event they donated sixteen copies of a book of Buddhist teachings to the chapel.[48] Here we see the counterpart to the hesitancy described above to let the community know about the temple and about individual members' Buddhist beliefs. There is a general strategy of avoiding publicity, but targeted interactions are sometimes pursued to expose non-Buddhists to Buddhism in a way that presents the temple as a normal, upstanding part of the community, educating outsiders about positive aspects of Buddhism and helping dispel misconceptions about the religion. These interactions tend to be tailored to the nature of the group being engaged with. For instance, at a Baptist church the presenter will give a very basic overview of Buddhism. At a liberal religious institution such as a Unitarian Universalist church, however, the engagement may be much more detailed. Ekoji has been a major participant in celebrations of the Buddha's birthday held at the First Unitarian Church of Richmond, with members of the various Ekoji groups describing their practices and leading the Unitarian Universalist congregation in chants and meditations. The impact of Buddhism on religious liberals such as these is potentially high, as some Unitarian Universalists, for instance, come away from these encounters with the intention to continue to practice Buddhist meditation on their own or to explore Buddhist beliefs more thoroughly. Religions with a syncretistic character can also be prone to absorbing new influences from Buddhism. Just as one example, the Voodoo Spiritual Temple in New Orleans has now incorporated buddha images into its altars.

Having Buddhists in one's city does not automatically increase the level of knowledge about Buddhism in the community, but over time it can lead to greater understanding among specific elements of the populace that have frequent interactions with Buddhists, as well as those who seek or are sought by the Buddhists for information. For example, Ekoji, along with the local Soka Gakkai chapter, helped provide Richmond hospital chaplains with information on how to deal with Buddhist patients. Students from high schools and universities are frequent attendees at Ekoji: often they have been sent there to conduct basic research as part of their religion courses. The high number of professors among Ekoji's members and supporters means that Buddhist events are sometimes organized on campus and that even in seemingly unrelated fields, such as courses on English literature, professors may bring up Buddhism in their classes or discuss it as somehow providing an illuminating perspective on the material being studied. And much larger projects have been conducted with the assistance

Members of Ekoji help the Sunday school children and congregation celebrate the Buddha's birthday at the First Unitarian Universalist Church of Richmond.

of Richmond's Buddhists as well—vcu's school of nursing has been especially active in this area. Dissertation research has been carried out among the area's Buddhists, including examination of meditators at Ekoji and the Still Water Zen Center (in nearby Carytown) to measure the effects of meditation on blood pressure and stress levels, and the impact of spirituality on Thai immigrants with diabetes.[49] These projects would have been impossible a few decades ago when Richmond lacked Buddhist institutions.

Richmond Buddhists can have their greatest impact on the people who are least favorably inclined toward them. As Buddhists move into the South, some evangelical Christians react by developing a mission attitude toward their new neighbors. The Vipassana group was meditating at Ekoji one evening when there was an aggressive knocking at the front door. Many participants were startled and some reacted with fear; no one got up to answer the pounding, which eventually stopped. When the leader of the group went out on the porch afterward to determine what had happened, he found that someone had left a jacket with literature in it belonging to the "Jesus Liberation Army." This was interpreted as an attempt at intimidation or conversion by a conservative Christian group, something that many of Ekoji's Buddhists had experience with.[50] In a similar mode, Ekoji was visited one afternoon by a contingent of students from one of the nearby seminaries. Their intent was to learn about Buddhism so that they could identify its flaws and develop programs to convert Buddhists to evangelical Christianity, a project they thought the Buddhists would be eager to assist them with. The future Baptist missionaries were shocked to find not only that the Buddhists did not eagerly welcome their Good News but also that not all Buddhists were Asians.[51]

The Buddhists do not leave their greatest mark, however, on groups such as the Jesus Liberation Army or institutions such as the International Mission Board (the primary overseas evangelical mission of the Southern Baptist Convention, headquartered in Richmond). Instead, it is in one-on-one conversations, as individual non-Buddhists come to learn of the Buddhist interests of their family members and friends, that Buddhism makes its largest impact on the South. While many Buddhists hide their practice from relatives they feel would disapprove, others have discussed it with their families. Sometimes this is not by choice: one practitioner, from a local Richmond family, told me about how he attended a visit by Tibetan monks to a local museum to make a sand mandala and was given the unusual opportunity to make cake offerings to the monks. "A month later I was sitting next to my aunt at a funeral, and she turned to me and said, 'Now we know [about your involvement with Buddhism].'" A news report of the event had been seen by the family, and he was no longer able to mask his defection from Christianity.[52] In other cases, Buddhists feel compelled to tell their family, even though they expect to receive a negative reaction. One Ekoji member decided not to hide her Buddhist interest while on a visit to relatives in Texas: "There's definitely fear and misunderstanding of Buddhism. I can tell you in my own family there's concern about my salvation. My family is conservative Christian. There is a genuine fear and almost an unwillingness to talk about it because they are so afraid, they can't ask any questions about it. One time I was getting a ride to Houston. So I was sandwiched in the truck between these two good ol' boys, and one of them saw my book by Thich Nhat Hanh, *Living Buddha, Living Christ*. He started challenging me on that. He got really aggressive. He said, 'Christ is a living God—how can you say that *Buddha* is living?'"[53]

The experience of one Zen Buddhist who attends Ekoji can serve as a case study of the sort of interactions that occur when a family learns of a member's Buddhism. Larry Johnston was thirty years old when I interviewed him one afternoon at Ekoji. Earnest and self-conscious, he is sometimes quiet at Ekoji meetings but brings frankness and insight to the discussions when he does decide to speak. He was born in Richmond, in a family that has deep roots in Virginia; he is related to George Washington on his mother's side. Johnston was raised in a Southern Baptist church and graduated from one of the local universities. His maternal grandfather was the minister of a fairly small, working-class church; Johnston's father had been a Catholic but converted to Baptism after meeting his mother. The home was a place of frequent and intense religious discussion. As a young man, Johnston was drawn into drug and alcohol abuse, which he eventually pulled himself out of, in part through the Buddhist practice he had first encountered in university courses. Today he is somewhat estranged from his father but has frequent contact with his mother's family, which has led them to learn of his Buddhist practice.

When I asked him if he has been affected by practicing as a Buddhist in the South, he said,

> The primary place it's affected me is in my family. My mom had a real hard time with it, because she felt that she had failed in some way in raising a good Christian boy. She'll say things like, "I keep praying that you come back to Jesus." I say, "Naw, it's not happening." [chuckles] I told a cousin of mine whom I'd been close to since we were small that I'm a Buddhist, and she rolled her eyes and said, "Oh God" [with a snort of disbelief]. Like she saw it as just a phase. There's been that sort of attitude that has come at me from every part of my family. I guess in some regards I'm fortunate that my grandparents are dead on my mother's side, because I don't know what they would think.

I nodded and prompted him a little further, commenting, "There's some resistance in the family, but you still go to family gatherings, so it hasn't broken that relationship."

"No, but it's made it strained at times," he replied. "My mom's sister was really upset about it at first. When she found out I was Buddhist she was convinced that I was going to Hell and that was that. She told my mom that. She was trying to convince my mom that she needed to convert me back and that it might weigh heavy on my mom, because my mom might go to Hell too if she didn't manage to bring me back. Because she'd failed as a mother."

Other family members exhibit a range of reactions: another aunt makes jokes about his Buddhism because she is uncomfortable with it; a cousin does not like it but tries to accept the situation and asks curious questions about Buddhism sometimes; an uncle seems OK with it; Johnston's older brother, who has drifted from the church, has actually tried some meditation. Johnston summed up the situation, "There's a lack of acceptance of it in my family in general. It's just a tolerance of it. 'We'll deal with it until he changes his mind' is how they're approaching it."

Despite this general disapproval, as we talked further it became clear that the family members most upset by his Buddhist practice are in fact the ones who have experienced the greatest change in their attitudes. Although his mother still prays for his return to Christianity, Johnston said that eventually she became accepting of his Buddhism because she remembered how her preacher father quoted from the Gospel of John — "No one gets to the truth but by me, for I am the way and the truth and the light" — and that he always emphasized "the way and the truth and the light," not the speaker (Jesus). "What she realized was that I'm following the way and the truth and the light, and it's not about this figure on a cross. My mom has grown to really love some of the changes that have come about in my life and in my interactions with her through the [Buddhist] practice."

The maternal aunt who thought he was going to Hell has also experienced a change in her thinking through her painful struggle with her own son. Raised with conservative Christian ideals, she was always vocally opposed to homosexuality. When her son finally told her that he was gay, she was shattered. She prayed about the matter for a long time. She finally had a breakthrough at church one Sunday, when a study group told her that they loved her son but hated who he was because of his homosexuality. The hypocrisy of this position enraged Johnston's aunt, who "flipped out" and told them that they could not possibly be good Christians and believe that. When she complained to her sister about the hatred directed at her son by the people at church, Johnston's mother turned to her and said, "That's how I felt when you said my son was going to Hell [for being Buddhist]." Brought up short, his aunt reexamined her own behavior. Now Johnston feels that she has become more accepting of his Buddhism.[54]

These sorts of interactions between Buddhists and non-Buddhists in the South do not capture headlines, but I believe it is here that Buddhism works some of its most significant changes on the region. As long as Buddhism is something "out there," a hypothesized "other" that southern Christians do not have personal contact with, it can be conceptualized as foreign, wrong, even immoral or evil. When a loved one becomes involved in Buddhism, the distant is suddenly revealed to be close at hand, and a crisis may be provoked. Immediate reactions from deeply conservative Christian relatives range from knee-jerk repugnance to bemused skepticism, while those with less commitment to Christianity may evidence bewildered curiosity or actual interest. For those most opposed to Buddhism, a process of reexamining one's Christian beliefs and values is set in motion. Christian teachings (and personal feelings) that emphasize filial love and integrity and stress open-heartedness and neighborliness are brought into conflict with other teachings that depict Christianity as the only source of genuine religion and consign non-Christians to everlasting torment in Hell. There is also social pressure exerted by other church members, family, and friends that may influence attitudes toward Buddhist family members.

Christians who have gone through this process, regardless of their ultimate conclusions, are changed by it: whether they continue to reject their Buddhist relatives or come to accept them, their beliefs are tested and sorted. Nor is the impact confined to the individual members of the family: as we saw with the anecdote about the church group and Johnston's gay cousin, conservative Christians live in a network of community relationships and frequently share their troubles with other Christians, seeking guidance or support. Just as the cousin's homosexuality became something the church as a whole had to think about, so too Johnston's Buddhism became a matter of discussion and reflection based on a real-world, not hypothetical, situation in their midst. Rejection of Buddhism from afar is reconsidered, and in some cases, these Christians have their understandings modified in ways they did not anticipate. In my opinion, these case-by-case alterations are a part of the story of Buddhism in America, and to the extent that these situations are noticeably common in the South, they can be legitimately considered to have a regional aspect.[55] So Buddhism is shaped by the South and in turn comes to shape the South in some ways, such as by influencing government agencies, by educating the community about Buddhism, and by provoking soul-searching by Christian relatives and acquaintances of Buddhists.

Conclusion

Works on southern religion have continued to appear over the last twenty-five years, but specialists sometimes notice a trend. Even as scholars publish on the subject, they often seem to demonstrate a level of anxiety about, or feel a need to apologize for, a perceived tenuousness of the South's continued existence as a definable region, and whether southern religion in a globalized age is still distinguishable in some perceptible way. As historian Corrie E. Norman pointed out in *Religion in the Contemporary South*, "It is no longer clear what the South is, what 'southern religion' is."[56] To those researchers who fear that the South is no longer a viable object for religious study, the Buddhists of America have a clear answer: Don't worry—from the minority perspective, the South remains very much a real, distinct place, and it has clear influence on the religious minorities within it.[57]

Buddhism is not the target of sustained, serious persecution by non-Buddhists, but it is nonetheless very much an outsider religion in the South. While their numbers are growing, Buddhists are poorly represented in the South as a whole, and they often must rely on teachers and support systems based in other parts of the country. Many Buddhists—especially those with strong local ties—feel that they must minimize their family's awareness of their religious interest, or they have experienced significant conflict with those relatives and other community members who do know about it. At the same time, Buddhists have been willing to push for their legal rights and to educate the public about Buddhism and the growing diversification of southern cities when the situation called for such action. Whether in prisons, homes, courts, or the streets, Buddhists are affected by the South and change the South and fellow southerners.

The Buddhists of Richmond, therefore, help to demonstrate the potential usefulness of bringing a regional perspective to the study of American Buddhism, and they also show why southern historians should pay greater attention to nondominant religious groups whose experiences may be distinctively southern and are a legitimate part of the overall story of the South. To further explore the issue of American Buddhist regionalism, the following chapter shifts from considering Richmond as a whole to zeroing in on one specific ritual event. How was this event a *southern* Buddhist practice? What attributes do such southern Buddhist activities display? We turn now to an analysis of Ekoji's slave trade meditation vigil to see precisely what the stakes are for the meeting of southern culture and Eastern religion.

The South is continually coming into being, continually being remade, continually struggling with its pasts.
—Edward L. Ayers, "What We Talk about When We Talk about the South,"
 All Over the Map, 1996

Chapter Six

THE REALITY OF OUR COLLECTIVE KARMA

Slave Trade Meditation Vigil as Southern Buddhist Ritual

Richmond remembers. It is a city of memory and pride, where the useful past is a treasure trove from which can be drawn resources for politics, religion, art, identity, and, especially, money-making. From Hollywood Cemetery to the Arthur Ashe Memorial, its landscape has been a site of memory and contestation carried out in the construction of artifacts and the performance of street rituals. Like all modern cities, it is constantly changing and reinventing itself, but nonetheless in spirit it is a place very different from New York City, which Michel de Certeau described as hour by hour throwing away its previous accomplishments and challenging the future.[1] Many Richmonders, by contrast, have tended to understand who they are by understanding or imagining who they have been.

In opening *Baptized in Blood*, Charles Reagan Wilson chose to illustrate the South's religion of the Lost Cause with a famous incident from "memory-fraught Richmond." On October 26, 1875, ten years after the end of the Civil War, the South's first statue of Confederate general Stonewall Jackson was dedicated before a crowd of many thousands. Uniformed Confederate veterans marched through the streets to the site of the statue, before which prayers were said and hymns sung. Speeches extolled the glories of the city's southern past, and Jackson's daughter laid a bouquet of flowers at the statue's pedestal. It was an emotional day that drew tears and applause from those who observed and participated in this sacred ceremony.[2]

Since then, many similar Confederate heritage parades have been held—indeed, they are still being held. They no longer draw the same crowds, however, and as Richmond has aged, diversified, and changed, newer street rituals have appeared to provide other readings of the meaning and sacredness of the city's history-haunted avenues.

In chapter 5, I laid out several broad ways that regionalism could be used to investigate the Buddhist phenomena in Richmond. In this final chapter, I shift my approach to focus on a single event as a case study for southern Buddhist ritual practice. I begin with a description of the 2008 slave trade meditation vigil organized in downtown Richmond by members of Ekoji Buddhist Sangha. I then discuss how the event was planned. From there, I investigate why people chose to participate and who the participants were, including their races, origins, and Buddhist orientations. I describe the effects that the vigil generated, and analyze the ritual actions themselves. Finally, I consider precisely how this was a *southern* event, a fitting final topic before concluding the book.

Slave Trade Meditation Vigil

It was a beautiful Saturday morning on April 19, 2008 (the middle of Confederate Heritage Month), as Cecelia Davidson drove into downtown Richmond toward the low-lying riverfront area known as Shockoe Bottom. She was not quite sure where her destination was, so she parked and approached two city sanitation employees working by the road. "Excuse me," she asked, "do y'all know where the Slavery Reconciliation statue is?" The two workers, both African American, paused, and one walked over to help the white lady out. He described where the statue was nearby, and Cecelia said, "Thank you very much. We're going to hold a meditation over there today, to witness to the past of slavery here, and for the slaves." To her surprise, the man began to cry. He told her they were doing a good thing, and she thought about the chance encounter as she drove away.[3]

Cecelia's friends from Ekoji, meanwhile, were gathering across the James River at Manchester Docks, on the river's southern bank. At eight in the morning most city folks were still at home, but some early risers were already out making the most of the weekend. Bobbers floated on the water as fishermen watched from the bank, and people were jogging, biking, and walking along the riverfront. The group from Ekoji did not draw much attention, though if anyone cared to look closer, they might have noticed that several participants wore rakusus—dark brown or blue cloth squares worn like bibs, which signified their commitment to the Zen Buddhist tradition. The dozen people gathered were mostly from Ekoji, though two had learned of the day's event from friends or family members who attend Ekoji, including one woman who had never done Buddhist meditation before. They were a mix of men and women, mostly in their middle years, with a single nonwhite participant: a younger woman of mixed Filipino and South American heritage.

As Cecilia pulled up, they prepared to start their daylong ritual. The group set off into the woods along a path marked "Manchester Slave Trade Trail." This was the first leg of the Richmond Slave Trail, a historic path established by the city in the 1990s. Beginning at Manchester Docks, where ships arrived with enslaved Africans, the trail winds across the river and into the city, following the path that disembarking slaves would have taken. In the woods the group from Ekoji fell into single file, with Zen priest Taigen Dan Leighton leading the way. In the green shade of the trees and wildflowers lining the path, the group walked quietly, meditating. For a time Leighton softly sang to himself, "Follow the Drinking Gourd," an old spiritual used on the Underground Railroad:

> The riverbank will make a very good road,
> The dead trees show you the way.
> Left foot, peg foot traveling on,
> Following the drinking gourd.

But he lapsed into thought as he recalled how the slaves who walked this trail were bound in leg irons, headed not toward freedom but toward the slave pen Lumpkin's Jail, known as "the Devil's Half Acre." Other participants also were contemplating those who walked the trail in earlier times. Cecilia and several others imagined themselves as slaves, bound and helpless, shuffling through the trees at night on the way to sale, attempting—as well as possible—to put themselves into the place of long-dead Africans. The other participants performed traditional Buddhist walking meditation, directing their attention to the feeling of the ground beneath their feet with each step and opening themselves to the passing moment without attachment.

The slave trail led them under the Interstate 95 overpass and through the woods and back out again, passing a historic marker for the slave trade at one point. As they reached Mayo Bridge, they met Lakshin, an Indian attendee of Ekoji, who waved and fell into line. Passing over the bridge, the group went by the Kanawha Canal, constructed—like much of eighteenth- and nineteenth-century Richmond—with slave labor. As they entered downtown Richmond the surrounding activity picked up, transitioning from walkers, joggers, and bikers along the river to shoppers and local business owners getting an early start on the weekend's activities. Step by step they moved through a district once thick with slave auction houses and jails, some of whose buildings still remained. Finally, after a walk of approximately a mile and a half, they reached their destination at the corner of Fifteenth and East Main. A year earlier, five thousand people had gathered here to celebrate the dedication of the Slave Trade Reconciliation Triangle. The site is a small, triangular space paved in bricks, with a larger triangular plot of grass behind it abutting a parking structure. A tall, abstract statue carved from black stone depicts two human figures embracing, perhaps as prelude to being sold apart, perhaps in reconciliation after the horrors of America's slave past have passed. Inscribed on it are words composed by Richmond schoolchildren: "Acknowledge and forgive the past—embrace the present—share the future of justice and equality." Plaques at the site describe Richmond's part as one corner of the triangular slave trade that connected Virginia with Benin, West Africa, and Liverpool, England; two identical statues now stand at those sites as well. At the epicenter of Richmond's slave past, the Slave Trade Reconciliation Triangle is part of the city's growing push to come to terms with its darker history and move into the future in a more positive manner. It is also part of a larger, centuries-old pattern of memorializing various aspects of the city's past, both to create local memory and to draw tourist dollars.

Several more participants greeted the walkers at the statue, including three women Buddhists who had driven in from West Virginia for the vigil, bringing the group's total number to eighteen. For the day, the statue became an altar, with the embracing black figures serving the role normally reserved for a buddha image in a temple worship hall. The group placed flowers at its base, along with an incense burner and a candle. Then they arranged themselves in a circle on the grass beside the statue, where they had set up cushions and chairs borrowed from the temple. By 9:00 A.M., Leighton had rung a bell and formal seated meditation practice began.

Almost directly overhead, the traffic on I-95 roared by—at the intersection of the interstate highway, the downtown expressway, several major local routes, and two different railroad tracks, this heavily trafficked area is known by locals as the "Spaghetti Works." The presence of the highway is another example of racial disparity in Richmond, as its establishment through this neighborhood in the mid-twentieth century was determined

The Slave Trade Reconciliation Triangle and statue at the busy intersection of East Main and Fifteenth Streets, with I-95 overhead. The strip club on the right-hand side of the photo sits next to a former slave auction site.

by racial forces and resulted in the displacement of thousands of African Americans and the destruction of a vital African American neighborhood. Directly across the street from the Slave Trade Reconciliation Triangle is Club Velvet, a strip club with a penchant for displaying large, racially offensive, right-wing posters that can provoke counterprotests.[4] The Reconciliation Triangle has no shade, and the mid-spring sun became hotter and hotter as the day progressed. But despite the less than ideal meditation conditions, the vigil continued. For several of the participants the sound of the traffic slowly receded until it was no longer even noticed, as a feeling of safety and peace settled over the participants meditating in the grass. Some sat following their breath, while others observed the feelings in their body and the thoughts flitting across their minds. One woman silently sent prayers of lovingkindness to those who suffer from racial oppression. Every thirty minutes the Zen priest rang the bell and the group did a few minutes of slow walking meditation in the grass before returning to sit some more. Throughout, people passed by in ones and twos, some stopping to look at the statue or gawk at the sitters. Most seemed to sense that something spe-

Participants meditating during the slave trade meditation vigil. Photograph by Sharon Russell, used with permission.

cial was going on and kept a respectful distance, but a few were intrigued and asked what was going on. A tourist couple from Michigan sat and meditated for thirty minutes, as did a young couple on bicycles and a woman in her forties.

After two hours, Leighton rang the bell and began to deliver a talk to those assembled. First, he laid out the historical significance of the site, describing the triangle trade, the huge numbers of slaves who passed through Richmond, and the experiences of those on the nearby auction blocks, who were literally "sold down the river." He described the area as a "power place" of concentrated suffering over the centuries. As he explained, the meditation vigil was designed to bear witness to this suffering, not to direct blame, make political statements, or demand redress. "We are all victims," he said. "The huge legacy of this place still haunts our society in many ways. Reconciliation must be based on acknowledging this painful past, on our willingness to face the reality of our collective karma." When he finished, the group returned to meditating for a while. The heat was increasing steadily. One participant, Serena Jenkins, became uncomfortable and contemplated leaving. As she thought about whether or not she should stay, it occurred to her that the slaves had not had any choice. If you were a slave you had to work in the hot sun. You were forced up the slave trail toward your destiny. For Jenkins, this was the moment when what the group was doing finally connected with the history of Richmond. And in the next moment she felt a flush of awakening, as she suddenly appreciated the gift of freedom that she enjoyed.

A little before noon, the group stopped their meditation to hold a service. Led by Leighton, they chanted a Buddhist scripture designed to generate lovingkindness for all beings:

> This is what should be accomplished by the one who is wise,
> who seeks the good and has obtained peace.
> Let one be strenuous, upright and sincere, without pride,
> easily contented and joyous.
> Let one not be submerged by the things of the world.
> Let one not take upon oneself the burden of riches.
> Let one's senses be controlled.
> Let one be wise but not puffed up,
> and let one not desire great possessions, even for one's family.
> Let one do nothing that is mean or that the wise would reprove.
> May all beings be happy.
> May they be joyous and live in safety.
> All living beings, whether weak or strong,
> in high or middle or low realms of existence,
> small or great, visible or invisible, near or far, born or to be born,
> may all beings be happy.
> Let no one deceive another, nor despise any being in any state;
> let none by anger or hatred wish harm to another.
> Even as a mother, at the risk of her own life,
> watches over and protects her only child,
> so with a boundless mind should one cherish all living things,
> suffusing love over the entire world —
> above, below, and all around without limit.
> So let one cultivate an infinite good will toward the whole world.
> Standing or walking, sitting or lying down, during all one's waking
>   hours,
> let one practice the way with gratitude.

Not holding to fixed views, abandoning vague discussions,
endowed with insight, freed from sense appetites,
one who achieves the way will be freed from the duality
of birth and death.[5]

Leighton dedicated the merit of their practice to all who suffered in Richmond's past and the pain that still remained in America and around the world due to the slave trade and its aftermath.

At this point, the group broke for lunch. Some had brought along picnic lunches, while others drifted away to downtown restaurants. Cecelia chatted with an African American woman who walked by, explaining what the group had been doing. The woman was curious but declined the offer to sit with the group in the afternoon. Serena went home, unable to continue due to the heat, and another participant was called away by commitments elsewhere. After lunch, the meditation began again. The participants from West Virginia sat on a low wall at the site, and a young man passing by sat down and joined in. Time passed slowly, measured in breaths and in intervals of sitting, walking, and sitting again. Toward the end, Cecelia's experience began to change. Instead of cars and trucks, she began to hear the screams and cries of slaves being separated from their loved ones, of whips cracking and striking bare flesh, of chains rattling, and harsh laughter from buyers and sellers gloating over their human commodities. She tried to turn her attention away, but it was if she was feeling the blows on her own body.

When Leighton rang the bell again at about four in the afternoon, he asked the participants to share their thoughts and experiences about the day. He began by talking about the effort he had exerted to get in touch with Richmond's history and learn the facts about the slave past. Henry, who had helped organize the event, said that he had had a nebulous idea of Richmond's slave history for a long time, but that the vigil had given him the impetus to look into it. The previous week he had read a biography of Frederick Douglass. "That gave a strong voice to the slave experience for me," he said.

Maria, a psychotherapist involved in social work, spoke about her own experiences with young women with shattered lives in Richmond. For her, their present-day problems stemmed from Richmond's slave history, and there was much healing that needed to take place. She choked up as she talked, bringing tears to Henry's eyes as well.

Several people mentioned the never-ending sound of traffic on the overpass above. Leighton related it to a river flowing above their heads. Henry nodded. "Yes, it's a constant flow of traffic that's powered by gasoline that comes from black crude oil drilled out of the earth. The wealth here comes from these extractions and exploitations. We make ourselves rich from it and then we turn away, we don't pay attention to it. We're unconscious about where our wealth and well-being come from."

The visitors from West Virginia said that they had come because the next year (2009) would be the 150th anniversary of John Brown's abolitionist raid at Harpers Ferry, the area they came from. They wanted to bear witness in Richmond as a way of beginning to commemorate that event.

After the discussion, the cushions and chairs were packed up, and people went home for dinner. The event continued in a different form the following morning. The Richmond Zen Group had its normal meditation and service at Ekoji on Sunday morning. But most of the attendees of the vigil were there, some at Leighton's explicit request; it was the first visit to a Buddhist temple for one of the participants. Leighton used his sermon to discuss the event and brought the meditation vigil up as a topic for the post-meditation discussion. Cecilia was still trying to deal with her experience of the previous day when she had heard and felt the slave trade for herself, an experience which had deepened as she reflected on it overnight. As she described it to the group, she felt overwhelmed by pain and collective torture, and finally broke down sobbing. She told them that it seemed like her own suffering joined with that of those who had been at the vigil site and with the whole world, until there was no definite person experiencing it anymore, just pain and suffering. "It was so powerful," she said. Several other people talked about their identification with the slaves and the pain they went through.

As the participants described their experiences, some of the people gathered at Ekoji who had not attended the vigil began to challenge them in various ways. One Ekoji member, Larry Johnston, who had wanted to go but was unable due to illness, asked if anyone felt any guilt over what had happened. Leighton stepped in and tried to deflect the use of the word "guilt," so Larry rephrased his question, asking if anyone felt identification with the slave traders. No one replied, and after a pause Leighton said that it had occurred to him and he had dealt with it. Also there that day was Bonnie, a first-time visitor to Ekoji and the only African American involved in the discussion. She had not attended the vigil either, and she was upset by what she was hearing. "What I'm hearing is a lot of privilege," she said. It struck her as disingenuous and a denial of the truth: that the people identifying with the slaves were really the slave masters, since they were all middle-class white people who thought they were "helping out blackie" with a little meditation vigil. Her comment seemed to suck the air out of the room at first. Then Brian, who had attended the vigil, talked about how he came from a small Virginia town where there were almost no African Americans. In that environment, he had never had to examine the racial ideas that were passed on to him. Now he lives in Richmond, a majority black city, though his neighborhood is white. For him, the vigil had unexpectedly brought his own unconscious feelings of racism to the surface, and now he had to deal with that.

When the discussion came to a close, many people expressed how grateful they were for the experience and hoped to repeat it again the next year. Thus far, the event has not been repeated, in part because Leighton is now teaching full-time in Chicago and no longer has time to come to Richmond. Despite the power that many felt in the experience, it is not clear if there is sufficient organization at Ekoji to hold another such slave trade meditation vigil, which may have to wait until the temple is able to attract a dedicated teacher interested in bearing witness to Richmond's troubled past.

Planning the Event

Meditation vigils to remember the American slave trade are not a traditional form of Buddhist practice, nor have they featured prominently in mainstream southern religion. How then did this 2008 event come about in Richmond? The genesis of the vigil lies in the Richmond Zen Group's attempts to entice a Zen priest to move to Richmond and minister to them full-time. During the first decade of the new millennium the Zen group invited many different teachers to visit Richmond and deliver talks at Ekoji. Most of these teachers came from the Suzuki lineage of Soto Zen and were flown in from the San Francisco Bay Area. One of the teachers who came most often, and whom the group was particularly interested in possibly forming a permanent relationship with, was Taigen Dan Leighton. Besides his vocation as a Zen priest, Leighton is also a scholar and translator with an interest in both Zen history and social movements in America.

During one of Leighton's visits in early 2007, Martin Boyd—a member of the Ekoji Pure Land group and one of the temple's lay leaders, took it on himself to drive Leighton around Richmond and show him some of the city's many historic sites, something he did for many of the temple's visiting teachers. Leighton was especially interested in Thomas Jefferson and his history in the city, as well as in Richmond's past as one of the most important places for the nineteenth-century slave trade. As Boyd drove his guest around Shockoe Bottom, he pointed out many historic buildings or newer buildings on plots that used to be connected to the slave trade, such as auction houses, slave jails, and quarters for slave traders. Boyd's knowledge of local history impressed Leighton, and when he saw how important the slave trade had been in Richmond, and that so many physical traces were still evident on the urban landscape, he began to contemplate holding some sort of event to recognize these facts. The model that immediately suggested itself was to hold a meditation retreat to bear witness.

Bearing witness in American Buddhism is a practice initiated by Bernard Glassman, a major American Zen teacher in the Maezumi lineage of Zen originally based at the Zen Center of Los Angeles. Glassman has had a long-standing interest in developing innovative programs that bring Buddhist practice to bear on social issues such as poverty, homelessness, hunger, violent conflict, and discrimination. In the early 1990s he began leading "homeless" meditation retreats on the streets of New York City, and in 1994 held the first of several bearing-witness retreats at the site of the Nazi death camp in Auschwitz, a model that has since been copied in order to bear witness to other tragedies around the world. Bearing-witness events involve silent seated meditation — Zen by default, though participants may come from any Buddhist lineage or be non-Buddhists — at sites of historical suffering. The idea is that meditating at such places acknowledges the pain of those who have experienced violence and injustice, and that this acknowledgment can lead to healing. Although these bearing-witness events have received significant press, especially in publications interested in "engaged Buddhism," they do not have a clear precedent in Zen history. They seem therefore to be a new practice created by Americans, with roots not only in Zen Buddhism but also in modern psychology, Glassman's Jewish ancestry, North American social activism, and New Age culture. These eclectic origins help ensure that Buddhists are not the only participants in many bearing-witness events; nonetheless, the ceremonies are typically initiated and led by Buddhist teachers and exist within a basic context of Buddhist meditation practice, philosophical orientation toward the issue of suffering, and specifically Zen concerns for the present moment as the time of salvation and bare awareness as the vehicle for religious awakening.

Leighton was well aware of such Zen-based bearing-witness vigils, both through his role as an American Zen priest and from his own history of activism. As a freshman at Columbia University in 1968 he had been involved in the student occupation of campus buildings. He was an anti-

Vietnam War activist, performing many acts of civil disobedience, some of which resulted in his arrest. He also participated in protest events in the San Francisco area against the Iraq War and often meditated along with protestors in front of the gates of the prison in San Quentin whenever a prisoner was due to be executed. Racial issues in America had always been of particular concern to him. So as his awareness of the slave history and legacy of Richmond increased, he felt it was natural that a bearing-witness meditation vigil like those held at Auschwitz should be held in downtown Richmond near the old auction houses.

Once he had decided to hold a meditation vigil, Leighton announced his desires to the Richmond Zen Group. Some people reacted with immediate enthusiasm, such as Henry Kelvin, a primary lay leader for the group. Others were unaware of bearing witness as a phenomenon, wondered about the appropriateness of the event, or had other reasons to hesitate in their commitment to it. Leighton could only come to Richmond about once each year, so much of the planning and publicity for the event was left to people at Ekoji. As the weeks passed and it became clear that the meditation vigil would indeed take place, more people became comfortable with the concept and began to commit to participating.

Officially, the event was sponsored by the Richmond, Virginia, Buddhist Peace Fellowship, a local chapter of the international Buddhist Peace Fellowship (BPF). Based in Berkeley, the BPF has a couple dozen chapters in the United States, most of them in the West and Midwest. In Richmond, the chapter was organized as a vehicle for protest against the military intervention in Iraq following the terrorist attacks of September 11, 2001. Besides marching in various protests, the Richmond BPF held monthly public meditation vigils for peace in Richmond's Monroe Park for many years (they were still continuing in 2008 when the slave trade vigil was held but had ceased by the time this book was completed). The small groups of meditators would sit for several hours in the park, with a sign that read "Richmond Buddhist Peace Fellowship." These vigils were sometimes disturbed by hecklers in passing cars who honked or yelled obscenities, and occasionally female participants were harassed by strange men. In some cases, the participants also gave basic meditation instruction to homeless people who live in the park.

While intended to give a pansectarian voice to Buddhists throughout Richmond, in actual practice the participants in the Richmond BPF chapter were almost exclusively members of Ekoji, especially the Zen group, with a fair number of people from the Vipassana group as well. At times over the years, a very small number of people from the Still Water Zen Center, a Korean Zen-based community of meditators that used to meet in Richmond, also participated. Depending on how one chooses to frame the situation, therefore, the slave trade meditation vigil could be plausibly described as an activity of the Richmond, Virginia, Buddhist Peace Fellowship; the Ekoji Buddhist Sangha of Richmond; or the Richmond Zen Group. The actual planning for the event was undertaken nearly exclusively by members of the Richmond Zen Group, especially Henry Kelvin, and Leighton. The time and place for the vigil were announced at the Ekoji Vipassana group and the Meditative Inquiry group; no one at the Ekoji Pure Land or Tibetan groups recalled any announcement about the event, although several learned of it through their personal contacts with members of the Zen group. Announcements were made via the international Buddhist Peace Fellowship (such as through its e-mail list and on its website), but no significant attempts appear to have been made to inform other Richmond Buddhist groups of the upcoming vigil.

Shortly after Leighton raised the possibility of a slave trade vigil, the Statue of Reconciliation was dedicated at the newly created Slave Trade Reconciliation Triangle. This struck Kelvin as the obvious place for such a retreat. As he explained: "[After the statue dedication] I told Taigen and I walked over to the site, and it was a lovely little corner downtown. I'd actually worked down there. So I said, 'OK, that would be the location to do it: there's a grassy lawn, and the statue is there, it's new, and we could call attention to the statue and our particular take on it.' Because [Leighton] didn't want to be political, he didn't want it to be shaming of whites and holding up blacks and arguing for reparations and stuff like that. It was just, 'Let's sit with this history and see what comes up.'"[6] Later, as he learned more about the slave trail as well, Kelvin suggested that they start by doing walking meditation along the trail and then sit in meditation at the statue downtown. Kelvin walked the trail with his girlfriend to learn the route, and Leighton came to check the statue out before the vigil.

When Leighton first saw the statue, he happened to mention his interest in holding the event to several African Americans who were visiting the sculpture. This conversation apparently went well and a number of people in the Richmond Zen Group took this as suggesting that they had the permission of Richmond's African American community to hold the event. There was in fact a fair amount of discussion about whether and how to reach out to the larger African American community and perhaps involve them, or at least inform them of the event. Little actual action was taken in the end, however. Ekoji has never had more than two or three African American participants at any one time; during the planning stages of the vigil there was just one regular African American attendee at the Zen meetings. It was months before he was specifically asked at a Zen discussion whether he as an African American would like to participate or have any feelings he wanted to share about the event; some members were appalled that it took so long for his feedback to be solicited, while others feared that singling him out as the sole nonwhite voice amounted to unfair pressure or "tokenism." His reaction, apparently, was positive, but he moved away from Richmond prior to the event and so ultimately was not a participant in the vigil. In the end no African Americans specifically came to participate in the vigil, although a few people who passed by the event did sit and meditate with the group for short periods of time.

More effort was put into reaching out to the peace activist and social justice community, which, in some cases in Richmond, includes overlap with the African American community. For example, phone calls were made and e-mails sent to Richmond Peace Center, attempting to inform them about the event and to have it announced to their membership. Little headway was made in this endeavor — the people at the Peace Center seemed not to understand clearly what the event was about, and although a promise was made to publicize the event via their e-mail listserv, no such announcement was actually made. The announcements via the parent Buddhist Peace Fellowship organization were more productive, as they brought the event to the attention of the three women in West Virginia who came to participate in the vigil.

To prepare, Leighton spent time reading about the history of the slave trade in Richmond, learning about how slaves became a major export commodity for Virginia in the nineteenth century after importation from Africa and the Caribbean was outlawed. Leighton's reading was designed both to increase his understanding of the historical events and to provide material for the talk he would deliver at the statue during the retreat. Kelvin also researched the subject, especially in order to help with his planning of the day's activities, but his decision to read a biography of Frederick Douglass was motivated by a desire to understand better the actual experiences of the slaves. Most of the other participants said they did not prepare for the event in any particular way.

Motivations for Participation

People who come to Ekoji have many reasons for being involved in Buddhism. Some are impressed by Buddhism's history as a relatively peaceful organized religion, or they respond positively to aspects of the Buddha's philosophy and cosmology. Many are especially interested in the practice of silent meditation, both for achieving spiritual insight and for its alleged psychological and physical health benefits, such as decreased stress, lower blood pressure, better sleep, and increased ability to manage troublesome emotions or handle difficult situations. None, however, have ever stated to me that their involvement in Buddhism was specifically related to dealing with issues of race and history. And some of those who participated in the vigil have at other times taken pains to conceal their Buddhist practice from their families and neighbors, out of fear of receiving prejudiced backlash. Why then did these people choose to spend a Saturday morning and afternoon sitting in the sweltering southern sun, exposing themselves in a very public way to the scrutiny of non-Buddhists in Richmond?

One reason that several people cited was simple curiosity about the process of bearing witness, since this was a novel practice that they had not been exposed to before in their explorations of Buddhism. As one informant put it, "I wanted to do something that was bearing witness. So I thought, why not this?"[7] Although she supports recognition of America's slave history and was in fact deeply affected by the event, her initial interest was not due to the fact that it was about slavery—any number of social issues or historical phenomena might have been memorialized, and her willingness to participate would still have been approximately the same. Many felt that it was likely to be an interesting, perhaps meaningful personal experience. In particular several people were intrigued by the slave trail walking meditation, imagining that it would be a highly spiritual experience to walk silently along the path through the green leaves with the group.

A second common reason was the desire to support the teacher, Taigen Dan Leighton. Many people in the Richmond Zen Group respect him and wanted to help him with the event. This motivation tended to be manifested in two slightly different forms. Some people feared that the event might not be successful, especially because the number of participants might be too low. Others were initially suspicious of Leighton's motives, and especially of the possibility of an outsider coming into the South and self-righteously judging the community. One member of the Zen group expressed this clearly:

I wanted to find out what Taigen's motivations were. He's an activist type, and I guess for myself I wanted to make sure that his motivations were in the right place, that they lined up with what I thought were the right reasons to do something like this. I had some questions around having someone come into the community from outside to stage an event like this—more specifically, about someone that was from the North coming to do an event like this in the South. I thought there would be a lot of issues around, "Who do you think you are?" I thought this has the opportunity to cause more negativity than there already is, or "Is it going to be an event that brings up things that people don't talk about?"[8]

When Leighton made it clear that he was going to hold the meditation vigil, even if it meant that he might have to sit there all day long next to the statue by himself, a number of people decided to attend as well so that he would not be alone. The motivation here was basically a desire not to see the Zen teacher embarrassed or insulted by being the only person to show up for the meditation vigil. A slightly different motivation was shown by those who were willing to participate because they trusted Leighton and thought that any event that he planned was probably worth supporting through their own participation. Thus even some people who were skeptical about the idea of using meditation to bear witness to Richmond's history with the slave trade nonetheless participated in the event out of loyalty to and trust in the visiting teacher. And those who were uncertain of the propriety of a nonsoutherner leading the event were eventually reassured of his intentions and, like the Ekoji member quoted above, became supporters of the events.

A third reason for participating that many people mentioned was connection to place. This form of motivation, unlike the previous ones, was explicitly linked to where the slave trade meditation vigil was occurring. For some, the Statue of Reconciliation was the specific focus. For example, one woman listed the fact that the statue was new as a reason to sit near it: the vigil would help to recognize it as an important part of Richmond. For others, it was not the statue that was the focus but the whole general area where so many slaves had been imprisoned and sold. Many informants repeatedly characterized it as a place of power, as if the collective suffering over the years had somehow built up a sort of spiritual battery charge that left the area pulsating with energy. As one put it, "It was a place of power, it was a place that holds a lot of our history, where a lot of our tragic events took place, and it's right here under our noses, right here in this city."[9] Another said: "That Shockoe Bottom area collects all the energy from around the city. And there's a lot of misery here in Richmond. You have slavery and then you have the Civil War. All the wounded in a seventy-mile radius were brought here to Richmond. There were hospitals and hospitals and hospitals. Homes and businesses were opened up to become hospitals, so we've got a lot of misery and sorrow going on. So all of that's gathering at Shockoe Bottom along with its history, that's right where they were selling the slaves. For me as a healing practitioner, it's not only the people, it's also the city, the land, everything."[10] Leighton summed up the feeling succinctly: "It seems like an important space to me — a sacred place."[11]

A further way that place was listed as a motivation was the fact that the vigil would take place outside of Ekoji's familiar environment. As one informant said, the vigil offered the opportunity to "bring spiritual practice to another part of the city."[12] By meditating publicly downtown it would help to establish more of the Richmond city environment as an appropriate place for Buddhist practice. One participant tied this to a practical matter, saying that meditation year after year in the same building can become somewhat stale, so meditating downtown and outside exposed to the elements was a way to refresh his Buddhist practice.

Of course, a major motivation for participating in the vigil was concern about the difficult racial past (and present) of the United States, and of Richmond in particular. Reasons related to race tended to fall into several different patterns. First, there were people who believed that participating in the slave trade meditation vigil would help to improve the state of racial tensions in Richmond and the region, and perhaps the country more generally. Some connected this to their own personal histories of civil rights activism in the South during earlier eras; Leighton also connected the meditation vigil to his activist activities in the North and on the West Coast.

How the event might actually bring about improvements in Richmond's racial situation was an issue that various participants conceptualized in different ways. In the activist sense, some felt that the public event would raise awareness of the site and therefore of Richmond's tragic past of slavery, segregation, and racial discrimination. As Cecilia put it when discussing why the event was important: "One of the challenges of the South is the culture. You have to wake people up."[13] Another informant implied that it wasn't simply lack of awareness but actual intentional forgetting that had to be overcome: "Monument Avenue glorifies the Civil War, and it's a very noble version of the Civil War. The monuments are beautiful, and I agree with the argument about state's rights, but ultimately the thing is that they really wanted the right to own slaves! Richmond has wanted to deny that dark part of its history and romanticize it in one way or another."[14] This sort of selective memory was a common theme. Henry Kelvin, the main local planner of the event, also expressed this in explaining why he felt the event should be held: "Richmond prides itself on its history, but only some of it. It prides itself on the Monument Avenue history of the rebel leaders who stood up to the government overreaching its bounds."[15] Another informant stressed that "this is a living history, yet it's buried or unknown."[16] Others talked about the vigil as a show of solidarity with and support for Richmond's African American community, acknowledging their historic sufferings and the injustices and obstacles many continue to face.

Beyond simply the public nature of the vigil as related to an activist-protest subculture, many felt that that the performance of Buddhist practices at this nexus of southern racial suffering would itself be effective. For example, Leighton said that he believes in "the power of awareness: it itself is transformative," and "just sitting and being with [that kind of suffering]" would have positive, though intangible, effects.[17] Maria, whose workplace encounters with struggling black women in Richmond and own experiences as a person of color impelled her to participate, spent much of the time sending Buddhist prayers of lovingkindness to those who suffered, an activity the entire group replicated in the liturgy of the service held at the vigil's midpoint. Traditionally, this sort of practice is connected to the Buddhist concept of sending merit to those who suffer, especially the deceased. This merit—often called "good karma" in the vernacular—can be envisioned as a sort of positive energy that is produced by positive actions (including meditation and sutra chanting), and which can be stored or transferred to those in need in order to improve their circumstances or futures, akin in some ways to the non-Buddhist idea of wishing someone good luck. Similar ideas exist beyond the formal boundaries of Buddhism in the New Age subculture of America, such as the view expressed by one of the non-Buddhist participants: "We went there with the intention of honoring all those people that were in that human drama. That was so important to me: the healing of Richmond. This is a big thing for Richmond, with all its racism—it's getting better, but this is still a big, big piece of it. That's the healing that this whole slave trade vigil was aimed at."[18] There is a sense that bearing witness to events is itself somehow positive and productive, beyond any other demonstrable results that people might wish to measure.

In general, motivations such as healing racism or ritually acknowledging the past tend to be externally oriented in nature. But another set of race-related motivations were more personal and inner directed. These related to each participant's desires to be changed as an individual by the process of the vigil. One Ekoji member who helped with the planning but was unable to attend due to illness on the day of the vigil said: "I wanted to bear witness to that suffering and that collective karma that I'm still a part of. I'm white in the South. I've got a lot of benefits just from those two facts. That brings up a lot of shitty things in you, and I wanted to touch that. I wanted to be present for that."[19] This informant, who participated in the discussion the next day at Ekoji, wanted to attend the vigil in order to deal with his own feelings of turmoil as a racially privileged person and the descendant of Virginia slave owners. Another informant offered similar sentiments: "I'm someone who does notice the biases against African Americans in my own mind. I'm not proud of it, but I picked it up osmotically. There's a little bit of fear. I wanted to confront that, and the vigil was one small way to do it."[20] By contrast, Maria, one of the few nonwhite participants, participated in part to deal with her own emotions surrounding the suffering she saw other people of color endure and that she herself experienced. Most of the participants were not as strongly conflicted as these informants, although many did acknowledge some abstract wish to heal or acknowledge racial conflicts that they believed impacted them in some way. Instead, they tended to express their motivation in terms of raising their own awareness about the events of Richmond's slave past. In other words, while some people sought spiritual healing or perhaps psychological therapy from the event, a larger number conceptualized the event's relationship to them as primarily educational: it would inform them about their city and perhaps give them greater knowledge of their role in its racial phenomena.

Vigil Participants

In analyzing the slave trade meditation vigil, we must pay attention to the demographics of the participants. Not including people who happened on the vigil and sat with the group for short periods of time, there were eighteen participants. Most of them took part in all the day's activities, although some went directly to the statue instead of walking the slave trail, and a few others went home early. The group was roughly even in terms of gender representation. The age range was less representative: nearly everyone was in their forties, fifties, or sixties, with only one older and one younger person who fell outside this span.

Given the racial nature of the history that the group was bearing witness to, it is natural to inquire into the racial makeup of the participants who meditated in the Reconciliation Triangle. The group was almost entirely white. One male participant was of South Asian birth, and one female participant was of mixed Filipino and South American heritage. Most notably, there were no African Americans present for the meditation vigil (again, not counting people who interacted briefly with the main participants at the statue). None, therefore, were compelled to participate out of feelings connected to their own ancestors' experiences of enslavement, or hardships experienced during the years of legal segregation in Richmond. Only a handful had experienced any sort of racial oppression or discrimination in their own lives, although many had secondhand accounts of observing or hearing about racial incidents involving friends or neighbors, and some had experienced hatred or even imprisonment as white civil rights activists.

At the same time, only one participant (to their knowledge) was descended from slave owners, and this fact did not form an important part of her motivation for participating in the slave trade meditation vigil. Thus, while this event was stimulated by the slave history of Richmond and was dedicated to bearing witness to the racial suffering of the area, almost none of the vigil's participants had a direct personal connection to either slavery or slave ownership; or, perhaps, few if any of the participants were aware of any such connections. We can say, therefore, that for most of the participants slavery was an abstraction whose presence in their city's history concerned and distressed them but was not of direct personal relevance. This is not meant to imply that they were in fact fully untouched by slavery: indeed, many participants talked about how slavery and discrimination's legacy has affected all Americans no matter what their race, both in the past and continuing in the present due to the unresolved racial problems of the country.

And what of regional background? Only two of the participants had been born or raised in the immediate Richmond area, while another six belonged to families that hailed from elsewhere in the South, such as North Carolina or West Virginia. The slightly larger portion of the participants, therefore, came from outside the South and had moved to the region as adults. Leighton was not a resident of Richmond at all; among the others, the most recent arrival had come to Virginia just a couple of years earlier, while some had lived in Richmond for several decades. There was no particular pattern to the origins of the nonnative southerners, whose backgrounds included the Midwest, Northeast, West Coast, and outside the United States. The group, therefore, was only partially rooted by ancestry in the South generally and Richmond specifically. Nearly all, however, lived in the South now and had taken on its history as an issue that they needed to grapple with for themselves. And those who were from the area were in some cases from very old southern families that stretched back well before the Civil War. One of the women meditating there in Shockoe Bottom, for example, was the great-great-great-great niece of Confederate president Jefferson Davis, whose White House lies just a half mile away from the site of the meditation vigil.[21]

Compared to the demographics of Richmond—which has a bare majority of African Americans and is overwhelmingly Christian and mostly southern-born—the group was not representative of the city, nor is there any reason to expect that it would be. What it does closely match, of course, is the Ekoji Buddhist Sangha of Richmond. Both the vigil participants and the Ekoji membership are largely white, with a few nonwhite attendees. Both are roughly equal gender-wise, and both draw on a mostly middle-aged, professional demographic, although Ekoji does have a minority of participants in their twenties who were not proportionately represented at the vigil. Ekoji's membership also includes a mix of people of old southern extraction, others who have lived in the South for much of their adult lives, and newer arrivals from outside the South. What was less representative was the mix of traditions represented at the vigil. In part because the event was not well publicized outside the Zen and Vipassana groups, those groups (especially Zen) made up the bulk of the participants, although all five of the temple's groups were represented in some fashion, whether by single-group participants or by people who attend the Zen meetings but also sometimes go to the Pure Land or Tibetan services as well. The facts that the vigil was initiated and led by a visiting Zen teacher and that the primary local planner was a lay leader of the Zen group also significantly impacted the profile of those who attended the vigil.

Limited publicity outside Ekoji is a primary reason that the demographics of vigil participants reflected those of the temple. We should note, however, the presence of several people who were *not* members of Ekoji and learned of the event through various channels. In addition to the three women from Harpers Ferry, West Virginia, another woman—also involved in Buddhism but not an Ekoji attendee—came after hearing about the vigil from a family member who goes to Ekoji. A fifth woman, who is not Buddhist, was invited by an Ekoji friend who knew that she was interested in healing the wounds of slavery and racism in Richmond.

Effects of the Vigil

It can be difficult for outside researchers to measure the effects of group meditation rituals such as the slave trade meditation vigil, but a number of possibilities came up in my interviews with the vigil participants and with Ekoji attendees who discussed the event the following day at the temple. Historian of American religion Thomas Tweed suggests that religion is often related to how practitioners conceptually map their landscape (as well as their place in the larger cosmos) and discusses how religions operate as forces that help people cross boundaries and establish dwellings in order to intensify joy and confront suffering. We can clearly see mapping strategies taking place in the meditation vigil, as participants overlaid their own Buddhist frameworks on the physical and historical characteristics of Richmond. By walking the slave trail and sitting by the slavery reconciliation statue, they inscribed Buddhist practice onto the cityscape and placed these sites within Buddhist conceptual maps that made the city and its history more personally familiar and meaningful. Shockoe Bottom "became a sacred place," one Ekoji member said. "It felt safe, protected, and sacred."[22] And the statue in particular took on a new significance for a number of participants. Previously just a generic part of downtown, the Reconciliation Triangle has become permanently meaningful for those who meditated there for a day, and passing through the area now can revive and reinforce those experiences and attitudes.

Much of the vigil's goal was "consciousness-raising," which was achieved in various ways. On the most superficial level, participants simply learned about Richmond's general slave history and the specifics of the places where the vigil occurred. Even life-long Richmond residents found that their knowledge of the past was enhanced by the event. As one said, "What was fascinating to me was I had been here, I had lived here, and I knew about the Civil War, but I didn't know anything about this site. I didn't know about the slave trail that's been there a long time or the history — we're not taught that, and it isn't brought up."[23] Another southerner concurred: "I actually learned a lot, there were a lot of things I didn't really know about Richmond and that specific location in the city. I felt like I really gained a lot."[24] Those who planned the event in particular developed a rather intricate knowledge of the practices of antebellum Richmond and the specifics of which local buildings had been used for various facets of the slave trade, and much of this information was conveyed to the participants at the vigil, as well as to attendees at Ekoji during various regular weekly gatherings both before and after the event. Several participants indicated that they had subsequently shared their knowledge and experiences with non-Buddhist friends, expanding the circle of education.

Beyond simple education about the past, Leighton hoped to increase awareness of racial issues and attitudes, and stimulate concern toward resolving these problems. The public nature of the event was one vehicle for this form of consciousness-raising, since the group sought to call the attention of the larger Richmond community to their bearing witness and invited Richmonders to reflect on the continuing effects of racial discrimination. Quite a number of people passed by over the course of the day and observed the group meditating next to the statue. Some passersby talked to participants and learned about the event, the site, and its importance to Richmond's past, and a few even participated themselves for a while. The event also informed some members of the Richmond community that there were Buddhists in the city and that they took the slave history seriously. This included not only the passersby but also members of the Richmond Peace Center, the city council, and other organizations that the group reached out to during the event's planning stages. Of course, the more immediate impact was on the participants themselves, who found their interest in racial issues heightened by the vigil experience. For a number of participants, the event brought to their attention the negative racial attitudes that they had been raised with, provoking soul-searching about whether they were more racist toward African Americans than they had realized. Others did not uncover personal feelings of racism but did come away with a greater understanding of how all people (themselves included) are enmeshed in webs of social stratification and systematic racial oppression.

Perhaps the greatest effects of the slave trade meditation vigil were emotional. Many participants indicated that they had been touched by and appreciated the experience, which they described as "moving," "powerful," "wonderful," or "great." It moved Richmond's slave past from a historical abstraction to a reality that vigil participants could empathize with in ways that they had not previously. One participant described it in the following terms:

The most important thing was that it had a greater impact that we weren't doing it in another city or even at Ekoji—we were doing it where these people actually went through these experiences of being sold. I think for me personally that had a really strong impact, that I was actually in that place. You think about how hot it's getting as you sit there without any shade. I guess I really hadn't thought that much about it, just the loss . . . [long pause as he chokes up and is unable to speak]. To be taken from your home . . . [long pause as he chokes up again]. To go through that pain . . . [pause] it was very emotional. For the people who did that practice, it was worth it. We just don't have that experience. To stop and do that experience for a day, it maybe *begins* to sink in, the whole experience of slavery.[25]

The experience created an emotional connection between many of the participants and the issue of slavery and its legacy. Cecelia's meditation, in which she heard the cries of slaves and felt the lash of whips, similarly underscores the emotions provoked by the vigil. Her experiences caused her to break down in tears both at the event and afterward, and for weeks afterward the feelings of the vigil remained with her. Recall also the revelation of Serena, who realized the freedom she enjoyed to be able to go home when she got too hot and the bondage that kept slaves from being able to make such choices. These sorts of emotional experiences increase the meaning of the event and heighten the relevance of racial issues to those who went through it, making it more likely that they will expend effort to educate others and work for racial reconciliation in the future.

The event also made an impact in ways not specifically related to race. Most of the participants enjoyed the opportunity to practice meditation, especially in a novel situation and with the guidance of the visiting Zen teacher. Despite the frequent allusion to emotions such as sorrow or pain, participants also indicated that they found aspects of the event pleasurable, such as the silent walk along the slave trail, the solidarity of sitting together as a group, and the extended length of the meditation session — much longer than the average session at Ekoji and therefore deeper, with the possibility of achieving levels of concentration, peace, and meditative insight usually unavailable at Ekoji. For one participant this was her first direct exposure to Buddhist meditation, and her visit to the temple the following day was her initial encounter with a Buddhist organization. Raised with a conservative Christian background, she had been drawn to liberal forms of Christianity and religion such as Unity and Unitarian Universalism as an adult. This taste of Buddhism led her to begin exploring the tradition by attending the Zen-based meditation group that meets at the First

Unitarian Church of Richmond and by reading Buddhist materials that she received at the church.

Most of the participants directly stated that the event was supposed to be "healing," but many left it ambiguous as to how exactly the meditation vigil was healing in effect, or who exactly was expected to be healed. The general impression presented by the participants was that acknowledging historical suffering would somehow, in an undefined manner, help ease lingering pain and sorrow. One informant called the performance of seated meditation in a public place "a wonderful gift to ourselves and everyone around us," but she was not specific about what that gift was precisely.[26] On the whole, the event seemed to be related to a general psychotherapeutic frame that is common in American society and has made a particularly significant impact on the practice of Buddhism in North America.[27] Just as on the therapist's couch suppressed or unacknowledged memories, experiences, and traumas are brought forward so that they can be recognized and dealt with by the patient, the slave trade meditation vigil seemed to be conceptualized (like bearing-witness events in general) as healing society by calling forth hidden or neglected pain so that it can be acknowledged and perhaps laid to rest. Most participants seemed to take this process rather metaphorically, rather than suggesting that the spirits of slaves might still be suffering in the present day. For example, one woman told me, "I think it helped somehow. They're not here. They're dead. But it might have released someone. I don't know."[28] This was actually among the *strongest* statements supporting a possible supernatural interpretation of the ritual, a clear indication of how little such beliefs figured in the participants' thinking about the event. We should be aware that this differs from many traditional approaches to Buddhism in Asia, where transfer of merit to spirits who have suffered and continue to suffer is a common occurrence, and meditation or chanting has often been undertaken for the sake of such languishing spirits (often, one's own ancestors).

The logic behind the meditation vigil does not seem to stem strongly from Buddhism itself, even though it occurred in a clearly Buddhist context as indicated by the practices performed and the self-identification of most of the participants. We could say that this reveals how closely aligned Buddhism and certain American cultural influences have become, such that Buddhists do not perceive notions derived from therapy as being non-Buddhist. Would this then be the therapeuticization of Buddhism or the Buddhification of therapy? Researchers may naturally be drawn to such questions, but they seem largely irrelevant to my informants and their pursuit of lived religion in modern America. Furthermore, one possible reading of the ritual ties it back to traditional Buddhist notions more directly. The largest amount of time at the vigil was spent in silent seated meditation. The leader and main organizers of the event, as well as the largest contingent of participants, all came from the Richmond Zen Group, which is a Soto Zen meditation group. In the Soto tradition, it is commonly taught that seated meditation does not *lead* to enlightenment: rather, sitting in meditation is itself the actualization of Buddhist awakening or Buddha-activity. In this school, therefore, there is a normative framework that interprets its central ritual (seated meditation) as the accomplishment of the activity's traditional goal. A similar logic may be at work in the bearing-witness model as well. It may be that participants (including, notably, the event's leader) were unable to clearly articulate how the vigil would bring about the healing of society because there was a baseline assumption that Zen rituals enact their goals. In other words, bearing witness does not transfer merit or raise awareness so that effort can be subsequently exerted in order to produce healing: bearing witness itself *is* the healing of society.

One final effect that should be explored is how the bearing-witness vigil also provoked negative reactions around race. Many people, both participants and those who listened to the participants discuss their experiences, felt that the event had gone well and was a positive thing. There were, however, other reactions. Maria, one of the only nonwhite participants, enjoyed the "warmth and camaraderie" during the silent meditation, but she was disappointed once people began to discuss their thoughts and feelings, both at the statue and the next day at Ekoji. In her opinion, the nearly all-white nature of the group meant that the discussions were pervaded by "white guilt" and negative interactions that put the onus on the nonwhite participants to somehow try and assuage such guilt rather than allowing them to focus on their own race-based pain and anger. This was a dynamic she had experienced before, and it had pushed her toward an awareness of how internalized racism and oppression "infect" all members of American society. Her response, in part, had been to organize separate groups for people of color and run workshops about unlearning racism. The slave trade meditation vigil once again confronted her with the difficulties of working with white people around issues of race and made her feel that "this group would have been better off segregated"—that is, that separate meditation vigils for white people and for people of color would have been more productive. These might have been a more useful way to proceed since they would allow each group to deal with its own race-specific issues, and, importantly, prevent white people from (intentionally or otherwise) oppressing nonwhite participants through their opinions or even their mere presence. As I discussed in the opening description of the event, Bonnie, an African American woman whose first visit to the temple occurred the day after the meditation vigil, was likewise unhappy with what she heard. She felt the participants were all speaking from a place of white privilege and did not really understand what the black experience in America was like. Even Maria was a target for such charges—when she tried to talk to an African American afterward she was shut down and basically told that she could not relate, something that she interpreted as "the Oppression Olympics or the competition to see who is the most oppressed."[29]

At least some people did seem to hear what the nonwhite participants were trying to communicate. One participant in that discussion, Larry Johnston, made this very clear:

> One thing that I found odd, and I actually asked this the day after, it didn't seem like anyone there had any identification with the slave traders. And that was part of what I was going there for. Those are my ancestors. Those are our ancestors. We're largely white, largely upper middle class, privileged people here in the Zen group. The vast majority of the Zen group is white, upper middle class. It's almost an anomaly when we have someone who isn't. We are direct descendents—in that time, that's who we would have been. We would have been holding the auction. I was just shocked that no one felt any identification with that. Everyone seemed to feel identification with the slaves. I understand that, that's where your compassion is naturally drawn toward: the one who is suffering, not the one who is causing the suffering. I wanted to go partly for that. That's the easy part. The hard part is that's where I come from, that's my collective history. That's my karmic history. And it's ours as a country. I wanted to bear witness to that, and maybe that's naive but I was hoping there would be some healing effect, some purging of that negativity that I've benefited from.[30]

Larry felt moved to discuss the entire situation further with some of his non-Buddhist, African American friends. One, a Muslim, said that she would be interested in participating if the vigil were held again.

Analysis of the Ritual

One of the first observations to make about the actual procedures of the slave trade meditation vigil is that they are basically Buddhist but have been intentionally modified in order to reduce sectarian specificity. Leighton and the other planners of the event drew on their Zen Buddhist training and familiarity, but, in line with a pluralistic Buddhist orientation (which I discussed in detail in chapter 4), they sought to open the rituals to participants who were not Zen practitioners, or even Buddhist. Therefore, Leighton did not insist on proper sitting posture as understood in the Soto Zen tradition, and he did not dictate what sort of meditation practices participants should do. The result is that some people sat in a very discernibly Zen posture, while others sat in forms more associated with the Vipassana movement or displayed no particular form at all (i.e., they simply sat comfortably at their leisure). Likewise, some participants carried out types of meditation common in Zen groups, such as counting their breaths or trying to be simply present and aware of their experience moment to moment, while others did non-Zen meditation practices, such as vipassana or metta (lovingkindness).[31] Sitting in a circle, as most of the group did, is not a traditional Zen form, and some people chose to sit in other arrangements, including perching on a low wall with their backs to the main group in the grass. In a Zen meditation context, proper form and correct meditation practice are strongly stressed—indeed, they are often ranked as more important than religious beliefs or moral actions. So the relaxation of such strictures here is significant: it indicates the importance accorded in this ritual to inclusivity and pluralism.

The activities were made more inclusive also by the decision not to use many of the liturgical elements common in the Zen services at Ekoji. While the Metta Sutta that the participants chanted is included in the Richmond Zen Group Chant Book, it is taken from the Theravada Buddhist tradition and has achieved a sort of quasi-nonsectarian status among many American Buddhist groups. This was seen, therefore, not as a Zen chant but simply as a generic (and appropriate) Buddhist one, and, importantly, one that does not include overtly Buddhist references. The merit dedication that Leighton crafted was similarly nondenominational. Other chants from the typical Zen service, such as the Heart Sutra, various dharani (esoteric chants), and the names of the lineal ancestors, were all deliberately left out, and even rituals such as the Three Refuges were not used, as they imply a type of Buddhist self-identification or commitment that not all participants might wish to affirm. No dress code was enforced and no restrictions or qualifications were announced for participation. In all, the Buddhist content was downplayed and tradition-specific forms were deemphasized.

Nonetheless, the event clearly retained a basic Buddhist framework. This began with the walking meditation from the riverside. Walking meditation is usually performed at a dedicated site for Buddhist meditation, typically interspersed with periods of seated meditation. If can also be applied to certain less common practices, such as takuhatsu, the ritual begging rounds that monastics perform.[32] In the twentieth century, some socially engaged Buddhist leaders adapted the walking meditation model to apply to other functions, such as the dhammayatras of Venerable Mahaghosananda in Cambodia and the peace walks of the Nipponzan Myohoji Buddhist order of Japan (which are also performed regularly in the United States). Thus there is some precedent for using walking meditation in the manner employed during the slave trade meditation vigil. The physical activity of walking through a space where suffering has occurred can be seen as acknowledging or hallowing the site. It helped the participants to relate to those they were there to remember, walking in the slaves' footprints, so to speak. It also had the effect of replicating a passage, as the group left the ordinary Richmond world of work and play and transitioned into a realm of bearing witness. This was augmented by the way the group moved through the alternating environments of woods and cityscape and crossed over the bridge to the site of the vigil.

The sitting meditation at the Slave Trade Reconciliation Triangle was another common Buddhist element, repurposed to serve the needs of the vigil. Historically, Buddhist meditation has not been used to carry out something called "bearing witness," but seated meditation has had many different applications and its meaning is readily adjusted to fit new circumstances such as those of contemporary bearing-witness events. For many Buddhists in the West, meditation is seen as the primary and most important practice of Buddhism, and performing it at the statue was a way of making the site sacred, or, it could be said, of proclaiming the site's already sacred nature. In Zen, the act of sitting is the expression or cause of enlightenment, and thus the meditation seat is sometimes conceptualized as the holiest of possible locations, the birthplace of new buddhas. Meditation was also a natural choice for the vigil because it is such a commonly shared practice among Ekoji's Buddhists, and it is what marks an event as Buddhist for many of them. Sitting silently allowed them to make a public witness to the suffering of the slave trade, yet without making any specific statement or imposing themselves on the neighborhood. It thus allowed participants to experience whatever thoughts or emotions arose for them as individuals and did not inconvenience or potentially anger nearby pedestrians, drivers, or businesses.

One of the most interesting elements of the ritual activities at the vigil is the way the group interacted with the statue. They chose to sit beside it, rather than in front of it, and to minimize their interaction with it so that they would not monopolize the site: Leighton was concerned that other visitors might want to see or touch the statue for themselves, and he did not want them inconvenienced by the meditating group. The statue, however, was not ignored. When the group arrived at the site they placed flowers at its base and lit a candle in front of it. These same gestures are used at the Ekoji altar; but in this case, the role of gohonzon (object of veneration) was played not by a buddha figure but by the representation of two embracing slaves. The flowers and candle became offerings to the departed spirits who were bought and sold in the nearby auction houses and to their descendants who suffered through slavery's ongoing legacy of poverty, discrimination, and violence. At the same time, the statue and the tragic events it represented were symbolically transformed into the source of the group's spiritual awakening, in the same manner that buddhas are enshrined and venerated for their enlightening teachings and powers. Whereas Confederate memorial ceremonies held in Richmond include uniformed citizens marching to Monument Avenue and leaving flowers at the statues of the defenders of the Confederacy and slavery, participants in the slave trade meditation vigil inscribed an opposing religious logic onto Richmond's streets by walking meditatively in their rakusus to the Statue of Reconciliation and placing flowers and a candle before it.

Southern Buddhist Ritual

Slavery was practiced in many parts of the United States, not just the South, and it is part of the inherited history of all Americans regardless of their location or race. As such, the slave trade meditation vigil might conceivably have been held anywhere in the country. Nor can any corner of America claim to be untarnished by racial tension, discrimination, and economic disparity. And yet the vigil was held in the South, and for good reason: it was in the South that slave ownership became not simply a form of economic exploitation but an entire social order unto itself, where slavery was transmuted from a necessary evil or neutral system of relations into an allegedly positive good designed to carry out God's plan for humanity. It was the Confederate states that fought a devastating war in part to retain their elite's rights to own other human beings, and it was in those formerly Confederate states that slavery's dismal legacy played out most vividly. And it is here that the misery of those who endured slavery has most often been obscured in favor of white narratives of past southern glory or victimization at the hands of northern aggression. Virginia specifically not only played a key role in the slave trade and the Confederacy, but it also was where the anti-integration policies of massive resistance were formulated. The topography of the South is mapped out in reference to slavery, the Civil War, and the struggle for African American civil rights in a manner far beyond any other region of the country, not only because of where important events took place but also because many white southerners chose to worship at the altar of the Lost Cause, while African Americans developed their own alternate civil religion.

One of the most interesting aspects of the slave trade meditation vigil is that it brings to the surface a theological or philosophical notion often unnoted in studies of American Buddhism. Time and again my informants talked about "collective karma" and "karmic history." Buddhism in America, especially among adult converts or sympathizers, is almost universally depicted as hyperindividualistic, with its model being the solo practitioner alone with his own thoughts on the cushion. American Buddhism is also generally portrayed as antimetaphysical, with many interpreters suggesting that common Buddhist ideas such as karma and rebirth are downplayed or even explicitly rejected. This ritual, however, suggests that some American Buddhists have a strong sense of themselves as participants in larger, collective dramas and are quite willing to employ traditional language and concepts, although these frames of reference are perhaps altered to meet the needs and attitudes of locals. Thus among many American Buddhists there is less focus on personal responsibility for actions in individual past lives as an explanation for current suffering, and less emphasis on moral behavior in order to avoid rebirth in the torturous hell realms, compared to traditional Buddhist approaches in Asia. But there is a clear belief in the more diffuse notion of the collective karma that is generated by groups and societies and that continues to manifest in the present in powerful ways. And just as traditional Buddhist rituals are often designed to purge or negate individual karma from the past, this new southern Buddhist ritual is intended to cleanse or heal collective karmic traumas of Richmond's slave history. These are not just ideas or concepts — they spur action that is played out in the public spaces of Richmond as Buddhists respond to their concerns and desires.

We should be clear that the logic embedded in this ritual is a somewhat new interpretation of Buddhism and the notion of karma. But we should also be cautious about labeling it therefore somehow inauthentic. Buddhists in Asia have continually reinterpreted Buddhism in order to meet the evolving needs of their various societies, and Buddhist rituals related to karma have changed many times as they crossed borders of time or culture long before the first Buddhists reached the United States. In this case, a group of American Buddhists in the South felt the need to ritually acknowledge and deal with their collective karma as southerners in an environment shaped and reshaped by racial suffering and oppression. This is an attitude that may well appear in many parts of the American Buddhist map. At the same time, we can detect the trace of a southern accent in this specific manifestation. Among people who struggle to define a particular southern attitude or mentality, one constant appears even more frequently than racial attitudes, evangelical orientations, or conservative ideas: the central place of memory. It has been pointed out many times that southerners are people of memory, and the South is held together as a distinct region by the way memory is deployed and re-created. Thus it is natural that a southern Buddhist ritual would cohere around the issue of memory of regional events and their lingering life in the present day.

As the slave trade meditation vigil shows, the memory-laden topography of Richmond and the concerns of newer players in the region can produce alternative religious readings and practices that challenge the historically dominant storyline that the South was the noble aggrieved victim of the Civil War, or the more recently ascendant southern narrative that slavery and segregation happened long ago and should be consigned to the dustbin of history so that we can get on with things. This meditation vigil was a southern Buddhist ritual because it was carried out in the South and was tied to specific places, economic histories, and social realities of the South. The ritual was designed to bear witness to and enhance awareness of these phenomena, and thereby to grapple with and transform the South's racial trajectory.[33]

This ritual was a good case study for regional Buddhism in America not only because it was so clearly tied to a specific area but also because it demonstrates the multifarious nature of regional Buddhism. The South — and other regions — never exist in isolation from other places, and Buddhism anywhere in the West is always a confluence of various local, regional, national, and transnational religious and cultural flows. Thus this southern Buddhist ritual was tied to a specific local place: Richmond, Virginia. It took place there, at a site chosen for its local relevance, and was planned and carried out primarily by Richmonders. It was also, importantly, regional: it was based on the cultural history of an entire region, and it stretched out to include participants from other parts of this region (such as West Virginia). It was national, too: the leader was a long-time resident of the West Coast, recently relocated to the Midwest. And its roots lay not only in the local Richmond soil but also in the transnational history of global migration and communication: the event officially took place under the auspices of the international engaged Buddhist movement, based on practices largely originating in Asia and refined at bearing-witness events in Europe. Regional Buddhism is never apart from forces operating at larger and smaller scales as well, and these forces must always be attended to if an accurate picture of a ritual, organization, idea, or other facet of Buddhism is to be understood in its regional manifestations.

Will the slave trade meditation vigil be repeated? Many people at Ekoji and their supporters in the wider community would like to see it become an annual event, but thus far it has not been held a second time. Just as regional forces produced it, other regional forces (such as the lack of a local teacher to keep the momentum going) constrain the ritual as well. But whether slave trade meditation vigils become common in the South or not, Buddhism has begun to establish deep roots in the southern soil, and in the process it is both transformed and transformative. Similar processes are happening at many other points on the American map, as global and regional forces come together to produce a diverse American Buddhist landscape. It is impossible to predict exactly what forms Buddhism will take in the future or what impacts it will have on the various regions where it is practiced. We can only say that as long as Dixie and other regions persist, the buddha-dharma will continue to manifest a southern accent.

I see NASCAR through the lens of Buddhism and Buddhism through the lens
of NASCAR because it is my makeup as a southerner and a Buddhist to do so.
It is as simple as that. Being a Buddhist helps me understand NASCAR on a deeper,
more profound level, and being a NASCAR fan helps bring to vivid life Buddhism's
sometimes academic theories.

—Arlynda Lee Boyer, *Buddha on the Backstretch*, 2009

Conclusion

BUDDHAS ON THE BACKSTRETCH

It is as simple as that: people in different parts of America experience Buddhism through lenses and circumstances supplied by the surrounding culture, and Buddhism impacts how those people navigate their regional culture. At root, that is this book's primary argument. Furthermore, Buddhism
is not an abstract philosophy but a fluid set of practices and attitudes enacted in specific places through the media of bodies and physical objects,
which can be used to produce new, multiple, and even competing Buddhisms. Values such as pluralism are instantiated in particular ways related
to the specificities of each situation and location, subject to the idiosyn-
crasies of individuals, the dynamics of groups, and the pressures of outside
forces. The unifying substrate to this book's twin themes of pluralism and
regionalism is the call for fine-grained attention to place (body, artifact,
room, building, neighborhood, region) as well as movement in the study of
American Buddhism. And it is my hope that those scholars who do know
the value of places—especially the southern historians—will see fit to explore more enthusiastically how the pluralizing changes in their favorite regions are not the death knell of their specialties but valuable new resources
for study. I close therefore by providing additional details for how regionalism can be explored in American Buddhism, including some suggestions
for possible future research.

American Buddhism can be studied by looking at regional distribution
patterns. In chapter 1, I highlighted ethnicity as one possible factor for in-

vestigation. We can also look specifically at race rather than ethnicity. For example, we might find it worth pondering that a large percentage of the well-known African American public faces of Buddhism — such as Jan Willis, Ralph Steele, Joseph Jarman, Alice Walker, bell hooks, Thulani Davis, Gaylon Ferguson, and Tina Turner — originally come from the South. Perhaps equally noteworthy, few of these individuals have chosen to remain in the South, and it typically was not in the South that they initially encountered Buddhism. Indeed, the South today is almost bare of African American Buddhist monks and priests.[1] Yet it would be foolhardy to dismiss the possibility that African American Buddhism (wherever it is actually found) carries more traces of southern cultural influence than does most Asian American or white Buddhism. And perhaps it is not coincidental that the South has produced the country's only African American Buddhist member of Congress: Hank Johnson, representative for Georgia's 4th District at the time of this writing.

There are many other potential forms of regional distribution to examine. *Tricycle: The Buddhist Review*, headquartered in Manhattan and one of the major American Buddhist periodicals, is sometimes characterized as an "East Coast" Buddhist magazine. Meanwhile *Tricycle*'s major competitors, *Shambhala Sun* and *Buddhadharma*, are both based even further east in Halifax, Nova Scotia, but are rarely accused of being Canadian or East Coast in nature. Why the distinction? Perhaps an analysis of the subscription lists for all three periodicals could provide a clue, revealing a larger East Coast audience for *Tricycle* and more Western or simply more dispersed home addresses for *Shambhala Sun* and *Buddhadharma* readers. Or perhaps it is simply a misperception shaped by anti–New York City sentiment, which might be clarified by such a study. Are nightstand Buddhists (who read books on Buddhism and perhaps meditate occasionally but are not affiliated with any Buddhist institution) uniformly distributed throughout the country, and does their ratio to "card-carrying Buddhists" differ from region to region?[2] Perhaps there are more such nightstand Buddhists in the central and southern states, where there are fewer local Buddhist groups and greater physical distances between temples and meditation centers (and this in regions that often lack effective public transportation). Similar factors might drive up online use of Buddhist resources or even membership in "cybersanghas" by solo Buddhists in the states with few options for contact with nearby Buddhist communities, such that online American Buddhism may be disproportionately southern and central in nature.[3] Where have American Buddhist pilgrimage routes been established? In

Many stupas have been erected across the South, but virtually all of them—like this stupa nestled in the hills of Appalachian Virginia—are away from roads and out of sight of the neighbors.

what areas do retreat centers tend to cluster? Where do Americans build stupas (monuments)? And, of course, beyond the simple numbers and concentration ratios, the important questions behind each of these projects will always be: Why do we see these regional differences? What are the factors driving them? Do they change over time?

In chapter 1, I suggested that climate and terrain can influence Buddhist practice. One example is the practice of buying animals that are destined to be slaughtered for food and releasing them back into the wild. Fish and turtles are particularly common objects of such compassionate action, undertaken in part as a strategy for generating good karma for the individual and community. But while this merit-making practice can be carried out year-round by communities on the Gulf Coast, northern Buddhists have to restrict their activities to those months when local lakes and rivers are not frozen over.[4] Warm weather and abundant coastline have drawn many Vietnamese Americans to southern coastal areas of the United States, where many became ensconced in the fishing industries of Texas and Louisiana, a major commercial sector back in Vietnam. Naturally, the erection of Buddhist temples in these areas has followed in the wake of such migration.[5]

Education can also be linked to regional phenomena. For many Americans who do not come from a Buddhist family background, college is where they first encounter Buddhism, whether in courses on religion, through a campus Buddhist group, or by meeting a new and more diverse circle of friends than they enjoyed as children. Since colleges and universities are not evenly distributed throughout the country, places with a high concentration of them (such as the Northeast) may produce relatively greater numbers of new Buddhists. Also, the exposure to various religions through classes, the diversity of campus populations, and the generally liberal atmosphere of many American universities means that Buddhism can flourish in college towns in parts of the country where Buddhism is otherwise a relatively rare phenomenon. This can have particular regional effects: the average Buddhist in a Buddhist-poor region, such as the Plains States, may be relatively more educated and more likely to be a recent convert than the average Buddhist in somewhere like Hawaii.

In Hawaii widespread devotion to the protector bodhisattva Jizo has altered the landscape itself, with many statues and markers erected in public spaces by Japanese American groups to protect and warn fishermen, swimmers, and surfers about the presence of dangerous currents and wave-prone beaches.[6] Public Buddhist monuments certainly do not occur with the same frequency in the American heartland, where crosses are omnipresent but Buddhist statues are decidedly rare.[7] Thus it is not simply that different regions affect their Buddhisms in diverse ways; the various Buddhisms within particular regions reciprocate in different ways as they in turn change what it means to live in Illinois, New York, or Hawaii. The Northeast is not the same as it was before Buddhists arrived, nor is the West Coast or the Midwest or anywhere else. In small and sometimes in large ways Buddhists have shifted the culture of the regions they have encountered. These encounters and changes were not and are not nationally uniform. Therefore we need to ask not only the common question of what impact Buddhism has made on America but also the less common one of what different impacts Buddhism has made in different parts of America.

Of course, we can find much overlap between these three modes of regional investigation. Buddhists distribute themselves differently in the United States as they are pulled toward or repelled by particular American cultural or environmental regions, and their level of concentration itself can impact the regions where they settle. Buddhist peace pilgrimages in the South, such as to Fort Benning in Georgia (site of the School of the Americas, infamous for graduating military officers who go on to become human

Jizo statue that protects swimmers, surfers, and fishermen in Hawaii.

rights abusers in their home countries) and Oak Ridge in Tennessee (site of uranium-enrichment facilities that helped produce the atomic bomb), are Buddhist responses to the local culture and themselves help to change the range of religious phenomena in the South. The point is not to depict these as three completely separate types of Buddhist regional phenomena but to raise them as different points of initial access for studies of American Buddhist regionalism. The best studies will of course bear their interdependency in mind.

In chapter 1, I indicated that regional differences within particular Buddhist lineages were an especially useful avenue of research. Let us use as an example the Jodo Shinshu tradition of the Buddhist Churches of America, since it is one of the few groups that receive some acknowledgement as having a regional identity. Geographically, the BCA can be largely divided into those temples west of the Rockies and those on the eastern side. Jodo Shinshu temples in California have a large pool of Japanese Americans (and new Japanese immigrants, workers, and students) to draw on. Demographically they are dominated by people of Japanese descent and many temples have a relatively traditional approach to Buddhist practice. This contrasts with Jodo Shinshu temples east of the Rocky Mountains, which have far fewer Japanese and Japanese Americans to work with. This has been a contributing factor to the disappearance of many eastern groups affiliated with the Buddhist Churches of America, such as the Pure Land groups that used to meet in St. Louis and Philadelphia, where the BCA no longer has any presence. The handful of surviving temples east of the Rockies are often those that managed to become much more racially and ethnically mixed than their Western counterparts—significantly, this is also the only area to have produced BCA groups founded on a non-Japanese American membership base (the Northampton Shin Sangha in Massachusetts and the original, prediversification Ekoji Buddhist Sangha of Richmond).

It is not just demographics that differ out East: these groups often display significantly more eclecticism in their practice and organization. It is in these eastern temples that new innovations such as quiet meditation in a Shinshu context (not a traditional practice for this denomination) and lay teachers (now called minister's assistants) have tended to first take root, and it is from the Eastern District that the BCA's first white president was produced, in part because being so far from the centers of power, he was a nonthreatening neutral party who was seen as not beholden to any particular faction. Indeed, so marked are regional variations within the Buddhist Churches of America that they can become a source of tension, with geographically based factions sometimes competing among themselves. Even on the West Coast the BCA's Southern District is sometimes seen as a self-sufficient, at times self-satisfied, enclave that does not need the Bay Area District and could leave the BCA should certain conditions arise, and the periodic election campaigns for BCA bishop often have a regional aspect as candidates draw on their local powerbases for support.

The issue of how the greater Japanese American population on the West Coast influences the Buddhist Churches of America demonstrates that the first three modes of regional interpretation — distribution, local culture, and Buddhist influence on regions — will often be key to intralineal regional analyses. Further evidence of this comes from the American Jodo Shinshu communities that are *not* part of the Japanese American dominated Buddhist Churches of America or the institutionally separate Honpa Hongwanji Mission of Hawaii. Beginning in 2001, white converts to Shin Buddhism began to organize their own groups completely outside the fold of the Buddhist Churches of America. And where did this happen? In West Hartford, Connecticut, a state with a small Japanese American population that has never been missionized by official representatives of Jodo Shinshu Buddhism. The founder of the Buddhist Faith Fellowship of Connecticut (BFFC) discovered Shin Buddhism through reading English-language books on the subject and decided to start a local group. He gathered other Connecticut residents who likewise did not have any access to a local Shin temple. The group they created is highly pluralistic, combining Shin teaching gleaned from books and occasional encounters with Shin communities in other states with practices and ideas taken from Zen, Vipassana, Tibetan, and other forms of Buddhism. This pluralism results from factors we explored in chapter 4, such as pluralistic attitudes, limited resources, low membership, contact with other Buddhist lineages, partial ignorance of more traditional patterns of Shin thought and behavior, and a fluid, open approach to Shin identity that disavows creeds or boundaries, some of which are connected to the fact that Connecticut is — for Shin Buddhism — the far frontier. And this pluralistic eclecticism allows Shin practitioners to promote themselves as something new on the scene (Jodo Shinshu) while incorporating elements of Buddhism already somewhat familiar in the area (such as meditation) so that they do not seem outré. Furthermore, this new lineage seeks to define itself in distinction to the Buddhist Churches of America, which it sees as too traditional and hierarchical (there is a notable anticlerical strain to the BFFC, hardly surprising for a group that exists completely outside the traditional teaching structure of Jodo Shinshu).

Recognizing its potential as a form of Shin Buddhism created by and adapted for non-Japanese Americans who have been ignored by official BCA missionary efforts, the BFFC has created a franchise model that is easily exported to other areas. Significantly, nearly all of the BFFC groups are in locations that have never had any BCA presence, such as Connecticut; Charlotte, North Carolina; Sarasota, Florida; and eastern Alabama. Failure by the Buddhist Churches of America to missionize the non-Japanese American population in general and these various eastern areas specifically has left them wide open for Shin new religious movements to expand into. Measured by membership, the BCA remains the main representative of Jodo Shinshu in the eastern United States—but measured by number of organizations, the Buddhist Faith Fellowship would be considered the primary form of Jodo Shinshu in the East, and with its greater number of sites for growth and its mission-oriented organizational structure, it may eventually come to dominate in membership numbers as well.[8] So American Jodo Shinshu is characterized by notable East-West differences of race, practice, and new institutional development, and even in the West subregional rivalries affect political and other decisions. This is a much richer, more interesting narrative than "Jodo Shinshu in America is a Japanese American Pure Land church, mostly found in California, end of story."

There are many such stories that we should be telling as we seek to understand Buddhism in the United States. Within the community of practitioners itself, it is not uncommon to encounter beliefs about the difference between Insight Meditation (Vipassana) on the East Coast versus the West Coast. Allegedly, East Coast Vipassana practitioners are more formal, rule-oriented, organized, and less expressive, especially in their New England incarnations at the Insight Meditation Society in Massachusetts. West Coast Insight Meditators are supposedly less formal, pay less attention to the precepts, are more heavily influenced by pop psychology, and more emotive, particularly at the Spirit Rock Meditation Center in California. In other words, East Coasters are stuck-up killjoys and West Coasters are self-absorbed hippies.[9] It is intriguing how this in-group narrative seems to mirror general stereotypes about these two regions. Is this story true? We will not know until someone undertakes a more systematic study. But either way, there is a noteworthy regional phenomenon going on here: either this is a case of regional culture actually altering Buddhist practice and experience or a case of regional loyalties influencing Buddhist self-perceptions where no measurable differentiation exists.

Many more examples can be found when we look for them. The central object of worship in the main hall of Shingon temples in the main-land United States is usually Dainichi Nyorai, the Japanese version of the Vairochana Buddha, or occasionally some other celestial buddha or bodhi-sattva. Vairochana is an anthropomorphic representation of the enlightened totality of the universe itself. But in Hawaiian Shingon temples the figure usually found in the main halls is Kobo Daishi, the semilegendary found-ing father of Shingon in Japan. The installation of this human figure is a sig-nificant difference in iconography and practice within the same tradition, based on regional factors that only become apparent when we pay attention to visual and material culture. How did this come about? Large-scale Japa-nese immigration began first in Hawaii. Most of the Japanese immigration to the Hawaiian Islands came from Jodo Shinshu–dominated areas, and it was the Honganji-ha sect of Shin Buddhism that sent missionaries to tend to the emigrant population. Shingon families represented a smaller contin-gent, but without missionaries of their own, they had to settle for attend-ing Jodo Shinshu temples and being part of the Pure Land community, rather than the esoteric Shingon one. Over the decades their memories of Shingon became attenuated, until by the time efforts were made to estab-lish permanent Shingon temples in Hawaii, the primary remaining vestige among these Shinshu-ized Shingonists was devotion to Kobo Daishi, a be-loved wonder-worker who commands loyalty and patronage even when other elements of Shingon have been abandoned. Shingon priests found that the usual worship figure Dainichi had few remaining followers, so they accommodated the lingering attachments to Kobo Daishi by installing him as the main object of worship in their Hawaiian temples, rather than Daini-chi, in an attempt to lure back ancestrally Shingon families who had assimi-lated into the Jodo Shinshu temples. The handful of mainland American temples, on the other hand, can assert their faithfulness to Shingon ortho-doxy by sticking with Dainichi or another more traditional figure, unlike their Shinshu-ized Hawaiian brethren.[10] Thus it is not just that regional-ism develops within the same lineage—regionalism then gives rise to alter-nate, even competing ways of understanding what the lineage should be in the first place. Naturally, these regionally based tensions are a prime factor that can lead eventually to schisms and the development of new Buddhist groups within America. Just as the Cumberland Presbyterian denomina-tion emerged from such regional differences, we may expect Buddhism in America to fissure at times due to regional tensions.

The final form of regional analysis I proposed in chapter 1 was atten-tion to the type of environment that any given Buddhist group exists in.

Shingon temple main altar with statue of Kobo Daishi in Hawaii.

Congressman Hank Johnson, mentioned above, is a member of SGI-USA, an organization that is famously multiracial. But all studies of racial composition within SGI-USA (such as David Chappell's essay in *Engaged Buddhism in the West*) have been conducted in major metropolises.[11] Does this racial integration hold true in smaller cities, in suburbs, and in rural areas? Even among major metropolitan areas one finds clear disparities in level of integration. Why is this, and do these constitute distinct regions within SGI-USA? For example, in San Francisco, often touted as one of the most progressive and accepting cities in America, SGI leadership is noticeably whiter than in cities such as Atlanta or Chicago. Maybe San Francisco is not as progressive as we thought? Does the high proportion of Japanese leadership in San Francisco inhibit African American leadership? Does the extreme availability of other alternative religious groups for African Americans keep their proportion in SGI San Francisco relatively low? Or is something else entirely going on? And if San Francisco is not representative of SGI-USA patterns generally, what other patterns in American Buddhism does it buck?

My case study has explored Buddhism in a modestly sized city. One area that needs far greater attention is American rural Buddhism. It may be that Thai Buddhism in Raleigh, North Carolina, has more in common with Chinese Buddhism in Honolulu, Hawaii, than it does with Thai Buddhism in Bolivia, North Carolina. Retreat centers in particular are often located in relatively rural locations, where they serve as escape destinations for urban and suburban Buddhists intent on getting away from the bustle and stress of their home and work spaces. As such, many rural Buddhist locations may operate on a more punctuated schedule than other American Buddhist places, alternating between relatively fallow periods, with few practitioners on site and little in the way of activities, and periods of sudden numerical and activity increase around national holidays or dates of significance to Buddhists in particular, such as the early December rohatsu sesshin retreat observed by many Zen Buddhists in America.[12]

We also need to pay attention to the built environment of Buddhist groups in Asia compared to the types of places they inhabit in America. If a Buddhist demographic or lineage was primarily rural in Asia and now exists mainly in urban spaces in the United States, what specific tensions or adaptations emerge? What practices have had to be abandoned, and what new activities have arisen to take their place? This applies to missionary figures as well. Is it significant, for instance, that Shunryu Suzuki, who ended up teaching Buddhism to urban Westerners in San Francisco, came from a

small village outside Yokohama? Would he have been as insistent on establishing the remote Tassajara Zen Center in Los Padres National Forest if he
had spent his childhood in bustling central Tokyo?

Regionalism in the Old Country can lead to differences, problems, or
schism in the New World. Regionalism can be temporary but have significant impact. Many Jodo Shinshu temples in Hawaii and North America
were organized in part around Japanese prefectural societies, and it is in
these groups that the ties of actual leadership were often created (and
people excluded from them lacked access to key networks). This pattern
repeated in a new way after World War II, with internment camp reunion
societies becoming important sources of support for the internal refugees
of the BCA, as well as sites for exclusive politicking and cliquishness. Japanese Americans from other camps typically could not join; non-Japanese
Americans definitely could never join. The patterns established within these
groups sometimes affected elections for bishop and president, appoint-
ments for treasurer and various positions, acceptance or rejection of specific ministers at local temples, and so on, for better and often for worse. Yet
these regional influences were also transient—today prefectural societies
and internment camp groups are much less important. Another example is
the presence of two separate Vietnamese American temples in Richmond.
They resulted from a schism over leadership styles, which appears to be
rooted partially in expectations based on the different areas in Vietnam
that various temple-members hailed from. Regionalism as an interpretative trope should be applied not only to current American phenomena but
also to their Asian antecedents as we seek to understand the transnational
element of local American Buddhisms.

Regions in Time

Regionalism is not simply about geography. It is also about time. The same
physical location may be part of various regions at different places along
its timeline, and the properties of any region or regions will almost certainly change over time. For example, from the European Christian colonial
perspective, southern New England was once the wild, untamed frontier.
Later, it was the stronghold of a town-based Puritan nation. Later still, it
was the land of urban Catholic dominance. Today it is, in part, a region of
strong public secularism. The geography remained the same, but (at least)
four different chronologically related regions can be discerned. This observation must be applied to Buddhist regions in the United States (and else-

where). The regions I laid out in chapter 1 are speculations for how to divide up the United States in 2012. Moving backward in time, some of these regions may exist in identifiable fashion, but others will disappear while ones not currently observed will emerge. Likewise, moving forward in time, the regions identified here will change some of their properties, borders will shift, and new regions will come into being while others cease to be definable entities. Buddhism's core observations that all things change and nothing has a permanent identity must be applied vigorously to the study of American Buddhist regionalism.

Because regions can be defined chronologically as well as geographically, we might apply a mode of analysis that identifies "chronological regions." This would mean treating regions as stages, rather than areas. For purposes of initial illustration, we could say that Buddhism in any given place potentially goes through five stages. The first is absence, when there is little or no Buddhism of any type to be found. From the Buddhist point of view, America in the year 1776 was basically one big region, a region of Buddhist absence. During this stage Buddhism is simply not a part of the larger social conversation.

The second stage is initial encounter, when the first notable numbers of Buddhists begin to move into an area or Buddhist elements tentatively begin to circulate in the wider culture. Initial encounter happens at very different times in different locations. Initial encounter occurred, approximately, for San Francisco in the 1840s, for the mountain West in the 1880s, for the Richmond area in the 1980s, and so on. The nature of the initial encounter matters as well in shaping chronological regions. Through whom or what did the encounter occur? An Asian immigrant group? Non-Asian new practitioners? Aspects of Buddhism floating in the pop culture? Mindfulness-Based Stress Reduction? Different chronological regions may be charted according to whether they first encountered Buddhists in the flesh or via intellectual ideas spread through print or other media. At this stage, Buddhism in the United States is still so novel and small that it is probably overlooked by most people and is treated as a curiosity by most of those who interact with it.

The third stage might be early growth. Here the number of Buddhists in an area has increased, or Buddhist practices, aesthetics, or ideas have gained a foothold in parts of the local culture. The first public Buddhist institutions begin to appear, such as a region's first temple or first meditation group that meets somewhere other than in a member's home. More visible on the landscape and still seen as foreign, Buddhism is likely to encounter greater opposition from non-Buddhists at this stage. The first systematic efforts to contain or eliminate Buddhism begin, such as racial restriction laws, unfair use of zoning codes, angry letters to the editor, or even violence against Buddhists or Buddhist institutions. Many Buddhists will react in ways that attempt to accommodate the outside pressure or demonstrate their compatibility with the region (such efforts have often been interpreted as "Americanization") while also beginning to develop a more coherent identity of themselves as *Buddhists* and to claim a right to live out such an identity. Ekoji clearly experienced these patterns in the 1990s, when the size of the temple membership increased and the city attempted to take over the temple.

The fourth stage would be inhabitation. No longer a novelty in whatever particular region is under study, Buddhists are now well-integrated into the community at large, and many non-Buddhists have been exposed to a degree of Buddhism, with some of them selectively appropriating the aspects that appeal to them as individuals. Conflict is not gone and serious confrontations may occasionally occur, but opposition becomes more muted as both insiders and outsiders reach an overall sense that the Buddhists have a claim to the area. With the pressure lower, Buddhist solidarity begins to break down and schisms may occur, resulting in new groups forming in the area. Richmond may be approaching this stage, but it seems too early to make a firm declaration on this point. More likely, Richmond is still in the stage of early Buddhist growth.

The fifth stage is diversification. Although still a minority, Buddhists have become a natural part of the landscape. Multiple types of Buddhist groups have appeared, producing a more complex local Buddhist ecology that serves various demographics. Liberal non-Buddhist religious groups in the area may have taken on aspects of Buddhism, such as meditation or beliefs about interconnectedness, and Buddhist statuary, books, meditation techniques, and so on can be found in non-Buddhist bookstores, gardening stores, health food shops, counseling practices, hospitals, and so on. This is clearly the situation in some of the nation's large urban areas, such as San Francisco, Los Angeles, Chicago, and New York City.

The same caveats that are applied to geographical regions must be applied to chronological ones as well. No two places will necessarily go through exactly the same process. The description here implies a linear progression, but an area may move forward or backward along the scale over time and display other possible stages instead. Events unconnected to Buddhism per se, such as the terrorist attacks of 9/11, will impact Buddhist regions at various stages in different ways. And microstages will be found to exist on further investigation: a region may overall be at the diversification stage, but in one particular neighborhood Buddhist encroachment may be entirely new and experiencing vigorous resistance. Buddhism may arrive in another area for the very first time, but due to particular aspects of that place at that time, it may experience immediate approval. Pluralistic cooperation among Buddhists in one area may be a survival strategy because they are at the stage of initial encounter or growth, while in another place it may be part of the diversification of Buddhism as a self-consciously ecumenical Buddhism arises among certain local Buddhists. Thus the same phenomenon (pluralism, for instance) may exist for different reasons related to regionalism (and other factors), and therefore if probed more deeply nuances between the manifestation of the phenomenon in different areas are likely to emerge.

Analyzing both American Buddhist pluralism and regions results in the creation of ideal types, which can hide as well as reveal. The interpretations offered here are not meant imperialistically but as creative ways to think about Buddhist and southern diversity. Researchers would do well to remember the logic of the Mahayana Diamond Sutra: Acknowledging that in reality things are not really things, we can then safely call them things in a provisional manner. Without language, labels, and words, conversation and exploration are impossible. With too much attachment to labels and concepts, reality is obscured. This is particularly important to note at the margins, because at the borders all categories begin to blend and break down, and because definitions arise out of context. The point of looking for regions in place or time is not to pigeonhole the Buddhist or the southern experience but to offer tools with which to analyze major trends and sniff out interesting or significant exceptions and countertrends. It is my hope, therefore, that future research will keep place in mind.

Appendix

Statistical Data and Questionnaire

To augment my observations at the temple, I distributed a questionnaire at the temple several times in 2004 and mailed copies to people on the membership list. Ekoji had fifty-three official members in 2004, of whom forty-nine returned the questionnaire— a response rate of 92.5 percent. Note that the Richmond Meditative Inquiry Group had not yet formed, so it is not represented in the questions or answers (although several of its core members are included here with the groups they were attending at the time, primarily the Zen and Pure Land groups at Ekoji). Much of the data was simply used to help me to get a better understanding of who the members of Ekoji were, how they arrived at the temple, and what practices they were involved in. But some of the data is directly relevant to this study and has been included—for example, the statistics provided in chapter 3. Of additional interest at this multidenominational temple are the dynamics of who attends which groups and how often. Therefore, I reproduce those results in six tables below, followed by the full text of the questionnaire that was distributed.

Table A1. Ekoji Groups That Members Have Visited

Ekoji Pure Land Group (%)	Richmond Zen Group (%)	Kagyu Shenpen Tharchin (%)	Ekoji Vipassana Group (%)
40.8	83.7	32.7	55.1

Note: Because people may visit more than one group, the sum of these percentages does not equal 100 percent.

Table A2. Ekoji Groups That Members Regularly Attend

Ekoji Pure Land Group (%)	Richmond Zen Group (%)	Kagyu Shenpen Tharchin (%)	Ekoji Vipassana Group (%)
22.5	46.9	8.2	36.7

Note: Because people may attend more than one group, the sum of these percentages does not equal 100 percent.

Table A3. Number of Ekoji Groups That Members Have Visited

Visited Only One Group (%)	Visited Two Groups (%)	Visited Three Groups (%)	Visited All Four Groups (%)
44.9	22.5	6.1	26.5

Note: Among respondents, 55.1 percent have visited more than one group.

Table A4. Number of Ekoji Groups That Members Regularly Attend

Attend Only One Group (%)	Attend Two Groups (%)	Attend Three Groups (%)	Attend All Four Groups (%)
69.4	16.3	4.1	0

Note: Because people may not attend any group regularly, the sum of these percentages does not equal 100 percent. Among respondents, 20.4 percent regularly attend more than one group. My questionnaire did not measure the additional number who *irregularly* attend a second, third, or fourth group.

Table A5. Number of Ekoji Members Who Have Attended Temple-wide Events

Dharma Movie Night (%)	Buddha's Birthday (%)	Buddha's Enlightment Day (%)
49	59.2	38.8

Note: Among respondents, 77.6 percent have attended at least one temple-wide event.

Table A6. Sectarian Identities of Members

Pure Land Buddhist (%)	Zen Buddhist (%)	Tibetan Buddhist (%)	Theravada/ Vipassana Buddhist (%)	Non-Sectarian Buddhist (%)	Other Buddhist (%)	Non-Buddhist (%)
20.4	40.8	12.2	30.6	12.2	2	10.2

Note: Because people may claim more than one sectarian affiliation, the sum of these percentages does not equal 100 percent. Theravada and Vipassana were separated on the questionnaire in an attempt to discern whether people conceived of these as separate entities. However, in follow-up interviews several people indicated that they checked off one and then proceeded to the next question but would have checked off both had they thought to continue examining the possible answers. Therefore some responses that only checked off one of these two were actually artifacts of the questionnaire and not reflective of the respondent's actual views. For this reason, the results of these two categories have been merged in this table. Among respondents, 18.4 percent claimed two or more sectarian affiliations.

Questionnaire

Hello, my name is Jeff Wilson, and I am a graduate student at UNC Chapel Hill. My area of study is Buddhism in America. I am doing a study of Ekoji Buddhist Temple in Richmond. Please take a few moments to fill out this questionnaire. All answers will be kept confidential. Your name and other contact information will not be published or revealed to anyone without your permission. Please feel free to use the back of the paper if you wish to make any additional comments. I can be contacted for further comments or concerns at: [address, phone, and email removed for publication]. Thank you very much for your help.

Name: Age: Gender: Ethnicity:

Address:

Phone: Email:

Today's date:

1) Have you ever attended any of these groups at Ekoji? Circle all that apply:
   a) Zen group b) Pure Land group c) Vipassana group d) Tibetan group
   e) Buddhist Peace Fellowship f) Vietnamese Buddhist group
   g) other _____

2) Do you attend any of these groups at Ekoji regularly? Circle all that apply:
   a) Zen group b) Pure Land group c) Vipassana group d) Tibetan group
   e) Buddhist Peace Fellowship f) other _____

3) When did you first visit Ekoji?

4) How did you hear about Ekoji?
   a) friend b) website c) newspaper d) walked by e) phonebook
   f) other _____

5) Do you consider yourself a Buddhist?   Yes No
   If yes, what is your sectarian identification? Circle all that apply:
   a) Zen b) Pure Land c) Vipassana d) Tibetan
   e) Theravada f) nonsectarian g) other _____

6) What is your religious background?
   a) Buddhist b) Protestant c) Catholic d) Jewish e) none
   f) other _____

7) Do you practice/follow any other religions besides Buddhism?   Yes No
   If yes, what are they? _____

8) Are you an official member of Ekoji?   Yes No

9) Have you attended any other Buddhist groups besides those at Ekoji?   Yes No
   If yes, which ones? _____

10) Have you attended any Ekoji special events? Circle all that apply:
    a) Movie night b) Buddha's Birthday c) Retreat
    d) Buddha's Enlightenment Day e) other _____

11) Have you attended the Ekoji prison ministry group?   Yes No

12) Do you practice Buddhism at home?   Yes No

13) What practices do you perform regularly? Circle all that apply:
    a) meditation b) chanting c) study d) precepts e) charity
    f) other _____

14) How did you get interested in Buddhism?

15) Are any of your family members Buddhist?   Yes No

16) What do you like best about Buddhism?

17) Would you be willing to have a longer conversation with the researcher (Jeff Wilson) about your activities at Ekoji?   Yes No

Notes

Introduction

1. The Prajnaparamita ("Perfection of wisdom") texts—of which the Heart Sutra (Mahaprajnaparamita-hridaya-sutra) is the shortest—are a large body of important Mahayana Buddhist scriptures. The Heart Sutra is included as an important liturgical component in many Mahayana lineages. Sutras (literally "threads") are canonical scriptures considered by Buddhists to record the utterances of enlightened beings. I have chosen to omit diacritical marks in this study: they are never employed by my consultants, few of whom pronounce non-English Buddhist terms in ways that faithfully mimic their Asian pronunciations. Diacritics would therefore misrepresent the actual oral and written practices of Ekoji.

2. Amitabha Buddha ("Infinite Light Buddha") is the central savior figure of Pure Land Buddhism. See chapters 2 and 3 for discussions of this branch of Buddhism. Nianfo ("Buddha-remembrance") is the practice of chanting the name of Amitabha Buddha, specifically in Chinese as "Namo Omitofo." In Japanese it is known as nembutsu, and Amitabha is called Amida.

3. Mara (literally "Murder") is the Buddhist archetype of evil and deluded attachment. According to legend, he attacked and tempted the future Buddha in an attempt to thwart his enlightenment.

4. A zafu (Japanese for "sitting cushion") is a round pillow stuffed with kapok, designed for seated meditation. In American Buddhist settings zafus are most often employed in Zen temples and meditation centers.

5. A zabuton (Japanese for "sitting mat") is a rectangular mat on which a zafu is typically placed.

6. Originally a term for the monastic community, in the American context *sangha* can also denote a Buddhist congregation.

7. Peter Williams, "How to Read a Church," 42–62.

8. Tyson, Peacock, and Patterson, *Diversities of Gifts*, 5.

9. Numrich, *Old Wisdom in the New World*.

10. Peter Williams, "How to Read a Church," 42–62.

11. Tweed, *Retelling U.S. Religious History*, 93.

12. Mahayana ("Great Vehicle") is one of the major branches of Buddhism. It first appears in sources from the first century BCE. There are many theories as to its origins; generally, Mahayana Buddhism can be characterized by a larger pantheon of enlightened beings compared to early sects, many additional scriptures (such as the Prajnaparamita texts), and adherence in some form to the bodhisattva ideal. Mahayana is usually contrasted with Theravada Buddhism, from which Vipassana derives. Shakya-

muni Buddha ("Sage of the Shakya people") is a common Mahayana name for the historical Buddha.

13. For instance, see Fields, "Divided Dharma," 183–95.

14. In general, the members at the temple expressed positive opinions about nearly every form of Buddhism and were eager to learn more about traditions other than their own. There were only two exceptions that occasionally violated this rule. At times, I heard some members disparage two Buddhist movements: the Soka Gakkai (which has a chapter in Richmond) and the New Kadampa Tradition. However, they were attacked specifically for being *sectarian*—that is to say, the reason these groups were characterized as "bad Buddhists" was that they themselves were perceived as prejudiced toward other forms of Buddhism and therefore as introducing dangerously exclusivist attitudes into Buddhism. This opposition seems to be mainly in the abstract: when some Soka Gakkai Buddhists paid a visit to the temple, they were warmly received.

15. Patricia Williams interview, March 4, 2011.

16. Hutchison, *Religious Pluralism in America*, 1. My understanding of pluralism as a religious ideology is informed by Hutchison's work. However, Hutchison himself appears to have promoted pluralism as a value, both within the academy and for society at large. My book does not take sides in the debate: pluralism here is observed as a fact of the community under study, not as an ideology to be either supported or decried.

17. Personality disputes, naturally enough, do occur at Ekoji—after all, the goal of eliminating ego-attachment is a Buddhist ideal, not an everyday reality. Some of these can be quite heated, and when there is reason to think that they relate in some way to the intergroup negotiations at Ekoji, my specific area of concern, I refer to them in the text. Those that seem to be purely between incompatible personalities I do not. That person A thinks person B is a jerk is good gossip but poor data.

18. Tweed, "Expanding the Study of U.S. Religion," 1–9.

19. Mathews, *Religion in the Old South*, xiii.

Chapter One

1. Mather, *Magnalia Christi Americana*.

2. Baird, *Religion in America*.

3. Turner, *The Frontier in American History*.

4. See, for example, Lippy, *Introducing American Religion*.

5. Numrich, *Old Wisdom in the New World*.

6. Mullen, *The American Occupation of Tibetan Buddhism*.

7. Cadge, *Heartwood*; Suh, *Being Buddhist in a Christian World*.

8. Carolyn Chen, *Getting Saved in America*.

9. Coleman, *The New Buddhism*.

10. Layman, *Buddhism in America*; Prebish, *American Buddhism*.

11. Prebish, *Luminous Passage*; Seager, *Buddhism in America*.

12. Prebish and Tanaka, *The Faces of Buddhism in America*; Williams and Queen, *American Buddhism*; Queen, *Engaged Buddhism in the West*; Prebish and Baumann, *Westward Dharma*; Numrich, *North American Buddhists in Social Context*.

13. Maffly-Kipp, "Eastward Ho!," 127–48.

14. Gaustad and Barlow, *A New Historical Atlas of Religion in America*, 262–67 (this is a new version of Gaustad's important earlier work, *Historical Atlas of Religion in America* [1962]); Carroll, *The Routledge Historical Atlas of Religion in America*.

15. Carroll also includes a map of Zen groups in the United States, though he does not indicate where his figures come from. Carroll's map of the BCA, while a laudable effort, also includes a number of errors, indicating the problems that arise when non-specialists are the only scholars attempting to work on regionalism in American Buddhism; Carroll, *The Routledge Historical Atlas of Religion in America*. Gaustad and Barlow use a catchall category, "Zen and Meditational Buddhism"; Gaustad and Barlow, *A New Historical Atlas of Religion in America*.

16. Significantly, Tweed has not published a major work on Buddhism in the South or carried out long-term ethnographic research there, though he has briefly raised the issue in some shorter works, including his introduction to a booklet he coauthored with the Buddhism in North Carolina Project, *Buddhism and Barbecue: A Guide to Buddhist Temples in North Carolina*; his essay "Our Lady of Guadeloupe Visits the Confederate Memorial"; and his less-than-one-page entry on "Buddhism" in the *Encyclopedia of Religion in the South*.

17. There have been a few, isolated works on Buddhism based on research conducted in the South, but none takes the fact of its subject's presence in *the South* as a dedicated object of focus. These works are concerned instead with their sites as generic transnational American Buddhist communities, rather than as *southern* American Buddhist communities. This trend holds true for studies in other regions as well. Examples of studies conducted in the South, but without attention to the specifically southern environment, include Lau, "The Temple Provides the Way"; Noel Yuan Lin, "Finding the Buddha in the West"; and Padgett, "The Translating Temple."

18. To be clear, this monk's support for conservative political figures and American military action is not necessarily *solely* a manifestation of regionalism. Many Cambodian refugees fled the murderous reign of the radical left-wing Khmer Rouge and thus often espouse anti-Communist or conservative social and religious agendas. Furthermore, any given Buddhist may of course hold virtually any political opinion imaginable. What I am suggesting is that regionalism is at least potentially *part* of the package, and that we should investigate these leads to determine regionalism's possible role in a way that we have thus far failed to do.

19. Zelinsky, "An Approach to the Religious Geography of the United States."

20. Carroll, *The Routledge Historical Atlas of Religion in America*, 131.

21. Gastil, *Cultural Regions of the United States*.

22. Garreau, *The Nine Nations of North America*.

23. Shortridge, "Patterns of Religion in the United States"; Shortridge, "A New Regionalization of American Religion."

24. Walsh and Silk, *Religion and Public Life in New England*; Balmer and Silk, *Religion and Public Life in the Middle Atlantic Region*; Barlow and Silk, *Religion and Public Life in the Midwest*; Shipps and Silk, *Religion and Public Life in the Mountain West*; Killen and Silk, *Religion and Public Life in the Pacific Northwest*; Roof and Silk, *Religion and Public Life in the Pacific Region*; Wilson and Silk, *Religion and Public Life in the South*; Lindsey

and Silk, *Religion and Public Life in the Southern Crossroads*; Silk and Walsh, *One Nation, Divisible*.

25. Fields, *How the Swans Came to the Lake*.

26. Carolyn Chen, *Getting Saved in America*.

27. Observations based on my own collection of data over more than twelve years of regional research into American Buddhism. For a partial, but still quite helpful, snapshot of the American Buddhist landscape and its various denominational concentrations, researchers may wish to consult the listings at DharmaNet International's InfoWeb page for the United States: http://www.dharmanet.org/listings/centres/country/United_States.

28. Notably, the East Coast houses the sect's peace pagodas in Leverett, Massachusetts, and Petersburg, New York, and the one under construction in eastern Tennessee, as well as the highly active Nipponzan Myohoji Atlanta Dojo and the Washington, DC, temple. The Southeast is also where Nipponzan Myohoji pilgrimage walks most regularly take place.

29. There are six Nichiren Shoshu temples in America, located in Kaneohe, Hawaii; San Francisco; Los Angeles; Chicago; New York City; and Washington, DC.

30. Prebish, "Varying the Vinaya," 65.

31. Shambhala Mountain Center, "The Great Stupa of Dharmakaya," http://www.shambhalamountain.org/stupa.html.

32. *Buddhist Churches of America: 75-Year History*, 57.

33. Siegel and Johnston, *Blue Collar and Buddha*.

34. Nakagaki, *Practice of Ahimsa in Buddhism*.

35. These comments come from my observations at San Francisco Zen Center and the Richmond Zen Group, as well as thoughts provoked by observations at Chapel Hill Zen Center and other local groups in the Suzuki lineage visited in various parts of the country. A further possibility that has occurred to me is that teachers from this lineage who do live in the far-flung regions away from the Bay Area may tend to exhibit relatively more diverse personal styles, since they are geographically distanced from the critical surveillance of their fellow lineage holders. However, I have not actively investigated this possibility and so include it here only as a potential direction for future research.

36. Community of Mindful Living, "Directory of Sanghas Practicing in the Plum Village Lineage," http://www.iamhome.org/USA_sangha.pdf. Observations about where and how members tend to encounter Thich Nhat Hanh's lineage come from discussions with practitioners over many years at different Community of Mindful Living groups, both urban and suburban and in various parts of the country.

37. Kingsbury, *Buddhism in Bellingham*, 59; emphasis added.

38. Killen and Silk, *Religion and Public Life in the Pacific Northwest*, 28. Note that the figures are not derived in exactly the same way: those for religious institutional membership contrast Oregon, Washington, and Alaska with the nation, while those for religious identity contrast only Oregon and Washington with the country as a whole.

39. In particular, see ibid., 155–64.

40. Morita, "Daimoku and the Sacred Pipe."

41. See the listings at DharmaNet International's InfoWeb http://www.dharmanet

.org/listings/centres/country/United_States; this information was supplemented with further online research at various websites for groups and temples in this region.

42. The website for the Buddhist Council of the Midwest is http://www.buddhist councilmidwest.org/.

43. Layman, *Buddhism in America*, 111–14. Shugendo is a form of syncretic tantric Japanese Buddhism based on mountain asceticism. At times it has been banned in Japan, and it is extremely rare outside of Japan.

44. A map of groups affiliated with the San Francisco Zen Center can be found at http://www.sfzc.org.

Chapter Two

1. Prothero, *The White Buddhist*.

2. He was born Takashi Tsuji. Kenryu is his Buddhist ordination name. In his early ministerial career Tsuji usually went by "Takashi Tsuji," or occasionally "Takashi Kenryu Tsuji." As he aged, however, he began to use his ordination name more frequently, calling himself "Kenryu Takashi Tsuji," and eventually simply "Kenryu T. Tsuji."

3. One publication that was released while this book was in production that includes some discussion of modern Shin priests in America is Ama, *Immigrants to the Pure Land*. Ama also notes some regional differences in the histories of Shin Buddhism in Hawaii and the continental United States.

4. Tsuji, *The Heart of the Buddha-Dharma*.

5. Layman, *Buddhism in America*.

6. "A Gift of Light: Ekoji." Tsuji also started Jodo Shinshu temples in three Canadian cities (Toronto, Hamilton, and Montreal), as well as mentoring Buddhist groups in five other southern locations (in Morganton, North Carolina; Augusta and Atlanta, Georgia; Florida; and Dallas, Texas). Besides the Northern Virginia Ekoji and the Richmond Ekoji, he also traveled to Seabrook Buddhist Temple in New Jersey to lead services. See Tsuji, *The Heart of the Buddha-Dharma*.

7. The Society of Friends is better known to the general public as the Quakers. Generally liberal in their approach to religion, Quakers in the "unprogrammed" tradition include meditative silence as a staple practice of many gatherings; not surprisingly, there seems to be some notable overlap in membership between Quaker and Buddhist congregations in the United States—in Richmond this can be observed in the hosting by the Richmond Friends Meetinghouse of several fledgling Buddhist groups at different times and in the participation of some Ekoji members in Richmond Friends religious services.

8. U.S. Department of Housing and Urban Development, *Settlement Statement*, June 3, 1985. Like Tsuji, Yehan Numata was a committed missionary for Buddhism, especially but not solely Jodo Shinshu Buddhism. The name Ekoji came from Numata, who helped found numerous Ekoji temples on at least three continents. Numata's endowments continue to fund numerous Buddhist organizations, such as Bukkyo Dendo Kyokai and the Numata Center, which provide substantial support for Buddhist activities in America and around the world. See "Introducing Mr. Numata," in Ekoji Buddhist Sangha of Richmond, *Dedication of the Temple*.

9. Yamaoka, letter to Joseph Tuttle.

10. Ekoji Buddhist Sangha of Richmond, *Dedication of the Temple.*

11. Ueba, letter to Tuttle.

12. Ibid.

13. Boyd interview, August 16, 2003; Suderman, letter to Ekoji Buddhist Sangha of Richmond.

14. Li Chen interview, January 11, 2003.

15. Galloway, "Dana and Ekoji Buddhist Sangha of Richmond . . . Revisited." *Yana,* as in *Mahayana,* means "vehicle." The words *zen* and *mahayana* are lowercased in Andrews's account. This version somewhat compresses events: in an interview in 2008, Galloway told me he actually attended a number of times before he told Tsuji about his Zen interest and received the key.

16. Ford interview, March 7, 2004.

17. Ford, "Ekoji Zen Group Formed."

18. Brown interview, August 19, 2003.

19. *Dharma Wheel,* issues from September 1994 to September–October 2002.

20. Brown, "Two New Groups at Ekoji." It is interesting to note that the Richmond Buddhist Association moved to its own temple, named Chua Hue Quang: "Temple of the Gift of Light." "Chua Hue Quang" is the Vietnamese pronunciation of the characters for Ekoji. When I made visits to Chua Hue Quang temple close to a decade later, members repeatedly expressed to me their gratitude to Tsuji and Ekoji Buddhist Sangha.

21. Ibid.

22. Grant interview, March 4, 2004.

23. Li Chen interview, January 24, 2004.

24. Tollifson, "Foreword," xi–xii.

25. Nguyen interview, June 12, 2003; Wolfson interview, October 20, 2003; field notes from visit to Buddhist Peace Fellowship on June 7, 2003.

26. Official City of Richmond, Virginia, website: http://www.richmondgov.com. In the Property Search engine, 3411 Grove Avenue is Map Reference Number W000 1599014 (http://eservices.ci.richmond.va.us/applications/propertysearch/). Neighborhoods are not always sharply defined in Richmond. This area can be considered part of either the Museum District or the Fan District, depending on the preferences of the speaker. The city officially designates 3411 Grove Avenue as part of the Museum District.

27. Silver, "The Changing Face of Neighborhoods in Memphis and Richmond." We should note that the overall whiteness of this part of Richmond, far from being accidental, is part of a larger racial strategy enacted by white Richmonders to funnel African Americans into other parts of the city while excluding them from this district.

28. Moeser and Silver, "Race, Social Stratification, and Politics."

29. U.S. Department of Housing and Urban Development, *Settlement Statement.*

30. McNeill interview, March 15, 2011.

31. Nakane, *Kyoto Gardens.*

32. For a time the temple also flew a string of small, colorful Tibetan prayer flags painted with mantras and images of protector deities. But Richmond experiences four

distinct seasons each year that bring rain, heat, wind, and snow, and the rapidly tattering prayer flags were deemed an eyesore. The Vietnamese group hung a large sign on the front of the building, but it was removed when they left.

33. This statue is more than two hundred years old. Damaged over the years by fire and incense smoke, the Buddha's body is now completely black, while his robes remain golden. The statue was donated by Shofukuji Temple near Kyoto, Japan. The "boat-shaped" nimbus, painted gold, was carved by Joseph Tuttle [pseudonym], one of Ekoji's earliest and most important members (he quit shortly after the temple's dedication, having been a principal force in bringing about that dedication). See Ekoji Buddhist Sangha of Richmond, "Immediate Release."

34. According to legend, when Mara made his final assault on the Buddha, the Buddha touched the earth, calling it to witness that he was worthy of enlightenment. Buddhist hand gestures usually have some encoded meaning—for instance, the right hand of Ekoji's Amitabha statue is raised in the gesture of welcoming, while the other is lowered in the gesture of bestowing teachings and blessings.

35. This is a typical arrangement for a Japanese altar, particularly a Jodo Shinshu one.

36. Seager, *Buddhism in America*.

37. Strauss interview, March 6, 2004; Noble interview, February 29, 2004.

38. Jeff Wilson, "Deeply Female and Universally Human." Guanyin is a frequent presence at Theravadin temples in Thailand these days as well, especially in areas influenced by Chinese Thai populations.

39. Peter Williams, "How to Read a Church."

40. Museum District Association, *The Columns* (Spring 2002).

41. Ekoji occasionally holds events at the synagogue when there is a need for a larger venue. Brown and Brown interview, February 22, 2004.

42. This figure is Budai, a Chinese monk identified in legend as an incarnation of the future Buddha, Maitreya.

43. Boyd interview, April 5, 2003.

44. Ibid.

45. Ibid.

46. The drinking of tea relates in some ways to the need for converts to imagine and enact Buddhist identity, a subject I discuss in the conclusion. Tea-drinking, an activity associated with "the Orient" in the Western imagination, follows most Ekoji services. Participants do not partake of other possible choices, such as coffee, soda, and so on. The origins of this activity do not lie entirely within the Western imagination, however: participants in the Pure Land services drank tea under Tsuji's supervision during his tenure.

47. Morreale, *The Complete Guide to Buddhist America*.

48. Boyd interview, January 12, 2003. Some lineages do take pains to demarcate their temple or monastery as a sacred, set-aside space of religious power. For discussion of the laying of sima stones and planting of bodhi trees at American Theravadin temples, see Numrich, *Old Wisdom in the New World*, 3, 16.

49. See Ekoji Buddhist Sangha of Richmond, *Dedication of the Temple*.

50. At the time of the attack on Pearl Harbor, the Canadian temples belonged to a national organization known as the Buddhist Churches of Canada (BCC). The BCC

had only been in existence for eight years at this point, having come into being during the summer of 1933. In December 1941 the previous director (*kantoku*) of the BCC, Zenyu Aoki, had just departed for Hawaii, and the director-designate, Ryuichi Hirahana, had not yet been able to step into the position officially. Before he could do so, Hirahana was interned along with four other ministers (Sukan Asaka, Dozan Katatsu, Renshin Tachibana, and Eon Mitsubayashi; Shinjo Ikuta and Yutetsu Kawamura went to Alberta to minister to the Japanese Canadians there). The BCC ceased to exist when the West Coast Japanese Canadian population was moved en masse into concentration camps far to the east. All of this left a vacuum of leadership, into which Tsuji was thrust because he was the only English-speaking minister and thus the vital link between the government and the mass of Buddhist internees. It should be noted, however, that Tsuji never held an official leadership position during this time period (indeed, there was no longer any official organization in which to hold leadership). Tsuji's leadership during this period must be seen as exceptionally unusual in context — as the youngest and newest minister, by normal BCC standards he should have been the most junior, taking instructions from and showing deference to the other ministers, rather than serving the publicly prominent role that he did.

51. "Bishop Tsuji Looking Forward to 100th Anniversary," San Francisco *Hokubei Mainichi*, 1.

52. Remarks by Tsuji at the BCA Minister's Conference, Oakland, CA, August 28, 1973, recorded in Kashima, *Buddhism in America*, 209.

53. Tsuji, "For Buddhism — A National Purpose," 11. Nembutsu is the recitation of "Namu Amida Butsu," which can be translated as "I take refuge in Amida Buddha." It is the central practice of Shin Buddhism.

54. Hatch, *The Democratization of American Christianity*, is a particularly salient source for understanding how such an authoritarian structure as the Methodist episcopacy was able to sustain a deeply lay-oriented, mission-fueled movement.

55. This list includes all five current Ekoji groups, the Chua Hue Quang temple, a second Vietnamese temple that split from Hue Quang, and the UU Buddhist meditation group at the First Unitarian Church of Richmond. Each of these groups exists only because of the space for Buddhist activities established by Tsuji in the mid-1980s.

56. "Canadian Minister Speaks Before Local Bussei," 1.

57. Tsuji, "Path of Freedom," 6.

58. Tsuji, "The Life to Come," 2.

59. Tsuji, "The True 'I,'" 10.

60. Tsuji, *An Outline of Buddhism*, 25.

61. Ibid., 28, 36.

62. Ibid., 38.

63. Tsuji, "Reincarnation: My Answer."

64. Tsuji, "For Buddhism — A National Purpose," 11.

65. Tsuji, *Three Lectures on the Tannisho*, 2.

66. Ibid., 2.

67. Ibid., 23.

68. Tsuji, *Gassho*, 3.

69. Tsuji, *The Heart of the Buddha-Dharma*, 42.

70. Tsuji, "The Essential Points of Jodo Shinshu." This document, which can be found in the archives at Ekoji Buddhist Sangha of Richmond, is apparently the text of a sermon, most likely delivered at Ekoji Buddhist Temple in Springfield, Virginia. It appears to have been produced in the 1980s.

71. Tsuji, *The Heart of the Buddha-Dharma*, 51.

72. Tsuji, *A Challenge for American Shin Buddhists*, 1.

73. Ibid., 2.

74. Ibid., 2.

75. Ibid., 8. All of these forms of Buddhism are quite different from Jodo Shinshu. Tsuji is essentially offering the equivalent of saying that, say, Roman Catholics need to learn from Quakers, Pentecostals, Mormons, and evangelical Baptists.

76. Tsuji, "Gassho to Amida," 120. *Gassho* is the Japanese word for the respectful or prayerful gesture of placing ones hands together and bowing.

77. Tsuji, *The Heart of the Buddha-Dharma*, 61.

78. Ibid., 75.

79. Ibid., 11.

80. Ibid., 72.

81. Ibid., 23–24.

82. The Zen in this case is sometimes stretched to include Chan Buddhism as approached by such teachers as Taixu or Thich Nhat Hanh.

83. Tsuji, *A Challenge for American Shin Buddhists*, 9.

84. Walsh and Silk, *Religion and Public Life in New England*, 37.

85. Ibid., 37.

86. The Religion by Region project in fact divides the South into two separate areas: the South and the Southern Crossroads, each of which is handled in a separate volume. However, both of these regions have a 0.5 percent Eastern religions makeup, so it is easy to combine them to produce an overall estimate of Eastern religion in the South. See Wilson and Silk, *Religion and Public Life in the South*, 29; and Lindsey and Silk, *Religion and Public Life in the Southern Crossroads*, 25.

87. Silk and Walsh, *One Nation, Divisible*, 5.

88. Tweed, "Our Lady of Guadeloupe Visits the Confederate Memorial," 142.

89. Reimers, "Asian Immigrants in the South," 107.

90. The discussion of demographics in the city of Richmond and Chesterfield and Henrico counties is informed by statistics taken from the American Community Survey, carried out by the U.S. Census Bureau, for the years 2006–8. Figures are taken from http://factfinder.census.gov. The category of "potentially Buddhist" used in this discussion includes those persons of Chinese, Japanese, Korean, and Vietnamese background, as well as the census category "Asian — Other." In other words, it is the same as the overall category for Asian Americans but with Asian Indians and Filipinos removed, since India (largely Hindu and Muslim) and the Philippines (mostly Christian) have very small Buddhist populations. "Asian — Other" includes populations with high Buddhist adherence (such as Cambodians) and very low Buddhist representation (such as Bangladeshis).

91. Lam interview, May 31, 2008. Ellwood Thompson is a grocery store located in Carytown, a mixed commercial and residential neighborhood of Richmond centered

on Cary Street, a few blocks from Ekoji. Carytown is a "progressive" neighborhood and Ellwood Thompson (located next to a yoga studio) stocks organic foods, soy products, and sometimes even meditation supplies. As such it serves as a mecca for Richmond's alternative lifestyles and politically liberal communities (this was the only site in Richmond where I could consistently expect to see Goddess-themed bumper stickers in the parking lot). Its bulletin board has been a significant resource for identifying Buddhist groups in Richmond during my research. It should be noted that the majority of Ellwood Thompson's clientele is Euro-American, as are most of the attendees at Ekoji (though the group that Lam attends is mixed). Thus he is saying that the only places he feels comfortable are nonetheless decidedly non–Asian American. This seems to indicate therefore that culture, not race, is the key: in these alternative spaces that are unlike the rest of Richmond, he does not feel like an outsider the way he does in the rest of the area.

92. Field notes from Richmond Buddhist Association, August 17, 2003.

93. Lam interview, May 31, 2008.

94. Bartholomeusz, "Real Life and Romance."

95. Nearly forty years later, the Richmond SGI-USA chapter has proven to be a permanent part of the city's religious diversity, but not a very large one. The chapter actually covers a "parish" of more than one thousand square miles, within which there are fewer than two hundred active Soka Gakkai members, who continue to meet in members' homes, as well as renting space once a month for a larger, world peace prayer service. History and statistics taken from conversations with the chapter's leader in summer 2006.

96. Larson interview, June 7, 2008.

97. Davidson interview, May 6, 2010.

98. Johnston interview, June 6, 2008.

99. Kelvin interview, May 25, 2008.

100. Johnston interview, June 6, 2008. Several of these comments were echoed in the analysis of the abbot of the Berkeley Zen Center, as conveyed to me via an Ekoji member's e-mail: "Several years back Mel Sojun Weissman came to visit us and met with just the core Zen folks one evening. This was during the time when we were looking to have a permanent teacher and while we interviewed many, and being told they all loved us, nobody wanted to come. I asked Sojun why? He said if he had his way, he would send someone, no questions asked. But with the way things are set up with [San Francisco Zen Center], he can't do this. He also said that people are scared. They have to find a job in unfamiliar territory, and one big factor: it's too comfortable in California and they don't want to leave." Davidson, "New Thoughts," May 7, 2010.

Chapter Three

1. Rogers interview, February 29, 2004.

2. Li Chen interview, January 24, 2004. Juseige is a relatively short sutra passage often performed in traditional Pure Land services. "I Gassho to Amida" is an original hymn written by Tsuji and performed to the tune of a traditional Shin chant, the Junirai.

3. The Three Refuges (Tisarana) are common to all branches of Buddhism, although their formulation differs slightly according to sectarian ideals. In the Pali chant used by the Pure Land group at Ekoji, devotees take refuge in the Buddha, the dharma, and the sangha, repeated three times. Pali is the canonical language of Theravada Buddhism. Pali elements were introduced into the Mahayana services of American Jodo Shinshu temples early in the twentieth century. See Tanabe, "Glorious Gathas."

4. Li Chen interview, January 24, 2004.

5. Ibid.

6. Ibid.

7. "Namo tassa bhagavato arahato sammasambuddhassa," ("Homage to the blessed one, the noble one, the perfectly enlightened one"). This chant opens most Theravadin rituals. It is interesting to note that the Pure Land group, a Mahayana congregation, uses this Pali chant, while the Vipassana group employs no regular liturgy at all.

8. Juseige is a section taken from the Larger Pure Land Sutra, one of the primary texts of Pure Land Buddhism. Ekoji uses the Americanized Jodo Shinshu translation from Tabrah, *Shin Sutras to Live By*, 1989. This translation was already available prior to 1989, because it was chanted at the dedication of the temple in 1986. Ekoji Buddhist Sangha of Richmond, *Dedication of the Temple*.

9. The Diamond Sutra (Vajracchedika Prajnaparamitasutra) is another important short Prajnaparamita text. A gatha is a Buddhist hymn or stanza.

10. Specifically, these are stanzas 18–27 from chapter 10 of the translation by the Padamakara Translation Group: Shantideva, *The Way of the Bodhisattva*, 164–66.

11. Li Chen interview, January 24, 2004. The manner in which the Chinese chanting of Amitabha's name is performed has varied over the years as the group has tried out methods derived from various Chinese lineages, introduced by visiting teachers or through tapes acquired from temples in other parts of the country.

12. Boyd interview, May 31, 2008.

13. This is a reference to Daiseishi, Amitabha's second bodhisattva helper, who is less widely known.

14. Li Chen interview, January 24, 2004. For information about Foguangshan, see Chandler, *Establishing a Pure Land on Earth*.

15. These estimates are based on my field observations in 2002–8.

16. See the appendix for information on these statistics.

17. Chimborazo Zen Group, "Chimborazo Zen Group—Information Packet." Chimborazo in Richmond is named after Mount Chimborazo in Ecuador, which until the nineteenth century was believed to be the highest mountain on Earth. It was considered to be a holy site by the pre-Columbian population of the Andes, similar to how mountains have been viewed religiously in Japan.

18. Wolfson interview, February 29, 2004.

19. Ford interview, March 7, 2004.

20. Loori is now deceased and Shimano has resigned.

21. Ford interview, March 7, 2004. Dai Bosatsu is a Rinzai Zen monastery in upstate New York. Atta Dipa is a Pali chant no longer performed by the Zen group at Ekoji. The other chants mentioned by Ford are Japanese Zen chants. See Grossman and Apfelbaum, *Daily Sutras*.

22. Ford interview, March 7, 2004.

23. Ibid. Oddly enough, these previous seating arrangements did not match those of the parent temples. This seems to be an example of small, regionally distant, lay-led branch groups either failing to understand the proper practice or not caring to align their practices with the parent temple.

24. An anonymous reviewer pointed out that Rinzai koan practice requires close supervision by a trained teacher, while Soto meditation can be more easily carried out without such guidance. No informant at Ekoji ever raised this as a motivating factor in the Zen group's realignment, but it certainly makes sense. With this in mind, we might expect that Soto Zen potentially would more easily penetrate American regions that lack Buddhist groups than Rinzai Zen.

25. Kelvin interview, January 30, 2004. The San Francisco Zen Center lineage is often called the Suzuki Roshi lineage, after its founder, the Soto Zen priest Shunryu Suzuki.

26. *Richmond Zen Group Newsletter*, June 2003.

27. The four bodhisattva vows are common Mahayana liturgical elements, expressing the wish to liberate all beings from suffering and master the Buddha's wisdom. The Richmond Zen Group uses the translation provided by San Francisco Zen Center. See Ekoji Buddhist Sangha, *Zen Service Book*.

28. Galloway interview, June 8, 2008.

29. Rogers interview, February 29, 2004.

30. Kelvin interview, March 8, 2011.

31. Ford interview, March 7, 2004.

32. Finney, "American Zen's 'Japan Connection.'"

33. Finke and Stark, *The Churching of America*.

34. These estimates are based on my field observations in 2003–8.

35. For information on these statistics, see the appendix.

36. Shungendo had a small number of American practice groups in the 1970s, but they are currently inactive.

37. Mullen, *The American Occupation of Tibetan Buddhism*.

38. Brown and Brown interview, February 22, 2004. This lama is Lama Norlha, the spiritual director of KST, whose framed picture sits on the fireplace mantle in Ekoji's hondo. He lives in Wappingers Falls, New York, but comes to Richmond each year.

39. Ekoji Buddhist Sangha of Richmond, *Kagyu Shenpen Tharchin*.

40. Chenrezi is the Tibetan form of Avalokiteshvara, the bodhisattva of compassion, just as Guanyin is the Chinese version.

41. Brown and Brown interview, February 22, 2004. Mahakala is a wrathful form of Chenrezi.

42. See *Dharma Wheel*, various issues.

43. Strauss interview, March 6, 2004.

44. These estimates are based on my field observations in 2003–8.

45. For information on these statistics, see the appendix.

46. There are currently no scholarly book-length treatments of the Vipassana movement, though Cadge's *Heartwood* does include extensive information on one Vipassana center in Cambridge, Massachusetts. For a short but useful description of the movement in the United States, see Fronsdal, "Insight Meditation in the United States."

47. Grant interview, March 4, 2004.

48. Ibid.

49. Ibid.

50. These estimates are based on my field observations in 2003–8.

51. For information on these statistics, see the appendix.

52. Harris interview, March 15, 2011.

53. My observations are mirrored by the findings of Carolina Kingsbury, who examined the multidenominational Bellingham Dharma Hall in 2004. As she noted, "One of the largest differences between the four Buddhist groups in Bellingham is esthetic, seen in the differential use of ritual, especially prostrations, chanting, and accoutrements such as incense, bells, and drums." Kingsbury, *Buddhism in Bellingham*, 48. Furthermore, if you read the minutes of the Bellingham Dharma Hall (some are provided in Kingsbury's book, and I have been receiving their minutes and announcements via e-mail from 2003 to the present), it soon becomes apparent that the most frequently expressed concerns among the groups are over practices and materials, not beliefs.

54. These comments are based on my field observations in 2002–8.

55. Boyd interview, August 16, 2003.

56. Li Chen interview, January 24, 2004.

57. The cosmic mudra is a hand posture: it consists of placing one hand on the other, palms up, with the thumbs touching, so that a circle is formed.

58. These observations are based on my field observations in 2003–4. See also Suzuki, *Zen Mind, Beginner's Mind*, 25.

59. Boyd interview, August 16, 2003.

60. Ford interview, March 7, 2004. DharmaCrafts is the largest marketer of Buddhist meditation supplies in the United States. For a discussion of the role of Zen-associated cushions, including the "hegemony" of the zafu, see Padgett, "'Americans Need Something to Sit On.'"

61. Kelvin interview, January 30, 2004.

62. Boyd interview, August 16, 2003. The Pure Land group appears not to have protested this change, although in discussion with several people it seemed that misgivings might linger over the preemptive manner in which the change was effected.

63. Ford interview, March 7, 2004.

64. Ibid.

65. Hack, "Collective Identity and Sacred Space."

66. Other Zen groups have decided to adopt extra rows of cushions, but this idea has not been approved in Richmond.

67. Danielson interview, March 7, 2003.

68. Fielding interview, March 6, 2004.

69. Danielson interview, January 24, 2004. *Gotama* is the most common Theravadin designation for the historical Buddha, who is more frequently called Shakaymuni in the Mahayana tradition.

70. The kneeling and the hands held to the front rather than the sides of the head are specific to Theravada. The anjali mudra is the classic "prayer position," with the two palms flat against one another, fingers pointing upward.

71. This was a constant theme of my interviews over the years. Informants expressed their feelings in nearly identical words to those used here, including in Larson interview, June 7, 2008. Kingsbury noted the same dynamic at her multidenominational field site: "Although there was about the same amount of ceremony and ritual as in the Shambhala group, Zen felt somewhat more formal." Kingsbury, *Buddhism in Bellingham*, 58.

72. Ford interview, April 9, 2006.

73. Thangkas are Vajrayana cloth paintings of important figures, such as Chenrezi or Amitabha Buddha.

74. *Pecha* is the term used by many members of the group; technically, pechas are specifically the texts themselves, as this is the Tibetan word for "book."

75. All information in this paragraph is from Strauss interview, March 6, 2004, and personal observations of practice in 2002–8.

76. "Om mani peme hung" is the Tibetan mantra of Chenrezi, more familiar to many as "Om mani padme hum" (the Sanskrit version). Mantras are collections of syllables associated with particular deities or enlightened beings.

77. Brown and Brown interview, February 22, 2004.

78. Tweed, *The American Encounter with Buddhism*, 69.

79. Lopez, *Prisoners of Shangri-La*.

80. Strauss interview, March 6, 2004.

81. Ibid., and confirmed by casual conversations with other temple attendees.

82. Strauss interview, March 6, 2004.

83. Kelvin interview, January 30, 2004.

84. Brown and Brown interview, February 22, 2004.

85. Ford interview, April 9, 2006.

86. Harris interview, April 5, 2006.

87. Boyd interview, April 8, 2006.

88. Ibid.

89. Larson interview, June 7, 2008.

90. Noble interview, April 9, 2006.

91. Brown interview, June 1, 2008.

92. Li Chen interview, April 8, 2006.

93. Kelvin interview, May 25, 2008.

94. Simpson interview, April 29, 2010; Davidson interview, May 6, 2010.

95. Nugent interview, May 31, 2008.

Chapter Four

1. Description is taken from field observations on January 11, 2003.

2. There were, however, implicit criticisms of the other groups that appeared in the form of the Zen group's desire for its own, solely Zen space.

3. Han and Han interview, February 28, 2004. Because some of the interviews quoted in this section were conducted prior to the creation of the Meditative Inquiry group, some refer to four groups at Ekoji, while later interviewees refer to five groups.

4. Li Chen interview, January 24, 2004.

5. Baine interview, February 7, 2004.

6. Simpson interview, March 7, 2004.

7. Brown and Brown interview, February 22, 2004. The Greensville sangha is a Buddhist prison ministry program that Ekoji conducts.

8. Strauss interview, March 7, 2004.

9. Grant interview, March 4, 2004.

10. Nugent interview, February 22, 2004.

11. McNeill interview, March 15, 2011.

12. Huntson interview, March 15, 2011.

13. Kraft interview, February 22, 2004.

14. Rogers interview, February 29, 2004.

15. Boyd interview, February 28, 2004. The five unforgivable acts that Boyd is referring to here are a traditional Buddhist formulation: to kill one's mother, to kill one's father, to kill an arhat (an enlightened monastic), to shed the blood of a Buddha, or to cause a schism in the sangha. Traditionally, the "sangha" under discussion here is the ordained monastic community. Boyd's use of the term indicates a degree of Americanization, with the word redefined to meet an egalitarian, congregation-based ethos — thus the name "Ekoji Buddhist *Sangha* of Richmond." And what would happen if the Zen group left? The history of Ekoji suggests that the other groups would adjust to the new circumstances and carry on, and furthermore that additional groups are likely to form at Ekoji in the future. Even if the temple were to fall apart altogether and disband at some point, according to the current bylaws the building would be returned to the Buddhist Churches of America, who might work to reestablish it as an active temple. Only time will tell whether the Zen group remains at Ekoji or secedes to establish a separate Zen center. Other groups have left Ekoji in the past, and despite the anxiety this engenders, the temple will likely survive the departure of yet another one. The important point here is that many members of the temple perceive its diversity to be a genuine asset, and they feel connected to a larger community beyond their own sectarian group.

16. Carl Becker, "Japanese Pure Land Buddhism in Christian America."

17. Boyd interview, August 16, 2003.

18. Ibid.

19. Li Chen interview, January 24, 2004. One intriguing possibility is that the practice of putting notes on the altar is derived from the influence of the Vietnamese Ekoji group, which eventually left to found its own temple. The origins of this practice are difficult to directly ascertain. Li Chen believes that it started when someone asked Tsuji what she could do about a sick loved one. The woman had a picture of the person, which Tsuji took and put on the altar. This seems to be the earliest record of what would become the current practice of putting notes about sick or deceased loved ones on the altar. The possible Vietnamese influence comes from the fact that the Richmond Buddhist Association had an entire second altar, housed in what is now the "Zen room," devoted to the photographs of deceased relatives. Did Tsuji take a cue from this practice? At this point it is impossible to offer anything more than speculations.

20. Brown interview, August 12, 2003.

21. Fielding interview, March 6, 2004.

22. Larson interview, January 31, 2004.

23. Grant interview, March 4, 2004.

24. Richard Kraft [pseudonym], quote taken from field notes, February 22, 2004.

25. Nugent interview, February 22, 2004.

26. Enmei Jukku Kannon Gyo is a chant contained in Ekoji Buddhist Sangha of Richmond, *Zen Service Book.*

27. Chod is a Tibetan visualization practice that involves picturing one's body being chopped into pieces.

28. The name of this practice has been omitted, in keeping with my informant's wishes. It denotes a type of tantric practice that is not supposed to be revealed to the general public.

29. Green Tara and Medicine Buddha are popular savior figures in the Tibetan pantheon. Tara is a female goddess who takes on many different forms; Medicine Buddha lives in the Eastern Pure Land and helps with all manner of afflictions.

30. A sesshin is a Zen meditation retreat.

31. Ngodro are preliminary exercises undertaken before receiving certain Tibetan empowerments or teachings. They vary slightly by tradition but typically include one hundred thousand full prostrations, one hundred thousand mantras, one hundred thousand visualizations of a deity, and so on.

32. Strauss interview, March 6, 2004.

33. Nugent, e-mail to Wilson, March 9, 2004. *Nembutsu* is the Japanese term for nianfo.

34. Boyd interview, January 12, 2003.

35. Danielson interview, January 24, 2004.

36. Noble interview, January 29, 2004.

37. These figures are all derived from a questionnaire I distributed to Ekoji members. See the appendix for details.

38. Many of these factors may also operate outside of the Buddhist context, leading to communities of hybrid Christians, hybrid Muslims, hybrid Hindus, and so on. But because I have not conducted research on such religions, and they may have features that mitigate the creation of hybridity, I do not wish to make a strong claim in this regard.

39. Observation based on field notes, January 23, 2004.

40. Description based on ibid.

41. Nguyen interview, June 12, 2003.

42. Numrich, "Local Inter-Buddhist Associations in North America."

43. Coleman, *The New Buddhism.*

44. For instance, see Matsunaga and Matsunaga, *Foundation of Japanese Buddhism.*

45. The U.S. Census Bureau also counts "metropolitan areas," which are entities far larger than actual cities. Metropolitan areas include suburbs, satellite cities, and sprawl that may range very far from the core cities themselves (for example, "New York–Northern New Jersey–Long Island, NY" and "Los Angeles–Long Beach–Santa Ana, CA"). By this formulation, the Richmond metropolitan area had 1,225,626 residents in 2008 (numbers from "Annual Estimates of the Population of Metropolitan and Micropolitan Statistical Areas: April 1, 2000 to July 1, 2008," http://www.census.gov/

popest/metro/CBSA-est2008-annual.html, accessed June 25, 2010). But this covers a very large geographic region, with many people who would be surprised to learn that they allegedly belonged to Richmond in some manner and who rarely venture into that city. I prefer, therefore, to focus on more commonsense metrics: the actual city itself and the suburban counties that directly touch it.

46. Of course, if the teacher is paid by the temple (not all teachers are), that in itself is a significant financial burden. A teacherless temple does not have this particular burden, but it still faces the universal hurdle of obtaining a place in which to meet.

47. Three decades ago, southern sociologist John Shelton Reed made an interesting observation that seems to apply here: "Southerners, I have said, incline to the view that churches are simply voluntary associations for the benefit, in the last analysis, of the individuals who make them up—a view so taken for granted that many Southerners cannot conceive that there is any other way to think of the church. The proposition 'Love it or leave it' seems perfectly reasonable to many Southern churchmen. From time to time groups *do* leave, to set up their own congregations or to found entirely new denominations. This mode of response results in both homogeneity and considerable group loyalty—in the new groups, obviously; but also in the old." Reed, "The Same Old Stand?," 26. Ekoji mirrors this in some ways: as circumstances have permitted, Ekoji has spun off more and more Buddhist groups, such as the Zen, Tibetan, and Meditative Inquiry groups, all of which were begun by attendees of other groups who successfully gathered enough like-minded fellows to found new groups closer in style to their own preferences. Yet Ekoji also shows the regional limitations of this phenomenon: there are enough people to create new groups based on significantly different forms of Buddhism, but not nearly enough to support several groups in the same basic tradition founded on fine gradations of style—that is, Richmond does not seem able to support a Zen group that is San Francisco Zen Center–based *and* a Zen group that is free-form *and* a Zen group that is Zen Mountain Monastery–based, and so on. Thus, whereas congregational homogeneity is a feature of the average southern Protestant church, heterogeneity may be a feature of the average southern Buddhist group, while relative homogeneity may be a feature of the average Buddhist group in some more "Buddhified" areas of the country, such as the San Francisco Bay Area.

48. Kelvin, Simpson, and Strauss interview, April 7, 2006.

49. Larson interview, January 31, 2004; Kelvin, Simpson, and Strauss interview, April 7, 2006.

50. Harris interview, March 15, 2011.

51. One Ekoji attendee does retain membership in the BCA, but while friendly with the Shin community he repudiates many basic aspects of Jodo Shinshu and does not consider himself a Shin Buddhist.

52. These themes came up time and again in my fieldwork. I have heard similar sentiments in other parts of the country, but there is a significant difference: in places with more Pure Land Buddhism, there are actual local Shin Buddhists who can serve as models of what Jodo Shinshu Buddhism is like, and these real-life practitioners are sometimes impressive enough that newcomers overcome their initial skepticism and explore Shin Buddhism further, a phenomenon rare in the extreme in Richmond.

53. Numrich, *Old Wisdom in the New World.*

54. Two other studies are also worth mentioning: Numrich, "Local Inter-Buddhist Associations in North America"; and Frieberger, "The Meeting of Traditions." Neither of these sources is directly applicable, as they both deal with regional inter-Buddhist organizations rather than specific contacts within the situation of a single temple. However, for further information about how different Buddhist groups in the West interact with one another, they are both useful.

55. See Ekoji Buddhist Sangha of Richmond, *Karmic Patterns in Our Lives.*

56. Harry Nugent [pseudonym], questionnaire, July 25, 2003.

57. For one representative discussion of this phenomenon, focused on the Japan context, see Teeuwen and Rambelli, *Buddhas and Kami in Japan.*

58. Even many of the Chinese Americans who attend the Pure Land group consider themselves to be adult converts to Buddhism.

Chapter Five

1. This does not mean that such features *never* impact Richmond Buddhism, only that their impact is slight and irregular. For instance, traveling Tibetan monks who make sand mandalas in the area dump their materials in the James River. Although this may be tangentially interesting, it is hardly a significantly impacting phenomenon.

2. These sorts of environmental influences can operate in easily unnoticed ways. For example, because the climate and soil conditions of central North Carolina provide the necessary conditions, Theravada Cambodian immigrants are able to grow traditional vegetables and herbs generally unavailable at local marketplaces, and they can use them at large religious and social ceremonies that help knit this refugee community together and to the homeland in Cambodia. In many places in the country it would not be possible to have these traditional dishes at important ceremonies. See Lau, "The Temple Provides the Way," 81.

3. These observations come from many years of fieldwork and discussion with temple members. Obviously these are general patterns, not always applicable. The Pure Land and Tibetan groups at Ekoji are more devotional than the Zen, Vipassana, and Meditative Inquiry groups; these two are also the smallest of the groups and even their participants often prefer relatively abstract interpretations of key motifs, such as describing Amitabha Buddha as one's own buddha-nature or describing the Tibetan deities in visualization practice as projections of the practitioner's mind, not autonomous, supernatural entities.

4. Nicholas Rogers [pseudonym], survey response, March 14, 2004.

5. This is true on a smaller scale for the other industries mentioned. The tobacco, financial, and energy sectors, as well as the growing high-tech industry in Richmond, draw skilled white-collar job seekers from outside Virginia. Some arrive as Buddhists; others are displaced from their familiar (often relatively politically and religiously liberal) networks and seek communities that will provide guidance and support consistent with their class and educational preferences.

6. Goldfield, *Region, Race and Cities,* 145.

7. Brown interview, June 1, 2008. The references to "terrorists" is apparently a confusion by the speaker, conflating Islam (often associated with terrorism in the American

mind) with Buddhism. I, too, have encountered people in the South who could not differentiate between these two religions.

8. Holmes interview, March 15, 2011.

9. Danielson interview, January 24, 2004.

10. Kelvin interview, June 8, 2008.

11. One informant, for instance, said that when she lived in another Virginia town she was often asked what church she went to (a very common question in the South, often asked in the course of strangers' first meeting). She would reply "none." If she trusted the questioner or had reason to think they might be sympathetic, she sometimes volunteered that she "meditated." Patricia Williams interview, March 4, 2011.

12. Simpson interview, April 29, 2010.

13. Troy Becker interview, March 14, 2011.

14. Osbourne, "Surviving High School," 257–59.

15. Story related by a close friend and fellow Tibetan group practitioner of Oliver Akerman [pseudonym] (Brown interview, June 1, 2008).

16. Johnston interview, June 6, 2008.

17. James interview, April 25, 2010.

18. Strauss interview, April 26, 2010.

19. Boyd interview, January 24, 2004; Li Chen interview, January 24, 2004.

20. Goldfield, *Region, Race, and Cities*, 54.

21. Huntson interview, March 15, 2011.

22. In fact, as this book was going to press, this contingent appeared to have finally triumphed, and plans were being made to erect a larger sign. Privately, other members have expressed discomfort at this development, but perhaps they were unwilling to make waves since some of the main temple's lay leaders were in favor of the sign.

23. Esse, "Turning the Wheel of the Dharma." The reference to the burning house is a parable from the famous Lotus Sutra, wherein a father gets his children to leave a burning house by promising them various prizes, then gives them something even better when they follow him out. The meaning is that the Buddha gets people to detach from the suffering of samsara through various paths, but ultimately there is only one supreme way of Buddhism.

24. Field notes from Ekoji Vipassana group, May 23, 2008.

25. Boyd interview, May 31, 2008.

26. Ashe and Rampersad, *Days of Grace*, 319, 340; Vecsey, "Arthur Ashe," B11.

27. Boyd interview, May 31, 2008.

28. *Magnum P.I.* was a popular television action and detective show that ran on CBS from 1980 to 1988.

29. Field notes from Richmond Zen Group, December 7, 2003.

30. Many other influences can be detected that are more subtle and less significant, but nonetheless interesting. Note, for example, how regional concepts and vocabulary frequently appear in the speech of my informants. When Buddhists frame their practice and experiences with the use of terms such as "Buddhist Confederacy," "Buddhist circuit rider," fear of being "lynched" for being Buddhist, and so forth, a type of regionalism is occurring. One of my favorite anecdotes in this vein was an Ekoji member's framing of Buddhism versus Christianity. Buddhism was like tofu, he asserted one day

during a discussion at the temple, whereas Christianity was like southern fried chicken. Because Buddhism, like tofu, does not have a strong, insistent flavor, it can take on the taste of whatever culture it comes into contact with. This was what had allowed it to adapt and change to fit a vast range of cultures — including now America's — without causing significant disruption and conflict. Christianity, in contrast, was like a strong dish that tried to overwhelm the senses without regard for the unique tastes of other dishes (cultures).

31. Brown, "Ekoji Buddhist Sangha," 2.

32. "Meditation Vigil to Bear Witness to the Slave Trade."

33. Ekoji's creation was preceded by that of the Richmond chapter of Soka Gakkai and the original Richmond Zen Group. But neither of these organizations held property: Soka Gakkai met in members' homes (and, when it grew large enough, occasionally rented spaces for monthly meetings), while the Zen group met in a room at a New Age store in the Carytown neighborhood. They thus never came into direct contact with the local government.

34. Discussion of the racial and economic dynamics of relations between Richmond and the counties is superbly handled in Silver, *Twentieth-Century Richmond*.

35. Much of the information in this discussion comes from several interviews with Ekoji board members (current and former): Boyd interviews, August 16, 2003, and May 31, 2008; Nugent interview, May 31, 2008; Brown interview, June 1, 2008; Galloway interview, June 8, 2008. The general correspondence between the temple and city supports my interpretation, especially the letter from Harty (assistant city assessor, City of Richmond) to Porfiri (lawyer, Coates and Davenport), the letter from Olsen (lawyer, Community Tax Law Project) to Lockhart (city assessor, City of Richmond), the highly detailed letters recording conversations between both sides sent from Olsen to Stutts (lawyer, Office of the City Attorney) dated October 13, 1995, and September 30, 1996, and the letter from Olsen to Young (mayor, City of Richmond), dated October 13, 1995, as well as the temple's second application for tax exemption: Tsuji, "Application for Exemption from Real Estate Taxation."

36. Information on race and tax issues comes from several sources, especially Shields, "The 'Tip of the Iceberg' in a Southern Suburban County"; Silver, "The Changing Face of Neighborhoods in Memphis and Richmond"; Silver, *Twentieth-Century Richmond*; Tyler-McGraw, *At the Falls*.

37. Boyd (Ekoji board trustee), letter to Brenner.

38. Olsen (lawyer, Community Tax Law Project), letter to Stutts (lawyer, Office of the City Attorney), August 30, 1996.

39. Robinson (assistant city attorney), letter to Wallace (clerk, General District Court), July 14, 1993. The letter indicates dismissal of Case No. GDC 92 — 106594 & 95.

40. Brown and Brown interview, February 22, 2004; Jabbar (supervising appraiser, Richmond City Tax Enforcement and Collections), letter to Olsen (lawyer, Community Tax Law Project), December 22, 1994.

41. "Delinquent Tax Statement," November 8, 1996.

42. Ryan, letter to Jacinto (president, Ekoji Buddhist Sangha of Richmond), undated (postmarked September 13, 1995); Brown interview, June 1, 2008.

43. Mallory-Jones (legal intern, Office of the City Attorney), letter to Olsen (lawyer, Community Tax Law Project), November 18, 1996.

44. "Ekoji Buddhist Sangha of Richmond Application for Exemption for Real Estate Taxation," September 22, 1994.

45. Richmond has long had minority populations of Jews and Unitarian Universalists (who may or may not be Christian on an individual basis). But these groups did not pose the same sort of challenge to the paradigms assumed by the city government as the increasing diversity of the late twentieth century did. Both Jews and Unitarian Universalists are organized on a congregational basis in Richmond essentially similar to the dominant Protestant churches, with formal membership rolls, boards of directors, and ordained clergy leaders.

46. Olsen (lawyer, Community Tax Law Project), letter to Stutts (lawyer, Office of the City Attorney), August 30, 1996.

47. Brown (Ekoji president), letter to Sadtler (chaplain, James River Correctional Center), October 11, 1995.

48. "Airport Interfaith Chapel Sutras," 1.

49. Terathongkum, "Relationships among Stress, Blood Pressure, and Heart Rate Variability in Meditators"; Thinganjana, "The Lived Experience of Spirituality among Thai Immigrants Who Are Living with Type 2 Diabetes." For the record, Terathongkum found that meditators have lower reported stress and that their blood pressure and heart rates are lower as well.

50. Davenport interview, April 28, 2010.

51. Boyd interview, May 31, 2008.

52. Brown interview, June 1, 2008.

53. Gibson interview, March 15, 2011.

54. Johnston interview, June 6, 2008. It would have been quite interesting to interview members of Johnston's family, as well as other non-Buddhists in Richmond dealing with their family members' Buddhism. However, I decided that this sort of research had too great a risk of stirring up trouble for my informants. As an ethnographer, I have a responsibility to see to it that my investigations do not negatively impact the people who are kind enough to share their time and experiences with me. Therefore, regrettably, I have had to rely on my Buddhist informants to report the feelings of their relatives and acquaintances. Perhaps eventually I will be able to develop a research model that allows for more direct access to these non-Buddhists without the risk of provoking increased conflict.

55. I wish to reiterate once again that I in no way consider conflict with Christian relatives to be confined to the South, nor do I assert that southern Christians uniformly act in the ways depicted here, or that all southern Buddhists have Christian relatives who must be dealt with. My argument is predicated on a series of observations: (1) in the South, there is a high percentage of evangelical Christians; (2) a large number of my informants had Christian relatives in the South and reported conflict or fear of conflict due to their Buddhist practice; and (3) my informants asserted a connection between the South and the sort of conservative Christianity that concerned them. Thus their Buddhism was shaped by their perception of regional forces that they felt

impacted them, and they believed the growth of Buddhism in the South in turn altered the character of their relationships with Christian family members who grappled with the implications of a diversifying South whose Christian nature they could no longer take for granted.

56. Norman and Armentrout, *Religion in the Contemporary South*, ix.

57. David Goldfield, a major historian of the South, made a similar observation about another religious minority: "If anyone doubts that the South is distinctive, then the place of Jews in the region and their relationship to their neighbors may serve as a corrective." Goldfield, *Region, Race, and Cities*, 12.

Chapter Six

1. De Certeau, *The Practice of Everyday Life*, 91.

2. See chapter 1, "Sacred Southern Ceremonies: Ritual of the Lost Cause," in Charles Reagan Wilson, *Baptized in Blood*. Note that this first statue, located in Capitol Square, is not the same as the well-known memorial on Monument Avenue, which was dedicated in 1919.

3. Description in this section recreated from interviews and print sources, as well as my own observations at the site (not on the day of the vigil): Kelvin interview, May 25, 2008; Nugent interview, May 31, 2008; Boyd interview, May 31, 2008; Johnston interview, June 6, 2008; Larson interview, June 7, 2008; Strauss interview, April 26, 2010; Jenkins interview, April 26, 2010; Leighton interview, April 29, 2010; Simpson interview, April 29, 2010; Davidson interview, May 6, 2010; Jasper interview, May 13, 2010; Sanchez interview, May 15, 2010; Harris interview, March 15, 2011; Leighton and Chester, "Facing the Legacy of Slavery"; "Meditation Vigil to Bear Witness to the Slave Trade"; "Richmond Slave Trail"; Ralph White, *Seeing the Scars of Slavery in the Natural Environment*.

4. In 2009, for example, the club displayed a huge poster of President Barack Obama in whiteface paint made to resemble the Joker from the Batman films; the poster's tagline read "Socialism." The NAACP held protests, while local radio shows and blogs filled with anti-Obama and anti-black comments, as well as angry denunciations of racism and conservatives.

5. *Metta Sutta* translated by Mel Weitsman (used with permission). Ekoji Buddhist Sangha of Richmond, *Zen Service Book*, 8.

6. Kelvin interview, May 25, 2008.

7. Davidson interview, May 6, 2010.

8. Simpson interview, April 29, 2010.

9. Larson interview, June 7, 2008.

10. Jasper interview, May 13, 2010. Note how Jasper conceptualizes the area both in terms of the specific events that took place there and the actual topography of the city as a whole: as the name implies, Shockoe Bottom—next to the river—is one of the lowest points in the city. Richmond is a city of hills and valleys, and Jasper imagines invisible energy flowing downhill like a fluid and collecting here by the James River in a natural spiritual reservoir (in this case, a pool of latent suffering).

11. Leighton interview, April 29, 2010.

12. Nugent interview, May 31, 2008.

13. Davidson interview, May 6, 2010.

14. Nugent interview, May 31, 2008.

15. Kelvin interview, May 25, 2008.

16. Harris interview, March 15, 2011.

17. Leighton interview, April 29, 2010.

18. Jasper interview, May 13, 2010.

19. Johnston interview, June 6, 2008.

20. Harris interview, March 15, 2011.

21. It is also relevant to mention that several Ekoji members told me they had considered attending or planned to attend the vigil but could not due to illness, schedule conflicts, or similar issues. Thus, on another day the vigil might have been larger and the demographics might have been slightly different. This group of almost-participants was comprised entirely of white southerners of old Richmond families. One was directly descended from slave owners, while others were uncertain of their family's possible involvement with slavery. Perhaps also noteworthy is that the almost-participants were all significantly older or younger than the average participant.

22. Davidson interview, May 6, 2010.

23. Jasper interview, May 13, 2010.

24. Simpson interview, April 29, 2010.

25. Ibid.

26. Jenkins interview, April 26, 2010.

27. For more on this issue, see the discussion in Jeff Wilson, *Mourning the Unborn Dead*.

28. Davidson interview, May 6, 2010.

29. Quotes in this paragraph come from Sanchez interview, May 13, 2010. The meaning of the comment about segregated groups is my own interpretation, based on Sanchez's comments and my own interactions with antiracism organizers. I appreciate Sanchez's sharing these conflicted feelings with me for the benefit of my research.

30. Johnston interview, June 6, 2008.

31. There are Zen groups in America that incorporate metta meditation into their procedures, but in general this is seen as a Theravada-derived form of Buddhist practice.

32. Takuhatsu is uncommon in Japan, the origin of the basic elements of this partially Zen-based slave trade meditation vigil. Begging rounds are somewhat more common in Southeast Asia, though hardly universal. It is a rare practice in America, where even Theravada monks are more likely to remain at their temples and be served by laypeople who bring them food.

33. There are many other ways in which this event can be analyzed regionally. Just for example, we can note that it occurred in April—not because that is Confederate Heritage Month (merely a coincidence), but because it was felt that any later in the year would be impossible due to the heat of southern summers. Another example is the group's nearly all-white racial makeup. Whether liberal or conservative, Christian or Buddhist, religious groups in the South have had a difficult time creating true integration.

Conclusion

1. This is not to say that the South is completely devoid of African American Buddhist clergy. For example, there is Lynda Myokei Caine Barrett, leader of the Houston-based Nichiren Buddhist Sangha of Texas. Barrett's mother is Japanese, while her father is African American.

2. Tweed, "Night-Stand Buddhists and Other Creatures."

3. For online Buddhism, see Prebish, "The Cybersangha"; and Veidlinger, "From Indra's Net to Internet."

4. Jeff Wilson, *The Buddhist Guide to New York*.

5. Do, *The Vietnamese-Americans*.

6. Clark, *Guardian of the Sea*.

7. The tallest outdoor Buddhist statue in America, however, is under construction in Tulsa. At fifty-seven feet tall, the image of Quan Am (Guanyin or Avalokiteshvara) will certainly make an impact on the local landscape.

8. The website for the Buddhist Faith Fellowship, including listings for its current chapters, is http://www.bffct.net/.

9. Observations on East versus West Coast differences based on personal fieldwork at multiple sites.

10. Kuki interview, August 25, 2008; Asahi interview, September 25, 2010; Sakamoto interview, October 24, 2010; personal observations at multiple field sites in Hawaii and North America.

11. Chappell, "Racial Diversity in the Soka Gakkai."

12. I have been thinking about these issues for a number of years, but some of the specifics came into greater clarity for me through discussion with Janet McLellan, who studies rural retreat centers. I thank her for sharing her insights with me and look forward to the much more sophisticated work in this area that she will eventually produce.

Bibliography

Interviews

Note: All interviews were conducted by Jeff Wilson.

Seicho Asahi at Koyasan Buddhist Temple in Los Angeles, September 25, 2010
Christina Baine [pseudonym], at Virginia Museum of Fine Arts in Richmond, March 7, 2004
Troy Becker [pseudonym], via telephone, March 14, 2011
Malcolm Boyd [pseudonym], at his home in Richmond, January 12, 2003
———, at his home in Richmond, February 22, 2003
———, at his home in Richmond, April 5, 2003
———, at his home in Richmond, August 16, 2003
———, at Ekoji Buddhist Sangha of Richmond, January 24, 2004
———, at his home in Richmond, February 28, 2004
———, at his home in Richmond, June 26, 2004
———, at his home in Richmond, April 8, 2006
———, at his home in Richmond, May 31, 2008
Fred Brown [pseudonym], at Ekoji Buddhist Sangha of Richmond, August 12, 2003
———, at Ekoji Buddhist Sangha of Richmond, August 19, 2003
———, at his home in Richmond, June 1, 2008
Fred Brown and Frances Brown [pseudonyms], at Capital Coffee in Richmond, February 22, 2004
Li Chen [pseudonym], at Ekoji Buddhist Sangha of Richmond, January 11, 2003
———, at Ekoji Buddhist Sangha of Richmond, January 24, 2004
———, at Ekoji Buddhist Sangha of Richmond, April 8, 2006
Sue Coates [pseudonym], at her home in Richmond, March 6, 2004
Yvonne Corazon [pseudonym], at her home in Richmond, March 6, 2004
Joel Danielson [pseudonym], at Ekoji Buddhist Sangha of Richmond, January 24, 2004
Ralph Darlow [pseudonym], via telephone, March 12, 2011
Walt Davenport [pseudonym], at his home in Richmond, February 29, 2004
———, via telephone, April 28, 2010
Cecelia Davidson [pseudonym], via telephone, May 6, 2010
Thomas Elliott [pseudonym], via telephone, March 9, 2011
Denise Fielding [pseudonym], at Ekoji Buddhist Sangha of Richmond, March 6, 2004
Brian Ford [pseudonym], at Ekoji Buddhist Sangha of Richmond, March 7, 2004
———, at Ekoji Buddhist Sangha of Richmond, April 9, 2006

Allen Galloway [pseudonym], at his home in Richmond, June 8, 2008

Rebecca Gibson [pseudonym], via telephone, March 15, 2011

Darren Grant [pseudonym], via telephone, March 4, 2004

Reggie Han and Gordon Han [pseudonyms], at Ekoji Buddhist Sangha of Richmond, February 28, 2004

Ben Harris [pseudonym], via telephone, April 5, 2006

———, via telephone, March 15, 2011

Meredith Holmes [pseudonym], via telephone, March 15, 2011

Garth Huntson [pseudonym], via telephone, March 15, 2011

Shelly James [pseudonym], via telephone, April 25, 2010

Lisa Jasper [pseudonym], via telephone, May 13, 2010

Serena Jenkins [pseudonym], via telephone, April 26, 2010

Larry Johnston [pseudonym], at Ekoji Buddhist Sangha of Richmond, June 6, 2008

Henry Kelvin [pseudonym], at his home in Richmond, January 30, 2004

———, at Crossroads Café in Richmond, May 25, 2008

———, at Harrison Coffee Shop in Richmond, June 8, 2008

———, via telephone, March 8, 2011

Henry Kelvin, David Simpson, and Sarah Strauss [pseudonyms], at Bread Crust Restaurant in Richmond, April 7, 2006

Amber Klein [pseudonym], at Crossroads Café in Richmond, March 6, 2004

Richard Kraft [pseudonym], at Ekoji Buddhist Sangha of Richmond, February 22, 2004

Sohko Kuki at Hilo Hooganji Mission in Hilo, HI, August 25, 2008

Andrew Lam [pseudonym], at Ekoji Buddhist Sangha of Richmond, May 31, 2008

Gail Larson [pseudonym], at Capital Coffee in Richmond, January 31, 2004

———, at House of India Restaurant in Richmond, June 7, 2008

Taigen Dan Leighton, via telephone, April 29, 2010

Trevor McNeill [pseudonym], via telephone, March 15, 2011

Dinh Nguyen [pseudonym], at Hue Quang Temple in Mechanicsville, VA, June 12, 2003

Julie Noble [pseudonym], at her home in Richmond, January 29, 2004

———, at her home in Richmond, February 29, 2004

———, at her home in Richmond, April 9, 2006

Harry Nugent [pseudonym], at Ekoji Buddhist Sangha of Richmond, February 22, 2004

———, at his home in Richmond, May 31, 2008

Nicholes Rogers [pseudonym], at his home in Richmond, February 29, 2004

Sumitoshi Sakamoto, at Hawaii Shingon Mission in Honolulu, October 24, 2010

Maria Sanchez [pseudonym], via e-mail, May 15, 2010

David Simpson [pseudonym], at Capital Coffee in Richmond, March 7, 2004

———, via telephone, April 29, 2010

———, via telephone, May 13, 2010

Sarah Strauss [pseudonym], at Ekoji Buddhist Sangha of Richmond, March 6, 2004

———, at Ekoji Buddhist Sangha of Richmond, March 7, 2004

———, via telephone, April 26, 2010

Elaine Summerfield [pseudonym], at Ekoji Buddhist Sangha of Richmond,
   February 29, 2004
Patricia Williams [pseudonym], via telephone, March 4, 2011
Jarrod Wolfson [pseudonym], at Ekoji Buddhist Sangha of Richmond, October 20,
   2003
————, at Ekoji Buddhist Sangha of Richmond, February 29, 2004

Books, Articles, Essays, and Theses

"Airport Interfaith Chapel Sutras." *Ekoji Buddhist Sangha of Richmond Monthly
   Information Letter* 2, no. 5 (July 3, 1999).
Albanese, Catherine. "Exchanging Selves, Exchanging Souls: Contact, Combination,
   and American Religious History." In *Retelling U.S. Religious History*, edited by
   Thomas A. Tweed, 200–226. Berkeley: University of California Press, 1997.
Ama, Michihiro. *Immigrants to the Pure Land: The Modernization, Acculturation, and
   Globalization of Shin Buddhism, 1898–1941.* Honolulu: University of Hawaii Press,
   2011.
Apple, Mary B. "Applying Faurian Critique to Gender Issues in Buddhist Practice at
   a Multi-sect Dharma Hall." M.A. thesis, Western Washington University, 2008.
Ashe, Arthur, and Arnold Rampersad. *Days of Grace: A Memoir.* New York:
   Ballantine, 1984.
Auge, Marc. *Non-places: Introduction to an Anthropology of Supermodernity.* New York:
   Verso, 1995.
Ayers, Edward L., Patricia Nelson Limerick, Stephen Nissenbaum, and Peter S. Onuf.
   All Over the Map. Baltimore: Johns Hopkins University Press, 1996.
Bailey, James Henry, II. *A History of the Diocese of Richmond.* Richmond, VA:
   Chancery Office, Diocese of Richmond, 1956.
Baird, Robert. *Religion in America: A Critical Abridgement of the 1844 Edition*, edited
   by Henry Warner Bowden. New York: Harper and Row, 1970.
Balmer, Randall, and Mark Silk, eds. *Religion and Public Life in the Middle Atlantic
   Region: The Fount of Diversity.* Walnut Creek, CA: AltaMira, 2006.
Barlow, Philip, and Mark Silk, eds. *Religion and Public Life in the Midwest: America's
   Common Denominator?* Walnut Creek, CA: AltaMira, 2004.
Bartholomeusz, Tessa. "Real Life and Romance: The Life of Miranda de Souza
   Canavarro." *Journal of Feminist Studies in Religion* 10, no. 2 (Fall 1994): 27–47.
Becker, Carl. "Japanese Pure Land Buddhism in Christian America." *Buddhist-
   Christian Studies* 10, 1990: 143–56.
Bell, Catherine. *Ritual: Perspectives and Dimensions.* New York: Oxford University
   Press, 1997.
Berman, Myron. *Richmond's Jewry, 1769–1976: Shabbat in Shockoe.* Charlottesville:
   University Press of Virginia, 1979.
Bhusan, Nalini, Jay L. Garfield, and Abraham Zablocki, eds. *TransBuddhism:
   Transmission, Translation, Transformation.* Amherst: University of Massachusetts
   Press, 2009.
"Bishop Tsuji Looking Forward to 100th Anniversary." San Francisco *Hokubei*

Mainichi, January 10, 1973. Copy located in the Buddhist Churches of America archive, 99.201, Japanese American National Museum, Los Angeles, CA.

Blanton, Wyndham Bolling. *The Making of a Downtown Church*. Richmond: John Knox, 1945.

Boles, John B., ed. *Autobiographical Reflections on Southern Religious History*. Athens: University of Georgia Press, 2001.

Boyd, Martin [pseudonym] (Ekoji board trustee). Letter to Phil Brenner (ACLU), July 1, 1993. Copy located in the Ekoji Buddhist Sangha of Richmond archives.

Boyer, Arlynda Lee. *Buddha on the Backstretch: The Spiritual Wisdom of Driving 200 MPH*. Macon, GA: Mercer University Press, 2009.

Brauer, Jerald C. "Regionalism and Religion in America." *Church History* 54 (1985): 366–78.

Brown, Fred [pseudonym] (Ekoji president). "Two New Groups at Ekoji." *Dharma Wheel*, April 1995.

———. Letter to Barbara Sadtler (chaplain, James River Correctional Center), October 11, 1995. Copy located in the Ekoji Buddhist Sangha of Richmond archives.

———. "Ekoji Buddhist Sangha." *Dharma Wheel*, Autumn 1996, 2.

Buddhist Churches of America: A Legacy of the First 100 Years. San Francisco: Buddhist Churches of America, 1998.

Buddhist Churches of America: Seventy-five-Year History, 1899–1974. Vol. 2. Chicago: Nobart, 1974.

Buddhist Council of the Midwest. http://www.buddhistcouncilmidwest.org/. Accessed March 15, 2010.

Buddhist Faith Fellowship. http://www.bffct.net/. Accessed March 15, 2010.

Butler, Jon, and Harry S. Stout, eds. *Religion in American History*. New York: Oxford University Press, 1998.

Cadge, Wendy. *Heartwood: The First Generation of Theravada Buddhism in America*. Chicago: University of Chicago Press, 2004.

"Canadian Minister Speaks before Local Bussei." *Midwest Dharma* 4, no. 3 (February 15, 1948): 2. Copy located in the Buddhist Churches of America archive, 99.201, Japanese American National Museum, Los Angeles, CA.

Carnes, Tony, and Fenggang Yang, eds. *Asian American Religions: The Making and Remaking of Borders and Boundaries*. New York: New York University Press, 2004.

Carroll, Bret E. *The Routledge Historical Atlas of Religion in America*. New York: Routledge, 2000.

———. "Reflections on Regionalism and U.S. Religious History." *Church History* 71, no. 1 (March 2002): 120–31.

Case, Keshia A. *Then and Now: Richmond*. Charleston, SC: Arcadia, 2006.

Chandler, Stuart. *Establishing a Pure Land on Earth: The Foguangshan Perspective on Modernization and Globalization*. Honolulu: University of Hawai'i Press, 2004.

Chappell, David W. "Racial Diversity in the Soka Gakkai." In *Engaged Buddhism in the West*, edited by Christopher S. Queen, 184–217. Boston: Wisdom, 2000.

Chen, Carolyn. *Getting Saved in America: Taiwanese Immigration and Religious Experience*. Princeton, NJ: Princeton University Press, 2008.

Chimborazo Zen Group. "Chimborazo Zen Group — Information Packet." November 2, 1990. Copy in the Ekoji Buddhist Sangha of Richmond archives.

Clark, John R. K. *Guardian of the Sea: Jizo in Hawai'i*. Honolulu: University of Hawai'i Press, 2007.

Cobb, James C., and William Stueck, eds. *Globalization and the American South*. Athens: University of Georgia Press, 2005: 107.

Cohen, Lucy M. *Chinese in the Post–Civil War South: A People without a History*. Baton Rouge: Louisiana State University Press, 1984.

Coleman, James William. *The New Buddhism: The Western Transformation of an Ancient Tradition*. Oxford: Oxford University Press, 2001.

Community of Mindful Living. "Directory of Sanghas Practicing in the Plum Village Lineage." http://www.iamhome.org/USA_sangha.pdf. Accessed March 15, 2010.

Dabney, Virginius. *Richmond: The Story of a City*. Charlottesville: University Press of Virginia, 1990.

Davidson, Cecelia [pseudonym]. "New Thoughts." E-mail to Jeff Wilson, May 7, 2010.

de Certeau, Michel. *The Practice of Everyday Life*. Berkeley: University of California Press, 1984.

"Delinquent Tax Statement." City of Richmond, Virginia, Division of Tax Collections, November 8, 1996. Copy located in the Ekoji Buddhist Sangha of Richmond archives.

DharmaNet International. *InfoWeb*. http://www.dharmanet.org/listings. Accessed March 15, 2010.

Do, Hien Duc. *The Vietnamese-Americans*. Westport, CT: Greenwood, 1999.

"Ekoji Buddhist Sangha of Richmond Application for Exemption for Real Estate Taxation." September 22, 1994. Copy located in the Ekoji Buddhist Sangha of Richmond archives.

Ekoji Buddhist Sangha of Richmond. *Dedication of the Temple*, May 17, 1986. Copy in the Ekoji Buddhist Sangha of Richmond archives.

———. "Immediate Release." Undated (circa May 1986). Copy in the Ekoji Buddhist Sangha of Richmond archives.

———. *Zen Service Book*, October 15, 2002. Copy in the Ekoji Buddhist Sangha of Richmond archives.

———. *Kagyu Shenpen Tharchin*, 2003. Copy in the Ekoji Buddhist Sangha of Richmond archives.

———. *Karmic Patterns in Our Lives*. Undated (circa February 2004). Copy in the Ekoji Buddhist Sangha of Richmond archives.

Esse, John. "Turning the Wheel of the Dharma: A Conference." 1990 [unpublished].

"EYBL Analyzes Buddhist Movement." *Midwest Dharma* 5, no. 3 (February 7, 1949): 1–2. Copy located in the Buddhist Churches of America archive, 99.201, Japanese American National Museum, Los Angeles, CA.

"EYBL Minister Schedule Mapped These: Propagation of Buddhism." *Midwest Dharma* 4, no. 10 (September 5, 1948): 1–2. Copy located in the Buddhist Churches of America archive, 99.201, Japanese American National Museum, Los Angeles, CA.

Farish, Hunter Dickinson. *The Circuit Rider Dismounts: A Social History of Southern Methodism, 1865–1900*. Richmond: Dietz, 1938.

Feldman, Glenn, ed. *Politics and Religion in the White South*. Lexington: University of Kentucky Press, 2005.

Fields, Rick. *How the Swans Came to the Lake: A Narrative History of Buddhism in America*. 3rd ed. Boston: Shambhala, 1992.

———. "Divided Dharma: White Buddhists, Ethnic Buddhists, and Racism." In *The Faces of Buddhism in America*, edited by Charles S. Prebish and Kenneth K. Tanaka, 183–95. Berkeley: University of California Press, 1998.

Fink, Leon. "New People of the Newest South: Prospects for Post-1980 Immigrants." *Journal of Southern History* 75, no. 3 (August 2009): 739–50.

Finke, Roger, and Rodney Stark. *The Churching of America, 1776–1990: Winners and Losers in Our Religious Economy*. New Brunswick, NJ: Rutgers University Press, 1992.

Finney, Henry. "American Zen's 'Japan Connection': A Critical Case Study of Zen Buddhism's Diffusion to the West." *Sociological Analysis* 52, no. 4 (Winter 1991): 379–96.

Ford, Brian [pseudonym]. "Ekoji Zen Group Formed." *Dharma Wheel*, April 1994.

Foster, Gaines M. *Ghosts of the Confederacy: Defeat, the Lost Cause, and the Emergence of the New South*. New York: Oxford University Press, 1987.

Frieberger, Oliver. "The Meeting of Traditions: Inter-Buddhist and Inter-religious Relations in the West." *Journal of Global Buddhism* 2 (2001): 59–71.

Fronsdal, Gil. "Insight Meditation in the United States: Life, Liberty, and the Pursuit of Happiness." In *The Faces of Buddhism in America*, edited by Charles Prebish and Kenneth Tanaka, 163–80. Berkeley: University of California Press, 1998.

Galloway, Allen [pseudonym]. "Dana and Ekoji Buddhist Sangha of Richmond . . . Revisited." *Dharma Wheel*, January 1995.

———. "A Gift of Light: Ekoji." *Dharma Wheel*, Spring 1996.

Garreau, Joel. *The Nine Nations of North America*. Boston: Houghton Mifflin, 1981.

Gastil, Raymond D. *Cultural Regions of the United States*. Seattle: University of Washington Press, 1975.

Gaston, Paul M. *The New South Creed: A Study in Southern Myth-Making*. Baton Rouge: Louisiana State University Press, 1970.

Gaustad, Edwin Scott. *Historical Atlas of Religion in America*. New York: Harper & Row, 1962.

———. "Regionalism in American Religion." In *Religion in the South*, edited by Charles Reagan Wilson 155–72. Oxford: University Press of Mississippi, 1985.

Gaustad, Edwin Scott, and Philip L. Barlow. *A New Historical Atlas of Religion in America*. New York: Oxford University Press, 2000.

Glassman, Bernie. *Bearing Witness: A Zen Master's Lessons in Making Peace*. New York: Bell Tower, 1998.

Goff, Philip, and Paul Harvey, eds. *Themes in Religion and American Culture*. Chapel Hill: University of North Carolina Press, 2004.

Goldfield, David. *Region, Race, and Cities: Interpreting the Urban South*. Baton Rouge: Louisiana State University Press, 1997.

Grossman, Daigyo Bill, and Marcy Apfelbaum. *Daily Sutras: For Chanting and Recitation*. New York: Zen Studies Society, 1982.

Hack, Sheryl. "Collective Identity and Sacred Space: A Study of Seven Zen Communities in Northern California." M.A. thesis, University of Delaware, 1989.

Hackett, David G, ed. *Religion and American Culture*. New York: Routledge, 2003.

Halttunen, Karen. "Groundwork: American Studies in Place — Presidential Address to the American Studies Association, November 4, 2005." *American Quarterly* 58 (March 2006): 1–14.

"Hamilton YBS Organized." *Midwest Dharma* 4, no. 3 (February 15, 1948): 8. Copy located in the Buddhist Churches of America archive, 99.201, Japanese American National Museum, Los Angeles, CA.

Harrell, David Edwin, Jr. "Religious Pluralism: Catholics, Jews, and Sectarians." In *Religion in the South*, edited by Charles Reagan Wilson, 59–82. Oxford: University Press of Mississippi, 1985.

Harty, Thomas R. (assistant city assessor, City of Richmond). Letter to Lynne T. Porfiri (lawyer, Coates and Davenport). Copy in the Ekoji Buddhist Sangha of Richmond archives.

Harvey, Paul. *Freedom's Coming: Religious Culture and the Shaping of the South from the Civil War through the Civil Rights Era*. Chapel Hill: University of North Carolina Press, 2005.

Hatch, Nathan O. *The Democratization of American Christianity*. New Haven, CT: Yale University Press, 1989.

Hill, Samuel S., ed. *Religion in the Southern States: A Historical Study*. Macon, GA: Mercer University Press, 1983.

Hunter, Louise H. *Buddhism in Hawaii: Its Impact on a Yankee Community*. Honolulu: University of Hawai'i Press, 1971.

Hutchison, William. *Religious Pluralism in America: The Contentious History of a Founding Ideal*. New Haven, CT: Yale University Press, 2003.

Isaac, Rhys. *The Transformation of Virginia, 1740–1790*. Chapel Hill: University of North Carolina Press, 1982.

Iwamura, Jame Naomi, and Paul Spickard, eds. *Revealing the Sacred in Asian and Pacific America*. New York: Routledge, 2003.

Jabbar, Robert A. (supervising appraiser, Richmond City Tax Enforcement and Collections). Letter to Nina E. Olson (lawyer, Community Tax Law Project), December 22, 1994. Copy located in the Ekoji Buddhist Sangha of Richmond archives.

Kapleau, Philip. *The Three Pillars of Zen: Teaching, Practice, and Enlightenment*. New York: Harper and Row, 1966.

Kashima, Testuden. *Buddhism in America: The Social Organization of an Ethnic Religious Institution*. Westpost, CT: Greenwood, 1977.

Kiblinger, Kristin Beise. *Buddhist Inclusivism: Attitudes toward Religious Others*. Burlington, VT: Ashgate, 2005.

Killen, Patricia O'Connell, and Mark Silk, eds. *Religion and Public Life in the Pacific Northwest: The None Zone*. Walnut Creek, CA: AltaMira, 2004.

Kimball, Gregg D. *American City, Southern Place: A Cultural History of Antebellum Richmond.* Athens: University of Georgia Press, 2000.

Kingsbury, Carolina. *Buddhism in Bellingham: Practice and Belief.* Ayrshire, UK: Hardinge Simpole, 2004.

Kollatz, Harry, Jr. *True Richmond Stories: Historic Tales from Virginia's Capital.* Charleston, SC: History Press, 2007.

Lau, Barbara. "The Temple Provides the Way: Cambodian Identity and Festival in Greensboro, North Carolina." M.A. thesis, University of North Carolina, 2000.

Layman, Emma McCloy. *Buddhism in America.* Chicago: Nelson-Hall, 1976.

Leighton, Taigen Dan, and Donna Chester. "Facing the Legacy of Slavery: BPF Witness in Richmond, Virginia." *Turning Wheel: Journal of Socially Engaged Buddhism,* Summer/Fall 2008, 7–8.

Lin, Noel Yuan. "Finding the Buddha in the West: An Ethnographic Study of a Chinese Buddhist Community in North Carolina." M.A. thesis, University of North Carolina, 2001.

Lin, Wan-Yu. "The Fitness of the Inward Landscape Design Ideal in Texas: Deviations in Chinese Temple Landscape Design." M.A. thesis, University of Texas at Arlington, 2001.

Lindsey, Alberta. "VCU Professor and Film Director Record Religious Diversity in Richmond." Associated Press, May 30, 2001.

Lindsey, William, and Mark Silk, eds. *Religion and Public Life in the Southern Crossroads: Showdown States.* Walnut Creek, CA: AltaMira, 2005.

Lippy, Charles H. *Pluralism Comes of Age: American Religious Culture in the Twentieth Century.* Armonk, NY: M. E. Sharpe, 2000.

——. *Introducing American Religion.* New York: Routledge, 2009.

Livezey, Lowell W., ed. *Public Religion and Urban Transformation: Faith in the City.* New York: New York University Press, 2000.

Loewen, James W. *The Mississippi Chinese: Between Black and White.* Cambridge: Harvard University Press, 1971.

Lopez, Donald S., Jr. *Prisoners of Shangri-La: Tibetan Buddhism and the West.* Chicago: University of Chicago Press, 1998.

——, ed. *A Modern Buddhist Bible: Essential Readings from East and West.* Boston: Beacon, 2002.

Maffly-Kipp, Laurie. "Eastward Ho! American Religion from the Perspective of the Pacific Rim." In *Retelling U.S. Religious History,* edited by Thomas A. Tweed, 127–48. Berkeley: University of California Press, 1997.

——. "If It's South Dakota You Must Be Episcopalian: Lies, Truth-Telling, and the Mapping of U.S. Religion." *Church History* 71 (March 2002): 132–42.

——. "Putting Religion on the Map." *Journal of American History* 94, no. 2 (September 2007): 522–29.

Mallory-Jones, Debbie (legal intern, Office of the City Attorney). Letter to Nina R. Olsen (lawyer, Community Tax Law Project), November 18, 1996. Copy located in the Ekoji Buddhist Sangha of Richmond archives.

Mather, Cotton. *Magnalia Christi Americana, or, The Ecclesiastical History of New-England.* London: Thomas Parkhurst, 1702.

Mathews, Donald G. *Religion in the Old South.* Chicago: University of Chicago Press, 1977.

———. "'We Have Left Undone Those Things Which We Ought to Have Done': Southern Religious History in Retrospect and Prospect." *Church History* 67, no. 2 (June 1998): 305–25.

Matsunaga, Daigan, and Alicia Matsunaga. *Foundation of Japanese Buddhism.* Vol. 2. Los Angeles: Buddhist Books International, 1976.

McAlister, Elizabeth. "Globalization and the Religious Production of Space." *Journal for the Scientific Study of Religion* 44, no. 3 (September 2005): 249–55.

McDannell, Colleen. *Material Christianity: Religion and Popular Culture in America.* New Haven, CT: Yale University Press, 1995.

McKern, Sharon. *Redneck Mothers, Good Ol' Girls, and Other Southern Belles: A Celebration of the Women of Dixie.* New York: Viking, 1979.

McMahan, David L. *The Making of Buddhist Modernism.* Oxford: Oxford University Press, 2008.

McPherson, Tara. *Reconstructing Dixie: Race, Gender, and Nostalgia in the Imagined South.* Durham, NC: Duke University Press, 2003.

"Meditation Vigil to Bear Witness to the Slave Trade." Richmond, Virginia, Buddhist Peace Fellowship Chapter, 2008.

Miller, Randall M., and George E. Pozzetta, eds. *Shades of the Sunbelt: Essays on Ethnicity, Race, and the Urban South.* New York: Greenwood, 1988.

Min, Pyong Gap, and Jung Ha Kim, eds. *Religions in Asian America: Building Faith Communities.* Walnut Creek, CA: AltaMira, 2002.

Mitchell, Mary H. *Hollywood Cemetery: The History of a Southern Shrine.* Richmond: Virginia State Library, 1985.

Moeser, John V., and Christopher Silver. "Race, Social Stratification, and Politics: The Case of Atlanta, Memphis, and Richmond." *Virginia Magazine of History and Biography* 102, no. 4 (October 1994): 519–50.

Mohl, Raymond A., ed. *Searching for the Sunbelt: Historical Perspectives on a Region.* Knoxville: University of Tennessee Press, 1990.

Morita, Yuri. "Daimoku and the Sacred Pipe: The Encounter of Buddhism with the Native American Indians." Ph.D. diss., Graduate Theological Union, 1981.

Morreale, Don. *The Complete Guide to Buddhist America.* Boston: Shambhala, 1998.

Mullen, Eve. *The American Occupation of Tibetan Buddhism: Tibetans and Their American Hosts in New York City.* New York: Waxman Munster, 2001.

Museum District Association. *The Columns.* Spring 2002.

Nagata, Brian K. "Former BCA Bishop Passes Away." *Wheel of Dharma* 31, no. 5 (May 2004): 1, 4.

Nakagaki, T. Kenjitsu. *Practice of Ahimsa in Buddhism.* New York: New York Buddhist Church, 2004.

Nakane, Kinsaku. *Kyoto Gardens.* Osaka: Hoikusha, 1978.

Neitz, Mary Jo. "Reflections on Religion and Place: Rural Churches and American Religion." *Journal for the Scientific Study of Religion* 44, no. 3 (September 2005): 243–47.

Nelson, Louis P., ed. *American Sanctuary: Understanding Sacred Spaces*. Bloomington: Indiana University Press, 2006.

"New Buddhist Temple." *Richmond Times-Dispatch*, April 21, 2003, B3.

"A New Place of Worship." *Richmond Times-Dispatch*, April 22, 2003, B4.

"News—Buddhist World." *American Buddhist* 12, no. 3 (March 1986): 2. Copy located in the Buddhist Churches of America archive, 99.201, Japanese American National Museum, Los Angeles, CA.

Norman, Corrie E., and Don S. Armentrout, eds. *Religion in the Contemporary South: Changes, Continuities, and Contexts*. Knoxville: University of Tennessee Press, 2005.

Nugent, Harry [pseudonym]. E-mail to Jeff Wilson. Subject: "Three items." March 9, 2004.

Numrich, Paul David. *Old Wisdom in the New World: Americanization in Two Immigrant Theravada Buddhist Temples*. Knoxville: University of Tennessee Press, 1996.

———. "Local Inter-Buddhist Associations in North America." In *American Buddhism: Methods and Findings in Recent Scholarship*, edited by Duncan Ryuken Williams and Christopher Queen, 117–42. Richmond, UK: Curzon, 1999.

———, ed. *North American Buddhists in Social Context*. Leiden, the Netherlands: Brill, 2008.

Official City of Richmond, Virginia, website: http://www.ci.richmond.va.us/index .asp. Accessed March 1, 2004.

Olsen, Nina E. (lawyer, Community Tax Law Project). Letter to Mack Lockhart (city assessor, City of Richmond), October 25, 1994. Copy in Ekoji Buddhist Sangha of Richmond archives.

———. Letter to Elizabeth Stutts (lawyer, Office of the City Attorney), October 13, 1995. Copy in Ekoji Buddhist Sangha of Richmond archives.

———. Letter to Leonidas Young (mayor, City of Richmond), October 13, 1995. Copy in Ekoji Buddhist Sangha of Richmond archives.

———. Letter to Elizabeth Stutts (lawyer, Office of the Richmond City Attorney), August 30, 1996. Copy in Ekoji Buddhist Sangha of Richmond archives.

Orsi, Robert A. "Everyday Miracles: The Study of Lived Religion." In *Lived Religion in America: Toward a History of Practice*, edited by David D. Hall, 3–21. Princeton, NJ: Princeton University Press, 1997.

———, ed. *Gods of the City: Religion and the American Urban Landscape*. Bloomington: Indiana University Press, 1999.

Osbourne, Christopher. "Surviving High School: A Gay Buddhist Graduates in the Heartland." *Queer Dharma: Voices of Gay Buddhists*, 2 vols., edited by Winston Leyland, 1:257–59. San Francisco: Gay Sunshine, 1998.

Packer, Toni. *The Light of Discovery*. Boston: Charles E. Tuttle, 1995.

Padgett, Douglas M. "'Americans Need Something to Sit On,' or, Zen Meditation Materials and Buddhist Diversity in North America." *Journal of Global Buddhism* 1 (2000): 61–81.

———. "The Translating Temple: Diasporic Buddhism in Florida." In *Westward Dharma: Buddhism beyond Asia*, edited by Charles S. Prebish and Martin Baumann, 201–17. Berkeley: University of California Press, 2002.

Peacock, James L., Harry L. Watson, and Carrie R. Mathews, eds. *The American South in a Global World*. Chapel Hill: University of North Carolina Press, 2005.

Porter, Jessica. "Buddhism Is an Eastern Way of Life Appealing to Westerners." *Ground Report*, January 27, 2010.

Prebish, Charles. *American Buddhism*. North Scituate, MA: Duxbury, 1979.

———. *Luminous Passage: The Practice and Study of Buddhism in America*. Berkeley: University of California Press, 1999.

———. "Varying the Vinaya: Creative Responses to Vinaya." In *Buddhism in the Modern World: Adaptations of an Ancient Tradition*, edited by Steven Heine and Charles S. Prebish, 45–73. Oxford: Oxford University Press, 2003.

———. "The Cybersangha: Buddhism on the Internet." In *Religion Online: Finding Faith on the Internet*, edited by Lorne L. Dawson and Douglas E. Cowan, 135–47. New York: Routledge, 2004.

Prebish, Charles, and Martin Baumann, eds. *Westward Dharma: Buddhism beyond Asia*. Berkeley: University of California Press, 2002.

Prebish, Charles, and Kenneth K. Tanaka, eds. *The Faces of Buddhism in America*. Berkeley: University of California Press, 1998.

"Progress in the Making." *Midwest Dharma* 4, no. 11 (October 15, 1948): 3.

Prothero, Stephen. *The White Buddhist: The Asian Odyssey of Henry Steel Olcott*. Bloomington: Indiana University Press, 1996.

Queen, Christopher, ed. *Engaged Buddhism in the West*. Somerville, MA: Wisdom, 2000.

Queen, Christopher, Charles Prebish, and Damien Keown, eds. *Action Dharma: New Studies in Engaged Buddhism*. London: Routledge Curzon, 2003.

Rambelli, Fabio. *Buddhist Materiality: A Cultural History of Objects in Japanese Buddhism*. Stanford, CA: Stanford University Press, 2007.

Ray, Celeste, and Luke Eric Lassiter, eds. *Signifying Serpents and Mardi Gras Runners: Representing Identity in Selected Souths*. Athens: University of Georgia Press, 2003.

Reed, John Shelton. *The Enduring South: Subcultural Persistence in Mass Society*. Lexington, MA: D. C. Heath, 1972.

———. "The Same Old Stand?" In *Why the South Will Survive*, edited by Clyde N. Wilson. Athens: University of Georgia Press, 1981.

Reimers, David M. "Asian Immigrants in the South." In *Globalization and the American South*, edited by James C. Cobb and William Strueck, 100–134. Athens: University of Georgia Press, 2005.

"Rev. Takashi Tsuji Accepts EYBL Traveling Minister Post." *Midwest Dharma* 4, no. 9 (August 7, 1948): 1–2. Copy located in the Buddhist Churches of America archive, 99.201, Japanese American National Museum, Los Angeles, CA.

"Rev. Tsuji Arrives in Chicago on EYBL Tour." *Midwest Dharma* 4, no. 11 (October 15, 1948): 1. Copy located in the Buddhist Churches of America archive, 99.201, Japanese American National Museum, Los Angeles, CA.

"Rev. Tsuji Spoke at Univ. of Oregon Program." *American Buddhist* 6, no. 1 (January 1962): 3. Copy located in the Buddhist Churches of America archive, 99.201, Japanese American National Museum, Los Angeles, CA.

"Richmond Slave Trail." Richmond Slave Trail Commission, [undated].

Richmond Zen Group Newsletter 1, no. 1 (June 2003).

Robinson, Sandra R. (assistant city attorney). Letter to Hon. Jean Wallace (clerk, General District Court), July 14, 1993. Copy located in the Ekoji Buddhist Sangha of Richmond archives.

Rogers, Nicholas. Survey response. March 14, 2004.

Roof, Wade Clark, and Mark Silk, eds. *Religion and Public Life in the Pacific Region: Fluid Identities.* Walnut Creek, CA: AltaMira, 2005.

Ryan, Mike, Jr. Letter to Mark Jacinto [pseudonym] (president, Ekoji Buddhist Sangha of Richmond), undated (postmarked September 13, 1995). Copy in the Ekoji Buddhist Sangha of Richmond archives.

San Francisco Zen Center. http://www.sfzc.org. Accessed March 15, 2010.

Schweiger, Beth Barton, and Donald G. Mathews, eds. *Religion in the American South: Protestants and Others in History and Culture.* Chapel Hill: University of North Carolina Press, 2004.

Seager, Richard Hughes. *Buddhism in America.* New York: Columbia University Press, 1999.

Sensbach, Jon F. *Separate Canaan: The Making of an Afro-Moravian World in North Carolina, 1763–1840.* Chapel Hill: University of North Carolina Press, 1998.

Shambhala Mountain Center. "The Great Stupa of Dharmakaya," http://www.shambhalamountain.org/stupa.html. Accessed March 15, 2010.

Shantideva. *The Way of the Bodhisattva.* Translated by Padmakara Translation Group. Boston: Shambhala, 1997.

Sharf, Robert H. "Buddhist Modernism and the Rhetoric of Meditative Experience." *Numen* 42 (1995): 228–81.

Shepherd, Samuel C., Jr. *Avenues of Faith: Shaping the Urban Religious Culture of Richmond, Virginia, 1900–1929.* Tuscaloosa: University of Alabama Press, 2001.

Shields, Thomas J. "The 'Tip of the Iceberg' in a Southern Suburban County: The Fight for a Martin Luther King, Jr., Holiday." *Journal of Black Studies* 33, no. 4 (March 2003): 499–519.

Shipps, Jan, and Mark Silk, eds. *Religion and Public Life in the Mountain West: Sacred Landscapes in Transition.* Walnut Creek, CA: AltaMira, 2004.

Shortridge, James R. "Patterns of Religion in the United States." *Geographical Review* 66, no. 4 (October 1976): 420–34.

———. "A New Regionalization of American Religion." *Journal for the Scientific Study of Religion* 16, no. 2 (1977): 143–53.

Siegel, Taggart, and Kati Johnston. *Blue Collar and Buddha* [film]. Collective Eye, 1987.

Silk, Mark. "Religion and Region in American Public Life." *Journal for the Scientific Study of Religion* 44, no. 3 (September 2005): 265–70.

Silk, Mark, and Andrew Walsh. *One Nation, Divisible: How Regional Religious Differences Shape American Politics.* Lanham, MD: Rowman and Littlefield, 2008.

Silver, Christopher. *Twentieth-Century Richmond.* Knoxville: University of Tennessee Press, 1984.

———. "The Changing Face of Neighborhoods in Memphis and Richmond, 1940–1985." In *Shades of the Sunbelt: Essays on Ethnicity, Race, and the Urban South*, edited by Randall M. Miller and George E. Pozzetta, 93–126. New York: Greenwood, 1988.

Snodgrass, Judith. *Presenting Japanese Buddhism to the West: Orientalism, Occidentalism, and the Columbian Exposition*. Chapel Hill: University of North Carolina, 2003.

Snyder, Gary. *The Gary Snyder Reader: Prose, Poetry, and Translations, 1952–1998*. Washington, D.C.: Counterpoint, 1999.

Suderman, Carrie [pseudonym]. Letter to Ekoji Buddhist Sangha of Richmond, December 9, 1995. Copy in the Ekoji Buddhist Sangha of Richmond files.

Suh, Sharon A. *Being Buddhist in a Christian World: Gender and Community in a Korean American Temple*. Seattle: University of Washington Press, 2004.

Suzuki, Shunryu. *Zen Mind, Beginner's Mind*. New York: Weatherhill, 1970.

Tabrah, Ruth. *Shin Sutras to Live By*. Honolulu, HI: Buddhist Study Center Press, 1989.

Tanabe, George, Jr. "Glorious Gathas: Americanization and Japanization in Honganji Hymns." In *Engaged Pure Land Buddhism: Essays in Honor of Professor Alfred Bloom*, edited by Kenneth Tanaka and Eisho Nasu, 221–37. Berkeley: Wisdom Ocean, 1998.

Taylor, George Rogers, ed. *The Turner Thesis: Concerning the Role of the Frontier in American History*. Lexington, MA: D. C. Heath, 1972.

Teeuwen, Mark, and Fabio Rambelli. *Buddhas and Kami in Japan: Honji Suijaku as a Combinatory Paradigm*. London: Routledge Curzon, 2003.

Terathongkum, Sangthong. "Relationships among Stress, Blood Pressure, and Heart Rate Variability in Meditators." Ph.D. diss., Virginia Commonwealth University, 2006.

Thinganjana, Wantana. "The Lived Experience of Spirituality among Thai Immigrants Who Are Living with Type 2 Diabetes." Ph.D. diss., Virginia Commonwealth University, 2007.

Tollifson, Joan. "Foreword." In *The Light of Discovery*, by Toni Packer, ix–xii. Boston: Charles E. Tuttle, 1995.

"Traveling Minister Program." *Midwest Dharma* 5, no. 11 (October 10, 1949): 6. Copy located in the Buddhist Churches of America archive, 99.201, Japanese American National Museum, Los Angeles, CA.

Troubetzkoy, Ulrich. *Richmond, City of Churches: A Short History of Richmond's Denominations and Faiths Issued Incident to America's 350th Birthday, 1607–1957*. Richmond: Richmond-Jamestown Festival Committee, 1957.

Tsuji, Kenryu. *An Outline of Buddhism*. 3rd ed. San Francisco: Buddhist Churches of America, 1979 [1954].

———. *Gassho*. San Francisco: Buddhist Churches of America, 1981. Copy located in the Buddhist Churches of America archive, 99.201, Japanese American National Museum, Los Angeles, CA.

———. "Gassho to Amida." *Pure Land*, n.s., no. 1 (December 1984): 119–21.

———. "Shin Buddhism in the West, Its Future as I See It." *Pure Land*, n.s., no. 1 (December 1984): 116–19.

————. *A Challenge for American Shin Buddhists.* San Francisco: Buddhist Churches of America, 1988.

————. "Application for Exemption from Real Estate Taxation." Submitted to the Assessor of Real Estate, City of Richmond, Virginia, May 7, 1990. Copy in the Ekoji Buddhist Sangha of Richmond archives.

————. *The Heart of the Buddha-Dharma: Following the Jodo Shinshu Path.* Berkeley: Ekoji Buddhist Temple and Numata Center for Buddhist Translation and Research, 2003.

———— [Takashi Tsuji]. "Path of Freedom." *Midwest Dharma* 5, no. 3 (February 7, 1949): 6. Copy located in the Buddhist Churches of America archive, 99.201, Japanese American National Museum, Los Angeles, CA.

———— [Takashi Tsuji]. "The Life to Come." *Midwest Dharma* 5, no. 8 (July 22, 1949): 3. Copy located in the Buddhist Churches of America archive, 99.201, Japanese American National Museum, Los Angeles, CA.

———— [Takashi Tsuji]. "The True 'I.'" *Midwest Dharma* 7, no. 1 (January 1951): 20. Copy located in the Buddhist Churches of America archive, 99.201, Japanese American National Museum, Los Angeles, CA.

———— [Takashi Tsuji]. "For Buddhism—A National Purpose." In *Buddhist Sermons no. 104* 10–11. San Francisco: Buddhist Churches of America, 1960.

———— [Takashi Tsuji]. *Three Lectures on the "Tannisho."* San Francisco: Buddhist Churches of America, 1967.

———— [Takashi Tsuji]. *Obon Odori.* Toronto: Eastern Canada Buddhist Publications [undated].

———— [Takashi Tsuji]. "Reincarnation: My Answer." San Francisco: Buddhist Churches of America [undated].

———— [Takashi Tsuji]. "The Religious Experience of Shinran Shonin." San Francisco: Buddhist Churches of America [undated].

Tuck, Donald R. *Buddhist Churches of America: Jodo Shinshu.* Lewiston/Queenston, NY: Edwin Mellon, 1987.

Turner, Frederick Jackson. *The Frontier in American History.* New York: Holt, 1921.

Tweed, Thomas A. "Night-Stand Buddhists and Other Creatures: Sympathizers, Adherents, and the Study of Religion." In *American Buddhism: Methods and Findings in Recent Scholarship,* edited by Duncan Ryuken Williams and Christopher S. Queen, 71–90. Surrey, UK: Curzon, 1999.

————. *The American Encounter with Buddhism, 1844–1912: Victorian Culture and the Limits of Dissent.* Chapel Hill: University of North Carolina, 2000.

————. "Buddhism." In *Encyclopedia of Religion in the South,* 2nd ed., edited by Samuel S. Hill and Charles H. Lippy, 149. Macon, GA: Mercer University Press, 2005.

————. "Our Lady of Guadeloupe Visits the Confederate Memorial: Latino and Asian Religions in the South." In *Religion in the Contemporary South: Changes, Continuities, and Contexts,* edited by Corrie E. Norman and Don S. Armentrout, 139–58. Knoxville: University of Tennessee Press, 2005.

————. *Crossing and Dwelling: A Theory of Religion.* Cambridge: Harvard University Press, 2006.

———. "Expanding the Study of U.S. Religion: Reflections on the State of a Subfield." *Religion* (2010): 1–9.

———, ed. *Retelling U.S. Religious History*. Berkeley: University of California Press, 1997.

Tweed, Thomas A., and Buddhism in North Carolina Project. *Buddhism and Barbecue: A Guide to Buddhist Temples in North Carolina*. Chapel Hill: University of North Carolina Press, 2001.

Tweed, Thomas A., and Stephen Prothero, eds. *Asian Religions in America: A Documentary History*. New York: Oxford University Press, 1999.

Tyler-McGraw, Mary. *At the Falls: Richmond, Virginia, and Its People*. Chapel Hill: University of North Carolina Press, 1994.

Tyson, Ruel W., James L. Peacock, and Daniel W. Patterson, eds. *Diversities of Gifts: Field Studies in Southern Religion*. Urbana: University of Illinois Press, 1988.

Ueba, Greg. Letter to Joseph Tuttle [pseudonym], undated [circa June 1986]. Located in Ekoji Buddhist Sangha of Richmond archives.

U.S. Census Bureau. http://factfinder.census.gov. Accessed June 21, 2010. And http://www.census.gov/popest/metro/CBSA-est2008-annual.html. Accessed June 25, 2010.

U.S. Department of Housing and Urban Development. *Settlement Statement*, Form no. 63-R-1301, "Sale of 3411 Grove Avenue by Edwin and Jean Kleinman to Numata Center for Buddhist Translation and Research, Inc." June 3, 1985. Copy located in the Ekoji Buddhist Sangha of Richmond archives.

Vecsey, George. "Arthur Ashe: A Life Dedicated to the Welfare of Others." *New York Times*, August 28, 2009, B11.

Veidlinger, Daniel. "From Indra's Net to Internet: The Effects of Social Networking Websites on the Acculturation of Buddhism in North America." Unpublished paper delivered March 18, 2010, at Buddhism without Borders Conferences, Institute for Buddhist Studies, Berkeley.

Walsh, Andrew, and Mark Silk, eds. *Religion and Public Life in New England: Steady Habits, Changing Slowly*. Walnut Creek, CA: AltaMira, 2004.

Ward, Jason Morgan. "No Jap Crow: Japanese Americans Encounter the World War II South." *Journal of Southern History* 73, no. 1 (February 2007): 75–104.

Watada, Terry. *Bukkyo Tozen: A History of Jodo Shinshu Buddhism in Canada, 1905–1995*. Toronto: HpF Press and Toronto Buddhist Church, 1996.

Weisinger, Minor T., Donald R. Traser, and E. Randolph Trice. *Not Hearers Only: A History of St. James's Episcopal Church*. Richmond: St. Paul's Episcopal Church, 1986.

White, Jeanne Carol Vosecky. "How Can I Make It Here? The Adaptation to Rural American Life by Lao Refugee Women." Ph.D. diss., University of Georgia, 2000.

White, O. Kendall, Jr., and Daryl White, eds. *Religion in the Contemporary South: Diversity, Community, and Identity*. Athens: University of Georgia Press, 1995.

White, Ralph R. *Seeing the Scars of Slavery in the Natural Environment: An Interpretive Guide to the Manchester Slave Trail along the James River in Richmond*. Richmond: James River Park System, 2002.

Williams, Duncan Ryuken, and Christopher S. Queen, eds. *American Buddhism: Methods and Findings in Recent Scholarship*. Surrey, UK: Curzon, 1999.

Williams, Peter W. *Houses of God: Region, Religion, and Architecture in the United States*. Urbana: University of Illinois Press, 1997.

———. "How to Read a Church." In *Art and the Religious Impulse*, edited by Eric Mazur, 42–61. Lewisburg, PA: Bucknell University Press, 2002.

Williams, Rhys H. "Introduction to a Forum on Religion and Place." *Journal for the Scientific Study of Religion* 44, no. 3 (September 2005): 239–42.

Wilson, Charles Reagan. *Baptized in Blood: The Religion of the Lost Cause, 1865–1920*. Athens: University of Georgia Press, 1980.

———, ed. *Religion in the South*. Jackson: University of Mississippi Press, 1985.

Wilson, Charles Reagan, and Mark Silk, eds. *Religion and Public Life in the South: In the Evangelical Mode*. Walnut Creek, CA: AltaMira, 2005.

Wilson, Clyde N., ed. *Why the South Will Survive*. Athens: University of Georgia Press, 1981.

Wilson, Jeff. *The Buddhist Guide to New York*. New York: St. Martin's, 2000.

———. "Deeply Female and Universally Human: The Rise of Kuan-yin Worship in America." *Journal of Contemporary Religion* 23, no. 3 (October 2008): 285–306.

———. *Mourning the Unborn Dead: A Buddhist Ritual Comes to America*. Oxford: Oxford University Press, 2009.

Woodward, Michael. "Ekoji Buddhist Sangha Supports Multi-denominational Practice on Grove Avenue." *Examiner.com*, March 21, 2010. Accessed April 29, 2010.

———. "Meditate for Haiti: A Benefit at Ekoji Buddhist Sangha." *Examiner.com*, March 23, 2010. Accessed April 29, 2010.

———. "Lama Chonam Leads Successful Meditation Benefit for Haiti." *Examiner.com*, March 30, 2010. Accessed April 29, 2010.

———. "Buddhists You Know: Richmond Zen Group's Anna West, Part One." *Examiner.com*, April 6, 2010. Accessed April 29, 2010.

———. "Buddhists You Know: Richmond Zen Group's Anna West, Part Two." *Examiner.com*, April 8, 2010. Accessed April 29, 2010.

———. "Buddha's Birthday Celebration Highlights Diversity, Foreshadows Change for Grove Ave. Temple." *Examiner.com*, April 11, 2010. Accessed April 29, 2010.

———. "Punk Rock Zen Priest Speaks to Packed Grove Ave. Temple." *Examiner.com*, April 14, 2010. Accessed April 29, 2010.

Wren, Benjamin Lee. *Zen among the Magnolias*. Lanham, MD: University Press of America, 1999.

Yamaoka, Seigen H. Letter to Joseph Tuttle [pseudonym]. October 8, 1985. Located in Ekoji Buddhist Sangha of Richmond archives.

Zelinsky, Wilbur. "An Approach to the Religious Geography of the United States: Patterns of Church Membership in 1952." *Annals of the Association of American Geographers* 51, no. 2 (June 1961): 139–93.

Index